SOCIAL CONTROL AND DEVIANCE

To:

ANDY,

FROM
Ali

WITH BEST REGARDS

7/6/2000

TREFOREST

TO THE LIVING MEMORY OF MY BELOVED LATE PARENTS -

ADAY AND *GULDADA*

Social Control and Deviance

A South Asian community in Scotland

ALI WARDAK
University of Glamorgan

Ashgate

Aldershot • Burlington USA • Singapore • Sydney

Published by
Ashgate Publishing Limited
Gower House
Croft Road
Aldershot
Hampshire GU11 3HR
England

Ashgate Publishing Company
131 Main Street
Burlington
Vermont 05401
USA

Ashgate website: http://www.ashgate.com

British Library Cataloguing in Publication Data
Wardak, Ali
  Social control and deviance : a South Asian community in
  Scotland. - (Interdisciplinary research series in ethnic,
  gender and class relations)
  1. South Asians - Scotland - Social life and customs 2. South
  Asians - Scotland - Social conditions 3. South Asians -
  Scotland - Family relationships 4. Marginality, Social -
  Scotland 5. Scotland - Race relations
  I. Title
  305.8'914'0411

Library of Congress Catalog Card Number: 00-130585

ISBN 1 84014 588 9

Printed and bound by Athenaeum Press, Ltd.,
Gateshead, Tyne & Wear.

Contents

List of Diagrams

List of Tables

Series Editor's Preface

I am very pleased to write this preface to a work that I witnessed in progress while the author and I were doctoral students under the supervision of Dr Peter Young at Edinburgh University. I fondly remember debating aspects of control theory (the framework of the book) with Dr Wardak as we walked from the university library in the early 1990s. I also remember him asking me the tricky question of what I considered the most important contribution to criminology in recent times and I remember how he smiled victoriously when I answered without hesitation that, without doubt, it was the development of gender awareness. He explained that he found my response amusing because, according to him, every doctoral student would identify the subject of his or her research as making the most important recent contribution to the field of knowledge. Needless to say, he was convinced that control theory was the best thing in criminology since sliced bread. I am pleased to welcome Dr Wardak's book to the same series in which my own research on Black Women and the Criminal Justice System was published. Indirectly, the two books will hopefully continue our intellectually stimulating debates.

Dr Wardak's book, I am proud to say, illustrates the theoretically informed style of work encouraged by the Edinburgh University's Centre for Law and Society. The author brings to this theoretical awareness, a methodological sophistication that offers an innovative analysis of social control and deviance. The title of the book gives the misleading impression that the author would dwell on the official discourse of social control and deviance but he is more interested in the phenomenology of how the Pakistani community in Edinburgh inter-subjectively make sense of both social control and deviance. This approach is intriguing because criminologists often assume that the state and its agencies have a monopoly over the definition of social control and deviance. By approaching the subject-matter from below, the author indirectly illustrates the theoretical importance of studying subordinate perspectives on reality without falling into the criminological trap of focusing exclusively on criminality.

Perhaps the author avoided the crime-centred pre-occupation of criminologists because the Pakistani youth he studied were not remarkably crime-prone, in spite of the self-reported criminality by some of them. The question that this raises for some criminologists is a controversial one: If Pakistanis in Scotland are excluded and marginalized like Africans in Scotland, how come they are not arrested as frequently as Africans by the official social control agents. The author did not raise this question directly probably because the number of Africans in the Scottish criminal justice system was not as large as their over-representation in England while Pakistanis appeared even more law abiding than the privileged native white people in both Scotland and England and Wales. It is a credit to the book that it is capable of provoking more research questions to be tackled in future works.

Other researchers who wish to follow-up on the implications of Dr Wardak's work could focus on non-migrant communities or on less peaceful ones. For example, the suggestion by control theory that those who are less committed to societal values, less involved in community rituals and less involved in religious observations would be more deviant could have a different interpretation if applied to troubled communities like Northern Ireland, The Kashmir Region or even to Mafia families with alternative notions of Izzet and Bizatti (honour and dishonour). Even when the Durkheimian collective conscience is not contentious, some researchers might wish to find out if there is anything that makes the Pakistani community in Edinburgh more capable of controlling deviance among its youth whereas the prisons in Pakistan are every bit as over-crowded as prisons everywhere in the world.

The author suggests that a possible explanation is that exclusionary practices by white employers have had the unintended consequence of making the Pakistani community more self-reliant and more likely to rely on self-employment as shopkeepers. This is probably a clue to the role of class relations on social control and the perception of deviance among the Pakistani in Edinburgh whereas in Pakistan, the majority of the citizens are relatively impoverished and consequently demonized by the official law enforcement agencies in Pakistan. Again, this is not a point directly raised in the book but one that can be provoked by the findings analyzed by the author.

Acknowledgements

It would not have been possible for me to travel the thousands of miles from Afghanistan to Scotland to study at the University of Edinburgh without the help of a number of individuals and institutions. First of all, I am very grateful to my elder brother, Dr. A. Wali Wardak, who helped me in the procedural processes of getting admission to the University of Edinburgh and travelling to Scotland. I am also very grateful to my parents and to my younger brother, Engineer A. Basir Wardak, who through many difficult days, gave the strong moral support necessary for me to continue in my search for knowledge. The loss of both my parents in 1998, while I was working on publishing this research as a book deeply shocked me – a shock that I am yet to come to terms with. However, as I knew that my beloved *Aday* and *Guldada* had always wanted me to be an academic and a writer, I was determined to complete publishing this book which I dedicate to their living memory that is deeply present in my conscience.

I have been very fortunate to be taught and supervised by distinguished scholars and academics and to have worked in the intellectually stimulating environment of the Centre for Law and Society, at the University of Edinburgh. I am especially very grateful to my supervisors Dr. Peter Young and the late Professor Frederick McClintock for their scholarly and invaluable supervision of my research. Dr. Peter Young particularly has been very kind in giving me considerable academic, social, and moral support in the various phases of my research. I express my deep gratitude to him and to his family. I also sincerely thank Dr. James Sheptycki for his supervision of this research while it was in its last stages of completion.

I was very privileged to have been given a scholarship by the Hugh Pilkington Charitable Trust for the completion of this doctoral research project. I particularly offer my most sincere gratitude and thanks to Mr. Roger Northcott, Mr. Robin Shawyer, and Mr. Jim Richardson – trustees of the Hugh Pilkington Charitable Trust – and to their families for their support throughout the process of my research. I also sincerely thank the School of Humanities and Social Sciences Research Committee, at Glamorgan University, for its financial support in the process of publishing this work. My special thanks go to Mrs. Anne Baik who helped me in the most crucial stages of the publication of the present book – without her help it would have never been in the shape in which it is now. I also wholeheartedly thank Dr. Frances Mannsaker, Professor David Dunkerley, Dr Sharif Gemie, Ms Patricia Clark, Professor Mike Maguire, Dr. Andrew Thompson, Dr. Fiona Brookman, Dr. Andrew Smith, Mr. Cennard Davies, and Mrs. Anne England for their support in various ways.

Mr. Abdul Latif Majothi, my colleague and great friend, deserves special thanks and my highest respects go to him. I would also like to acknowledge the helpful contribution of Dr. Malory and Mrs. Alexandra Nye to my research; their friendship has been a rich source of intellectual and moral support throughout the process of this research.

There have been many other persons who have given me academic, statistical and other forms of advice and help. My sincere thanks are due to Professor David Garland, Professor Neil MacCormick, Professor Beverley Brown, Professor Colin Bell, Dr. Biko Agozino, Dr. Bob Hodgart, Mr. Tom McGlew, Miss Frances Provan, Mr. Alec Robertson, Dr. Francis and Mrs Debbie Watkins, Mr. Peter Bell, Mrs. Patricia Bell, Miss Claire Bell and Miss Susan Bell. I very sincerely thank all these individuals for whom I have great respect.

I am wholeheartedly grateful to all members of Edinburgh's Pakistani community and to the leaders of the Pakistan Association, particularly, Mr. Yousaf Inait, Mr. Khaled Meir, and Mr. Mohammed Aslam, as well as to *Hafiz Sahib* Abdul Ghafoor, the *Imam* of the Pilrig Mosque. My sincere thanks are also due to Mr. M. Ishaq Khan of Edinburgh's Pakistan Society. Finally I express my deeply felt gratitude and respect to the Pilrig boys without whose co-operation and friendship this research would have never been accomplished. I hope that this study will be of some interest and benefit to the young Pilrig boys, to their parents and to Edinburgh's Pakistani community. I also hope that the study will provide some insight for members of the wider Scottish society into the fears, problems, and hopes of the British-born Pakistanis and of the Pakistani community in Edinburgh.

Finally, and as always, I am very grateful to Masuda for her constant encouragement and support in difficult times.

A.A. W.

General Introduction

After the end of World War Two Scotland became home for relatively large Asian populations. Since the late 1950s, increasingly stable Pakistani, Bangladeshi, Hindu, Sikh, and Chinese (including those from Hong Kong) communities have emerged in the major Scottish cities and towns. These Asian communities, which form the bulk of the Scottish ethnic minority population are a clearly visible feature of Scottish society, particularly of its urban life. Pakistani, Indian, Bangladeshi and Chinese shops and retail stores, restaurants, and other businesses contribute vigorously to the commercial and economic life of Scotland; the relatively recent emergence of mosques, temples and *gurdwaras*, and the quietly developing Asian arts scene, including music, dance and fashion, enrich the social and cultural life of Scottish society.

Among the Scottish ethnic minority populations, Pakistanis, who are predominantly Muslims, are the largest ethnic minority group (33% of the total Scottish minority population) in the country. The Scottish Pakistani community as a whole, and its various branches in different Scottish cities and towns, have developed their own cultural, religious, economic and political institutions which give structure to various aspects of their members' lives. These communities, which are gradually emerging as small-scale societies within the wider Scottish society, have recently become the subject of increasing interest and debates among politicians, policy-makers, academics and the general public. Events such as the publication of Salman Rushdie's *Satanic Verses*, the establishment of 'The Muslim Parliament of Great Britain' and the increase of racial violence against members of ethnic communities, particularly against Pakistanis, have further stimulated the debate. But despite all this the Scottish Pakistani/Muslim community is the least researched and therefore (I believe) the least understood.

The existing small body of research on Scotland's Pakistani population relates mainly to their history of migration and to their experiences of racial discrimination and exclusion. Much of the research that I will refer to in Chapter I discusses Scottish Pakistanis under the general categories of 'Asians', 'South Asians' and 'people from the Indian sub-continent'. Studies that focus more specifically on Scotland's Pakistanis include occasional surveys by the Scottish Office, the Commission for Racial Equality (CRE) and a few studies by Scottish Universities. However, this research, by and large, relates to the areas of housing, employment, education and racial violence. Interestingly, the only relatively credible research that focuses on Pakistani communities in Scotland are three small studies. They include an MA dissertation on the Pakistani community in Glasgow by Elahi (1967); a paper on a Pakistani community in Dundee by Jones and

Davenport (1972); and another study on the aspects of the Asian community (mainly Pakistani) in Glasgow by Strivastava (1975). However, none of these studies involve an in-depth analysis of the social organisation and social institutional structures of the Pakistani communities in Scotland. As far as the study of social control or deviance is concerned, there is no single study on these subjects in Scotland and in the United Kingdom as a whole. This is confirmed by the most recent Social Sciences Citation Index (S.S.C.I). All this clearly points to a gap in the existing body of knowledge about the social institutional structures of the Scottish Pakistani communities, their social and normative orders, and the way(s) such orders are maintained. The present study of social control and deviance in a south Asian (Pakistani) community in Scotland is a small step in the direction of filling the existing gap.

As its title suggests, this book is divided into two main parts: Social Control (Part One) and Deviance (Part Two). Part One deals with the historical development of the Pakistani community in Scotland, its social organisation and the way(s) its various social institutions operate as agencies of social control. In Part One, the analysis of the various processes and mechanisms of social control is preceded by a general introductory chapter that provides a structural framework for the book. This chapter, after describing the historical and demographic background of the Pakistani community in Scotland with a special focus on Edinburgh, examines the reaction of the wider Scottish society to the presence of the South Asian migrants since their arrival in Scotland. The extent of discrimination against these 'coloured' migrants, and their exclusion from the social, cultural and political life of the wider society is examined in the light of empirical evidence. The central questions that follow from this discussion are: what are the implications of these exclusionary practices for the Pakistani population of Edinburgh? And what are the social responses of Edinburgh's Pakistanis to the exclusion and discrimination that they experience in the host society?

After attempting to answer the first question, the concept of 'community' is examined from a theoretical point of view. It is asserted that Edinburgh's Pakistani population see themselves as members of a Pakistani community on three different levels: sometimes, they identify themselves with the wider Pakistani/Muslim community, on a national level; on other occasions they identify with and refer to the local Pakistani community as 'us' on an intermediate local city or town level; occasionally Pakistanis in Edinburgh more closely relate to each other as a community on a narrower kinship or *Biraderi* level. Thus the phrase 'Edinburgh's Pakistani community', in this book, may refer to any or all of these three levels depending on the context of analysis. However, it is used to refer more directly and frequently to the level of community that is between the local level (all Pakistanis in Edinburgh) and the narrower level of *Biraderi*. It refers to the participants and also to the institutional arrangements of the Pilrig Mosque and Community Centre, where the majority of Edinburgh's Pakistani residents socially interact, exhibit a sense of community and social belonging, and have common social bonds (See Chapter I, Section III). Following this definition, a strong reactive element in the development of this particular community is emphasised. This analysis that describes Edinburgh's Pakistani community as a 'closed' community deals with the second of the two questions - responses to exclusion

Discussion of the historical and demographic background of Edinburgh's Pakistani community and the social processes that have led to its development into a relatively stable and cohesive social group raises a central question: how is this community socially organised, and how is its social order produced and maintained?

The question of the maintenance of order is essentially a question of social control. In the light of the intellectual history of the notion of social control, it is operationally defined in the context of Edinburgh's Pakistani community as the extent to which the community's social institutions promote order and regulate behaviour through the social bonding of members to its moral and social order.

To try to answer the central question about social order and its maintenance in the community, Chapters II and III examine the fundamental social institutions of Edinburgh's Pakistani community and the ways they operate as agencies of social control. These social institutions or agencies of social control are: the family, the *Biraderi* (social network of kinship/friendship relationship), the mosque, and the Pakistan Association, Edinburgh and the East of Scotland (P.A.E.E.S.).

In Chapter II the Pakistani family in Edinburgh, particularly its major mechanisms of social control, form the main focus of discussion. This discussion examines the socialisation process of the British-born Pakistani children and its role in these children's social bonding to the moral and social order of the community. The discussion is further extended to the relationships between 'parental authority' and the socialisation process. The main question that is asked is: how do the two separately and conjointly operate as mechanisms of social control within the Pakistani family in Edinburgh?

Just as the Pakistani family provides a fundamental social framework for close relationships among parents, children and some other close relatives, the *Biraderi* constitutes such a framework for social relationships among kin and friends on a broader level. Thus, the process of the social bonding of members of the community to its social and moral order is further examined in the context of the *Biraderi*. *Lina Dina* (taking and giving), or a form of institutionalised reciprocity among kin and friends that creates and recreates mutual moral and social obligations among both donors and recipients, constitutes the central theme of discussion. It is argued that it is within the communitarian social structure of the *Biraderi* where members are interdependent and have obligations to one another that *Izzet* and *Bizati* (Honour and Dishonour) operate as important mechanisms of social control. The main point of analysis in this context is why and how do *Izzet* and *Bizati* operate as effective mechanisms of social control in Edinburgh's Pakistani community?

The processes of the social bonding of the community's members within the family and the *Biraderi* further extends and finds practical expressions in the mosque and in the P.A.E.E.S. The context of such processes in the mosque is basically moral and spiritual where religious education/preaching and collective worship operate as major mechanisms of social bonding of the members to a shared and sacred moral order. *Sabaq* (Mosque-based Islamic education) and its role in the socialisation of the British-born Pakistani children in the Islamic belief system and rituals forms the focus of discussion. The main point of analysis is the implication of this religious socialisation of the young Pakistanis for their active participation in the collective worship, ceremonies and rituals of the community. At this point the discussion extends to the collective expression of shared Islamic beliefs in the congregational prayers of *Jom'a* (Friday) and *Eid* (the Islamic festival that marks the first day after the fasting month of *Ramadan*). The main question that is examined is: how and to what extent do congregational worship and its related rituals lead to the creation of a sense of a moral community among members, and what are the implications of this for social control?

The P.A.E.E.S, which is responsible for the general organisation of the social, cultural, educational and religious activities within Edinburgh's Pakistani community, and which represents the community to the outside world, is the fourth social institution that is examined as an agency of social control; it is viewed, in the present study, as a semi-formal agency of social control of the community. The organisational structure of the P.A.E.E.S. and its leaders' bases of power are descriptively examined. The main question concerning social control that is examined is: what are the main spheres of the exercise of authority by the leaders of the P.A.E.E.S., and what are its limits?

What has been so far said constitutes a general introduction to the first part of the book - social control - in Edinburgh's Pakistani community. The second part of the book is concerned with deviance. The two parts of the book are as closely connected to each other as social control and deviance are. Social control and deviance are considered two fundamental aspects of social organisation: social control defines what deviance is, and specifies how it should be dealt with (see Black 1976 : 105). In the context of the present study, the family, the mosque, the *Biraderi* and the P.A.E.E.S. define what is 'right' and what is 'wrong'; what is 'morality' and what is 'immorality', what is 'normality' and what is 'deviance'; and what behaviour is to be sanctioned positively (rewarded) and what negatively (punished).

Thus the second part of the book examines what the community's agencies of social control define as deviance. Deviance (as a sociological category) is examined in a sample of sixty British-born Pakistani boys who regularly attended their *Sabaq*-classes in a mosque/community centre that is situated on Pilrig Street, in the Leith area of Edinburgh (I shall refer to these boys as 'The Pilrig Boys', or 'The Pilrig sample' throughout this book). The bulk of this part of the book deals with the theoretical and empirical examination of deviance in the Pilrig sample. However, prior to the theoretical and empirical analysis of deviance in Chapters V and VI, Chapter IV gives a general introductory and descriptive account of the Pilrig Boys and their deviance. Following a description of the general 'sample characteristics', the main question that is examined is: what is deviance in the social and normative context of the present study?

After the examination of deviance from a theoretical point of view, it is defined as violation of the social norms of Edinburgh's Pakistani community by its members. In the context of the Pilrig sample, deviance and its various degrees are determined on the basis of the frequency of violation of seven fundamental norms of the mosque-school and the Pakistani community that are applicable to the behaviour of young people. Analysis of the quantitative data about the frequency of violation of these norms by individual boys demonstrates a continuum of four degrees of deviance in the Pilrig sample – from the least to the most deviant boys. In the light of ethnographic data about every individual boy in each of the four categories, the continuum is further developed into a four-fold typology of the Pilrig boys: conformists, accommodationists, part-time conformists, and rebels. Although individuals in each of the four categories deviated to various degrees from the norms/rules of the mosque-school and the community, it is argued that boys in the first two categories are considered in the Pakistani community of Edinburgh as 'non-deviants'; boys in the last two are considered as 'deviants'. This typology is further supported by the results of self-reported delinquency data. These results, based on data collected by the use of a self-reported delinquency scale, show strong positive correlations between the frequency of 'breaking windows/damaging property', 'leaving a cafe without paying', 'theft of more than £5' and the level of deviance in the Pilrig sample. There are weak positive correlations between the frequency of 'using force or its threat for getting money or other valuables' and of 'participation in group fight' and the level of deviance. However, the frequency of 'knocking someone down on purpose' is not correlated with the degree of **deviance** among the Pilrig boys. (However, as a main focus of the present study is deviance - a sociological category - self-reported delinquency data are not used in this book.)

In order to explain deviance in the Pilrig sample of deviant and non-deviant boys, Travis Hirschi's (1969) version of social control theory is used as a theoretical framework for the present study. According to this theory an individual is more likely to get involved in crime and deviance when his/her social bond to the conventional order of society/community is weak or broken. Social bond, Hirschi argues, consists of four fundamental elements. They are: attachment, commitment, involvement, and belief. The central hypothesis is that the less attached, committed, involved and believing individual is more likely to break the rules and norms of the society/community.

Thus, Chapter V deals with the empirical examination of Attachment, defined as an individual's emotional involvement in (significant) others and therefore sensitivity to their feelings, wishes and expectations. The main question that is examined is: is attachment to parents, teachers and (conventional) friends related to deviance in the Pilrig sample? In addition, relationships between various forms of parental supervision and discipline ('too strict', 'moderate', 'neglectful') and deviance in the Pilrig sample are analysed in this chapter.

Chapter VI deals with the empirical examination of relationships between the other three elements of the social bond – Commitment, Involvement, Belief – and deviance among the sixty Pilrig boys. Commitment is defined as an individual's investment in conventional behaviour. Thus, the following question is the focus of analysis in this context: are scholastic performance, family *Izzet* (honour), and aspirations for higher/professional education related to deviance among the Pilrig Boys?

Involvement is defined as an individual's participation in conventional activities - the extent of an individual's engrossment in doing legitimate activities so that he/she has no opportunity for committing criminal/deviant acts. The question that is examined in the second part of Chapter VI is: do spending time on homework, participation in school-related and on Mosque/community-related activities, and the 'feeling of nothing to do', have any relationship with deviance among the Pilrig Boys?

Belief, which is understood as the individual's sense of the moral validity of society/community's norms, and its links with deviance in the Pilrig sample is the subject of analysis in the last part of this chapter. The main question that is examined is: does belief in Islamic teachings, in the moral values of society, and feeling of guilt (after behaving dishonestly) control deviance among the Pilrig Boys?

The relationships between each of the four elements of the social bond are then statistically examined. The statistical results of the quantitative data are, in many cases, complemented by and interpreted in the light of qualitative data.

Finally, the major findings of both parts of the book are summarised and concluded. The interconnections between the various institutional mechanisms of social control within Edinburgh's Pakistani community are explored and illustrated. These illustrations show that certain mechanisms of social control play more central part in maintaining the social and normative order of Edinburgh's Pakistani community than others. Likewise the relative strength of relationships between the various indices of the four elements of the social bond and deviance in the Pilrig sample are illustrated and compared. The comparisons reveal that certain social control variables are more effective in controlling deviance among the Pilrig boys than others. The overall conclusion of the book clearly suggest that social control and social deviance are inextricably interlinked as two fundamental aspects of the social organisation of Edinburgh's Pakistani community.

PART ONE: SOCIAL CONTROL

Introduction to Part One

This introduction examines a general intellectual history and theoretical background of the notion of social control. It will focus mainly on the contributions of macrosociology and social psychology to the general theory of social control which have dominated the debate over the subject for more than one hundred years.

Although the notion of 'social control', as a sociological concept on its own right, entered sociological theory only about the turn of the century, it had been central to the thinking of most 'Classical' social theorists, in an indirect way. Most 19th century sociologists when discussing 'social order' – the most central problem of sociology – also discussed its maintenance. These sociologists, in attempting to explain how patterns of social relationships developed and formed the whole (society), at the same time gave detailed explanations of how the whole was maintained (social control). Maine's categories of 'Status and Contract' (1861), Tonnies' 'Gemeinschaft and Gesellschaft' (1887) and Durkheim's 'Mechanical and Organic Solidarity' (1984 [1893]) offer a few examples.

It was after the publication of Edward Alswarth Ross's *Social Control* in 1901 that the notion and concept of social control directly entered sociological theory and became one of sociology's central themes. The question that Ross endeavoured to answer was not different, in essence, from that of mainstream Classical social theory – the possibility of society and its orderly functioning. Ross (1901 : 3) wondered how men and women 'are brought to live closely together and associate their efforts with that degree of harmony that we see about us'.

For Ross this was possible through 'Social control' which he described as 'Intended social ascendancy'. 'Social ascendancy' refers to the various processes and mechanisms whereby society attains a superordinate position over the individual and moulds his/her feelings, desires and attitudes in accordance to its conventional rules and expectations. Ross (1901 : 320) gave detailed descriptions of the various means of social control that he also called 'Engines of social control'. According to Ross the principal means of social control are : 'Public opinion', 'Law', 'Belief', 'Social suggestion', 'Education', 'Custom', 'Social Religion', 'Personality', 'Ideals', 'Ceremony', 'Art', 'Enlightenment', 'Illusion', 'Social evaluations', and certain 'Ethical' elements. Most of these 'Engines of social control' that are by and large externally exercised over the individual contain strong elements of coercion.

Although Ross's list indicates that coercion is only one possibility, the rest of his other 'means' of social control are also 'external' to the individual. Normative considerations, persuasion, suggestion, social and psychological manipulation and the actual use of force and coercion are all forms of 'external control': they are designed to subject the individual to society's conventional norms/rules. 'Self-control' or 'Internal control' mechanisms have only a marginal place in Ross's work. Ross concedes that social control is more effective when it is 'diffused' and takes place spontaneously from within the individual. But he does not explain how the mechanisms of 'internal control' operate.

It appears that the centrality of 'social ascendancy' in Ross's theory of social control is based on his basic assumption about human nature. Ross (1901 : 5) says that, 'It is a common delusion that order is to be explained by the person's inherited equipment for good conduct, rather than by any control that society exercised over him'. Ross implies that human nature is constituted by the individual's (selfish) complex of drives and impulses. In order to ensure a degree of harmony and order among the conflicting desires and impulses of individuals in society, the latter has to control them (mainly) externally.

In the last part of his classic work, *Social Control*, Ross explains that how the various 'means' in his broad list of social control mechanisms can be linked to what he refers to as a 'system of social control'. For Ross, the various means of social control complement each other. He defends the broadness of his list as sufficiently varied and elastic to suit different situations and differed social groups. Moreover, Ross asserts that this can explain the degree of social control, in terms of 'more' or 'less', 'strong' or 'weak' and 'rigid' or 'elastic', in various societies.

Ross's interest in 'external control' to regulate and mould the individual's desires and feelings according to society's expectations and rules was also shared by his contemporary, the prominent sociologist William Graham Sumner. Five years after the publication of Ross's *Social Control*, Sumner in his famous work *Folkways* (1906 : iii-iv) asserted that 'Folkways are habits and customs of the society, . . . Then they become regulative and imperative for succeeding generations, . . . While they are in vigour, they very largely control individual and social undertakings'. Sumner maintains that all social norms exercise coercive power over the individual and control his/her conduct. He further explains that their degree of coercion varies according to the degree of the centrality of the various forms of these norms to the orderly functioning and well-being of the community/society. For example, the relatively peripheral norms that Sumner calls 'Folkways' encounter only mild sanctions for their non-observance. But 'Mores' that are relatively more central to the well-being of community/society are enforced by more stringent sanctions when they are infringed. Finally, core societal 'values' and beliefs that are the most central for the well-being and even survival of society invoke the most severe sanctions when violated. Sumner adds that it is because of the vital importance of societal core values/beliefs for the well-being of society that most of them often become formal legal norms - laws.

Sumner, like Ross, views social control as society's regulative mechanism 'external' to the individual and largely controlling conduct from without. However, unlike Ross, Sumner argues that society's social control mechanisms are not intentionally designed to control the individual's conduct – social norms emerge naturally out of the needs of social groups for their social functioning and survival; even most legal norms, he argues, first emerge as social norms, outside the domain of the state.

Other prominent social theorists and philosophers have placed even stronger emphasis than Ross and Sumner on the regulative mechanisms of social control from without (external social control) in particular Roscoe Pound. For Pound, the individual's conduct is primarily and largely regulated by society's controls and constraints so that it suits the needs and expectations of the social order:

> The pressure upon each man brought to bear by his fellowmen in order to constrain him to do his part upholding civilised society and to deter him from anti-social conduct, that is, conduct at variance with the postulates of social order. (Pound 1942: 17-18)

Pound's use of legally orientated terminology not only implies that social control is basically legal control, but he explicitly states in his influential work, *Social Control Through Law* (1942:20-25) that 'In the modern world, law has become the paramount agency of social control.. Social control is primarily the function of the state.'.

Despite the fact that Pound's assertion has been criticised as an exaggeration by many legal anthropologists and sociologists of law, his work has greatly influenced modern legal theory and jurisprudence. This is not the place to go into the controversy over this subject, it is sufficient to say that social control, for Pound, is mainly 'External control'.

The works of Pound, Sumner and Ross and their emphasis on external social control mechanisms to regulate individual and social undertakings and to maintain social order have greatly influenced the modern sociology of social control. However, they failed to explain how 'External controls' were incorporated into the individual's personality; how individual conduct comes to be (to a significant extent) controlled from within through 'internal control' mechanisms. These scholars' fundamental assumptions about the superordinating role of society over the individual are criticised as 'one-sided' and deficient.

The macro sociology of social control of Ross, Sumner and Pound was particularly criticised after the popularity of the works of Charles Harton Cooley and George Herbert Mead – the two founding fathers of modern social psychology. Cooley and Mead both rejected the idea of separation between the individual and society, and therefore the 'social ascendancy' of the latter over the former. Mead profoundly shared Cooley's view (1909 : 350) that 'individual and society were twin-born'. Known as 'Social inter-actionists', Cooley and Mead believed that the individual and society continuously interacted in a two-way-relationships. In the process of their social interaction the individual projects himself/herself to the surrounding social environment, affecting those in the very process of projection who, at the same time, affect him/her. The two are involved in a process of reciprocal relationships that spontaneously produces and reproduces social order and, at the same time maintains it. More importantly, this process may also involve revolt against some existing social norms. Thus, social control for Cooley and Mead does not only involve processes that both produce and maintain social order but the same processes move the vehicle of social change.

Cooley's three influential works, *Human Nature and Social Order* (1902), *Social Organisation* (1909), and *Social Process* (1918) emerged after Ross's *Social Control* (1901). In none of these three books did Cooley directly formulate a theory of social control or even much use the term. However, he indirectly addressed the question of how internalisation of society's values and norms by its individual members resulted in the maintenance of social order.

Central to Cooley's view of social control is his concept of 'Social self' to which he also referred as 'Social feelings' or the 'looking-glass self'. For Cooley the 'Looking-glass self' develops in three phases of the individual's social interaction with society: the first phase involves the individual's appearance to other persons in his/her surrounding social environment such as the family, the peer-group and, in a general vague sense, to the whole society. In the second phase the other persons judge the individual as they appear - approval or disapproval, admiration or contempt, like or dislike etc. In the third phase the individual takes on the judgements of the other persons and develops a feeling about his/her 'Looking-glass self'. It is the development of one's looking-glass or social self that places one in another person's mind, and one thus enters a state with the other which Cooley (1902:102) calls 'Communion'. Thus, living in each other's mind, so to speak, operates as a powerful mechanism of 'internal control' over the conduct of the individual in society. The most suitable social contexts for the development of Cooley's 'Social self' are what he calls 'Primary groups' – individuals' familiar associations, i.e. the family, peer group, neighbourhood.

The ideal that grows up in a familiar situation may be said to be part of human nature itself. In the most general form it is that part of a moral whole or community wherein individual minds are merged and the higher capacities of the members find total and adequate expression. And it grows up because familiar associations fill our minds with imaginations of the thoughts and feelings of other members of the group, and the group as a whole, so that for many purposes, we really make them a part of ourselves and identify our self-feeling with them (Cooley 1909 : 23).

Thus, according to Cooley's theory, social control operates spontaneously from within the individual. He explains a social-psychological process that operates as an inexpensive but powerful mechanism of social control.

Cooley's view of social control as an internal social-psychological mechanism that operates in the process of the individual's social interaction with the society is profoundly shared by George Herbert Mead (1925; 1934). For Mead the 'self' developed in two phases of the individual's social interaction with the community/society. These two phases are identified as the 'I' and the 'Me'. The 'Me' represents what Mead called the attitude of the 'Generalised Other' – of other persons in the community/society. The 'I' represents the response of the individual to the attitudes of the 'Generalised Other'. 'Self' emerges in the process of the 'fusion' between the 'I': and the 'Me' that in turn results in the entrance of the community into the individual's 'mind'. This process produces and reproduces the social order and operates as an important mechanism of social control:

> It is in the form of the generalised other that the social process influences the behaviour of the individuals involved in it and carrying it on, i.e., that the community exercises control over the conduct of its individual members; for it is in this form that the social process or the community enters as a determining factor into the individual's thinking. (Mead 1934 : 155)

Mead implies that the community places itself as a determining factor only in 'the individual's thinking'; it does not necessarily, determine his/her behaviour in an intended direction. That is the individual does not take the attitude of the 'generalised other' for granted. The 'reflexiveness' that the 'Me' and the 'I' brings to the emergence of the 'self' requires that before the individual takes on the attitude of the 'Generalised Other' (the community/society), he/she examines and judges it. Then the individual's response comes as an 'I' that is both 'object' and 'subject', at once, affected by the community, and affecting it, at the same time. Thus far from being shaped and conditioned by the attitude of the 'generalised other', the individual and the society are both actively involved in producing and in maintaining the social order. More importantly, the 'individuality' of the individual is a fundamental aspect of the process of social control, as nicely put by Mead:

> Social control, so far from tending to crash out the human individual or obliterate his self-conscious individuality is, on the contrary, constitutive of and inextricably associated with that individuality; for the individual is what he is, as a conscious and individual personality, just as he is a member of society, involved in the social process of experience and activity, and thereby socially controlled by it. (Mead 1934 : 255)

What has been so far been said about the general theory of social control, clearly indicates that, unlike Ross, Sumner, Pound and their followers, who defined social control as the super-ordination of society over the individual, for Mead and Cooley it is a two way relationship: a reciprocal relationship between the individual and society in the process of which the two actively create the social order and simultaneously develop mechanisms for maintaining it. Mead however, places even more emphasis than does Cooley over the creative and active role of the individual in the process of his/her social interaction with society. Mead's theory of the 'Self' is, in fact, a refinement of Cooley's formulation of the development of 'Social self'.

While the 'internal' mechanisms of social control have been studied by other well known scholars such as Jean Piaget, John Devey, Sigmund Freud and even by Emile Durkheim, Cooley and Mead's contributions dominate contemporary debate on the subject. However, it must be said that Cooley and Mead largely ignored the elements of inequality and imbalance in the relationship between individuals and the individual and the social order. Development of the 'self' in the process of social interaction between individuals and society cannot be satisfactorily explained without the considerations of power relationships in this very process. Power may rarely manifest as a factual force in social relationships in modern (or post-modern) society. But it is vigorously at work in political and economic terms, and more importantly through manipulative means. By the latter, I mean the power of propaganda, modern advertisement and of the general mass-media that exercise invisible control over individuals. It is a form of 'latent' control: we may not be aware that our minds are 'invaded' and our wills covertly and skilfully manipulated, and, hence, controlled.

What has been said so far shows that despite certain theoretical advances regarding the concept (and notion) of social control in the past hundred years, problems of its generality and complexity remain unresolved. The overlapping relationship among the forms, kinds, agencies, mechanisms and instruments of social control, and even whether the concept is viewed and studied as an independent, or dependent variable (or both) add both to the complexity and even vagueness of the notion. Likewise the multi-dimensional and overlapping relationship between social order and social control make it hard to draw a clear-cut dividing line between the two.

All this has led students of the sociology of social control to acknowledge the complexity of the notion and the lack of a definitive understanding of the concept of social control. One prominent scholar, Stanley Cohen (1985 :2) commented that the concept of social control has become 'something of Mickey Mouse concept'. Indeed, social control (both as a concept and a notion) is currently interpreted in different ways in different academic disciplines, and is utilised for a variety of purposes (see Gorwich 1945; Janovitz 1975; Meir 1982; Edwards 1988; Krienken 1991).

Nevertheless, empirical research on social control could significantly contribute towards the refinement of the general theory and towards making more clear-cut distinctions among the various overlapping aspects of the notion. Thus, I would suggest that social researchers, in order to reach more concrete conclusions, must bear three fundamental points in mind: first, the researcher must specify whether he/she studies social control as a dependent variable (as a reaction to deviant behaviour); or as an independent variable (as a kind of influence and the extent to which it has an impact on human behaviour); or both (as a process that basically operates as an influence but is readily activated against deviant behaviour should it take place) (see Gibbs 1981 Ch. 6: Black 1984 : 4-6). Second, the various levels of social control-*macro*, *intermediate* or *micro* - must be distinguished. That is, whether social control is studied on the level of a society, community, or on a primary group's level (for example, social control in a family). Third, and most importantly, the researcher must specify the social context of and pay considerable attention to the type of social organisation in which he/she studies social control. Since social control is a fundamental aspect of social organisation, it is crucial for the researcher to pay specific attention to the type of organisation in which social control operates. Here we can draw on the work of Amitai Etzioni.

In his influential work, *A Comparative Analysis of Complex Organisations* (1964) Etzioni categorises social organisations according to their predominant compliance patterns into three fundamental types: 'coercive', 'utilitarian' and 'normative' organisations. In 'coercive' organisation, according to Etzioni, the predominant means of social control is factual force or its threat over the subordinate participants. This type of organisation may have different 'manifest' aims but their 'latent' (and actual) aim is to keep the participants in. Chief examples of coercive organisations are: concentration camps, prisons, correctional institutions and prisoner-of-war camps. An important feature of coercive organisations is the 'behavioural conformity' of participants as opposed to 'attitudinal conformity'. The second refers to conformity that is based on internal conviction and a sense of moral obligation, whereas the first form is largely ensured through the use or threat of force (see Merton 1959, Rose Laub Coser 1961). Since very little internalisation of norms takes place in a coercive organisational setting the participants (actually inmates) would leave, if they were not constrained.

In 'utilitarian' organisations, lower and even middle-ranking participants are predominantly controlled through remuneration, mainly in terms of material rewards. Examples are most capitalist organisations that employ various categories of white-collar, professional and blue-collar workers. The participants predominantly exhibit 'behavioural conformity' to organisational rules/norms; some high-ranking and well-established participants may exhibit 'attitudinal conformity' too. Thus social control in 'utilitarian' organisation is largely dependent on the rewards that the lower and middle-ranking participants receive.

In contrast to both 'coercive' and 'utilitarian' organisations, in 'normative' organisations social control operates mainly through the internalisation of norms and moral/ideological commitment. Religious/cultural organisations, ideologically orientated political parties, and some voluntary organisations are some examples. Because participants internalise the norms/rules of the organisation, their conformity is 'attitudinal' (and behavioural too) because it springs from their inner convictions and beliefs.

Despite the fact that there is a degree of overlap between the three types of organisations, and between their corresponding forms of social control, the typology provides a very useful framework for empirical research projects, particularly about the study of a specific form of social control in a specific organisational setting. It guides the researcher to specify the organisational context of social control, its forms, agencies, and mechanisms.

Thus, in the light of Etzioni's typology Edinburgh's Pakistani community is a 'normative' organisation; it is basically a cultural/religious community whose participants (or members) are socially bonded to each other by their shared values, traditions and beliefs. Therefore, internalisation of community's values, beliefs and norms operates as the predominant (though not the only) form of social control within it; and the main patterns of compliance to the community's norms are 'attitudinal'. Within this particular organisational setting, agencies of social control and the various mechanisms in each agency are clearly identifiable.

With this specification of the fundamental aspects of social control, it is now more possible to define social control, operationally within the 'normative' organisational context of Edinburgh's Pakistani community. Social control in this specific community refers to: *the extent to which the community's social institutions (or agencies of social control) promote order and regulate behaviour through the social bonding of members/participants to its moral and social order.*

The above definition is commensurate with empirical observation. It not only applies to and suits the organisational setting of the community under study on an operational level it is also both comprehensive and inclusive on a theoretical level. The individual's social bonding and the regulation of his/her behaviour may take place in the process of social interaction, spontaneously resulting in the development of 'social self' and 'internal social control', as Cooley and Mead argued. At the same time the process of social bonding may be accompanied and/or backed-up by 'external controls' including social and psychological manipulation, positive and negative economic, social and religious sanctions and by factual coercion or threat of it, as argued by Ross, Sumner, Pound and other macro sociologists of social control.

Finally it must be mentioned that the concepts of social order and social control in the present study are looked at as two fundamental and closely interrelated aspects of social organisation. According to some writers the former refers to the relatively stable and established patterns of social relationships, and the latter to the processes and mechanisms that maintain the established patterns and the whole they form (see Young 1987). However, the two are not separated in the present study as they are inextricably interlinked in Edinburgh's Pakistani community.

After this lengthy but necessary theoretical introduction to the notion of social control, and defining it operationally in the context of the present study, it is now appropriate to examine the ways its various mechanisms contribute to the maintenance of social order in Edinburgh's Pakistani community. This examination will focus on the analysis of the fundamental social institutions of the community - the family, the *Biraderi*, the mosque, the P.A.E.E.S. - in Chapters II and III, but first, it is important to look at the historical development of these institutions (or agencies of social control) and the Pakistani community of Edinburgh as a whole in Chapter I.

1 Migration, Exclusion and the Making of a 'Closed' Community

Introduction

This chapter consists of three different but closely interrelated parts. In the first part the history of migration from the Indian sub-continent to Scotland and Britain since the late 19th century up to the present is traced. The large-scale migration from the Indian subcontinent to Great Britain is considered as the legacy of the latter's long colonial rule of the former. Then the size of the Pakistani population alongside other ethnic minority populations in Britain and in Scotland is numerically illustrated. In the light of the 1991 Census for Scotland, the distribution of Pakistani population in the various regions of the country with a special focus on the Lothian Region and Edinburgh city is statistically examined.

The response of the wider Scottish/British society to the presence of migrants from the Indian sub-continent since their arrival in the country is the theme of the second part of the chapter. In the light of documented historical evidence, it is argued that these immigrants were discriminated against and largely excluded from the social, cultural and political life of the wider society. This argument is followed and is supported by more recent empirical evidence: a substantive body of existing research shows that ethnic minority populations, particularly Pakistanis, in Scotland and in Britain have been largely excluded from the social, cultural and the political life of the wider society. Employment, housing, sports and social/cultural entertainment, politics and racial harassment are the main areas that are examined.

In the third and last part of the chapter the responses of the Pakistani population to their exclusion from the social, cultural and political life of the wider society is discussed. In the light of ethnographic evidence about Edinburgh's Pakistani population, it is argued that the latter have responded to their exclusion and sense of alienation from the wider society defensively: by drawing sharper and more dividing social boundaries which are reflections of an increasingly inward-looking community. This has led to the making of a 'closed' Pakistani community in Edinburgh – a small-scale society within the wider Scottish society. This argument is, furthermore, supported by the recent social and political events, eg. the Salman Rushdie affair, and the establishment of 'the Muslim Parliament of Great Britain' and their social consequences for Britain's Pakistani/Muslim community and its relationship with the wider British society.

I: Migration to Britain

Britain has long been a country of both emigration and migration. On the one hand, adventurers, curious discoverers and traders from the British Isles travelled to remote parts of the world. Some of them returned to Britain with interesting tales about other cultures, people and about the places they visited; a few even wrote extensively about the 'other cultures' and pioneered British Social Anthropology; others found the lands and the people they visited as promising places and 'partners' for trade and business; still other curious and brave adventurers from the British Isles were able to discover 'New World(s)' – the unknown continent of America. Thus, hundreds of men and women from the British Isles emigrated to America, Australia, Africa and Asia. In most of these parts of the world, people from the British Isles lived and worked as colonial rulers and soldiers, traders and permanent settlers. As I will discuss later in this chapter, it was mainly the British colonial connection with these lands, particularly with Africa and Asia which resulted in the mid-twentieth century large-scale migration to the British Isles.

On the other hand, the last five hundred years have also witnessed migration of various kinds of people, belonging to different cultures, religions and colours to the British Isles: the Flemings and Huguenots, the Irish, Jews from Spain and from Germany, Italians, Hungarians, Poles and other East-Europeans and more recently, migrants from the New Commonwealth countries (India, Pakistan, Bangladesh, Hong Kong, Africa and the West Indies).

The bulk of the later category of migrants in Britain came from British colonies/ex-colonies; they were mainly brought to Britain as 'migrant labourers' after the second world war, particularly during the late 1950s and 1960s. Unlike the bulk of the first category of migrants to Britain, those who belong to the later category are predominantly 'coloured', non-Christian and of non-European cultural background. Interestingly, it is only people who belong to the later group of migrants in Britain who are officially referred to as 'migrants' and members of 'ethnic' and 'racial' groups!

According to the most recent government census (1991), 5.5 percent of the British resident population belong to 'ethnic' groups (other than 'white'). The remaining 94.5 percent belong to the white group. Table 1 shows the exact numbers and percentages of Britain's ethnic minority groups.

According to Table 1 the largest ethnic minority group in Britain is Indian; this forms 1.5 percent of the total population, or 27.9 percent of the total ethnic minority population. The second largest ethnic minority groups in Britain is the Black Caribbean, forming 0.9 percent of the total population and 16.6 percent of the whole ethnic groups population, the Pakistanis

Table 1 - 1991 Census: Resident Ethnic Population – Great Britain

Ethnic Group	Number (thousands)	% of total population	% of population in 'Other Groups'
All Groups	54,889	100.0	n/a
White	51,874	94.5	n/a
Other Groups	3,015	5.5	100.0
Black Caribbean	500	0.9	16.6
Black African	212	0.4	7.0
Black Other	178	0.3	5.9
Black Total	891	1.6	29.5
Indian	840	1.5	27.9
Pakistani	477	0.9	15.8
Bangladeshi	163	0.3	5.4
Chinese	157	0.3	5.2
Other Groups - Asian	198	0.4	6.6
Other - (non-Asian)	290	0.5	9.6

Source: 'Population Trends' (1993:13): No. 72, Office of the Population Census and Services (OPCS)

constitute the third largest ethnic group in Britain: 0.9 percent of the total British population and 15.8 percent percent of the ethnic minority population as a whole. As the present research is about a Pakistani community in Scotland, I will go into the details of Scotland's Pakistani population and their geographical distribution in various regions, in later pages. First, it is important to look at the history of migration from the Indian sub-continent to Scotland.

A Brief History of Migration from the Indian Sub-continent to Scotland

The relatively recent history of overseas migration to Scotland is very similar to what was briefly mentioned earlier about migration to Britain in general. This particularly applies to the large-scale overseas migrations during the 18th and 19th centuries to this country. During these two centuries significant numbers of Irish, Jews, Italians, Lithuanians, and Poles migrated to both England and to Scotland. These predominantly European migrants who settled in Scotland have largely assimilated into the wider Scottish society and are not officially considered as members of specific ethnic minority groups at present. Similarly the bulk of migrants from the new commonwealth countries, (both those from the Indian sub-continent and from Africa), from China and Hong Kong, Africa and from the Caribbean to England and Scotland took place almost at the same period: late 1950s and 1960s.

As was pointed out the origin of large-scale migration from the Indian sub-continent to Scotland is closely linked with the long British colonial rule of the Indian sub-continent that had a strong Scottish connection (see Cage 1985; Muirhead 1986; Cain 1986; Miles and Dunlop 1987; Dunlop 1988; Armstrong 1989; Maan 1992). Most of the first Indian migrants (from India, Pakistan and Bangladesh, as these were all one country until August 1947) came to Scotland mainly as colonial seamen with the (British) East India Company; others were brought as servants by the returning British military and political officers in India, and later as indentured wage-labourers by British industrial companies. Some of the seamen who were poorly paid and ill-treated by their officers on board ships escaped after the arrival of their ships at the Scottish ports of Edinburgh, Glasgow and Dundee (see Visram 1986; Dunlop & Miles 1990; Maan 1992). Then they stayed in the Scottish cities and searched for work. Since the Indian seamen were British subjects they had the right to stay in Scotland temporarily, and even permanently. The pattern of leaving the ships was gradually followed by many more seamen. It is assumed that by mid 19th century a sizeable number of Indian (ex-) seamen lived in Scottish port-cities. Salter, a British missionary, documented the presence of Indians in Scotland and England in the second half of the 19th century:

> At this time [c. 1871] about 250 Asiatics . . were constantly visiting in the provincial towns. . . . These disciples of the prophet of Mecca wander from Plymouth to Ben Lomond and from Aberdeen to Hastings. (Salter 1873 : 221)

The phrase 'disciples of the prophet of Mecca' in the above passage indicates that the Indians that Salter visited were Muslims (probably from the predominantly Muslim part of India which is now Pakistan and Bangladesh). Salter (1873) also mention the presence of these Indians in the major Scottish cities of Glasgow and Edinburgh. It is documented that the Indians in large Scottish cities were accommodated in special residential centres that were called 'sailors' homes'. Probably the first of such 'homes' was situated in Broomie Law area, in the centre of Glasgow, during the second half of the 19th century. For example, the tenth 'Annual Report Of The Glasgow Sailors' Home' (1867) said that: 'the conduct of the seaman has been as satisfactory as it could be expected, taking into account the vicious influences of the shore.' The report suggests that these Indians lived a kind of institutional life at this time, and were yet to develop their own relatively independent individual and community life.

Another category of Indians who lived at this period in Scotland were servants; they were brought to the country by high-ranking Scottish colonial political and military officers in India. Though no documented evidence about the presence of Indian servants (as a separate category) in Scotland appears to be available, it is, however, recorded that Indian servants were brought from India to Scotland. For example, the author of 'Continental and Colonial Servants in the Eighteenth Century' writes that:

> High civil and military officials who had acquired wealth in service of the East India Company returned home to establish themselves in luxury and splendour, and carried native servants with them. (Hetch 1954:52)

The above passage indicates, by implication, that the Indian servants did live in Scotland. Maan (1992 : 83-84) suggests that the apparent lack of documented evidence about the presence of this category of Indian residents in Scotland may be due to their relatively smaller number and also of their scatteredness throughout Scotland. Therefore, they might have converted to Christianity, married local women and were consequently absorbed by the wider society. Maan adds that it is equally possible for these servants to have joined the then existent groups of Indians, after the end of their contracts or the death of their masters. Then, because of the similarity of the features of the servants and the seamen, they all might have been called Indian seamen - a well known category.

These former Indian seamen and servants worked hard to enter the Scottish labour market. Some of them worked as unskilled wage labourers in the large Scottish cities; others did some 'odd jobs', and still few others begged on the streets of Edinburgh and Glasgow. A few of these Indian residents in Scotland were able to afford to rent cheap property; they converted the rented premises into lodging/boarding houses. The houses that were situated close to each other were used for the accommodation of most of the Indian residents in the Scottish major city ports; they were also used for the accommodation of other Indians who were in transit. These houses gradually started becoming small colonies of the Indian residents, (see Maan 1992 : 85-86). However the emergence of relatively stable and independent Indian communities in the major Scottish cities had yet to emerge.

In the aftermath of the abolition of slavery in 1834, thousands of Indians were recruited as indentured labourers in India and were then transferred to other British colonies such as South Africa, Trinidad, Mauritius and Fiji. While the overwhelming majority of these labourers were sent to the British colonies, some of them were also brought to Scotland and England to serve the booming British industry at that time. Many of these indentured labourers did not return home; instead they joined the former Indian seamen and servants who worked as unskilled labourers in Scotland's open labour mar-

ket. This development significantly increased the size of the already existing small colonies of Indian residents in Scotland, particularly in Edinburgh
and Glasgow. The Indians, or in Salter's words the 'Asiatics' and their small
'colonies' became part of the Scottish city life. Some of the Indians even
became well-known persons among the local people. The well known Indian
residents in Edinburgh at this time were Roshan Khan, Khuda Baksh,
Sheikh Roshan and Mir Jan. Interestingly these names indicate that all the
four Indians were Muslims. The most famous of Edinburgh's Indian residents, however, was Roshan Khan about whom Salter wrote:

> A well known character, and long-resident at the Scottish capital. He has
> long-enjoyed the fame of supplying savour pipes to the lovers of smoke;
> and he attends the High Street near the Castle Hill, every Friday for that
> purpose . . . I entered his room one September evening . . . and call it a
> room only because he was found there, for it was occupied by twenty
> others as destitute as him. (Salter 1873 : 235)

The arrival and the subsequent residence of native Indian students (other
than the sons and daughters of British civil and military officers in India) in
the early 1880s was an important development that contributed a great deal
to the organisation of the small 'colonies' of Indian residents in Glasgow
and Edinburgh. Most of the native Indian students attended the University
of Edinburgh to study medicine; some of these students attended the universities of Glasgow and St. Andrews as well. With only six members, the
Indian students at Edinburgh University, founded the first 'Indian Students'
Society' (now called the 'Edinburgh Indian Students Association'). The
main aim of Indian Students Society was to look after the wider interests of
their fellow students. The society looked after the general welfare of their
fellow students and also made arrangements for the provision of Indian food
for them. Moreover, the Indian students in Edinburgh took an active interest in the Indian National politics, especially in the campaign for the independence of India from the British rule.

What is of particular importance to the present discussion is that the
activities of the Indian Students' Society extended into the social and cultural life of the rest of Indian residents in Edinburgh and Glasgow. The students not only enriched the social and cultural life of these Indian residents
but they also contributed to the social organisation of their community. This
happened, particularly, when the students became part of this community
and worked as doctors after receiving their medical qualification. Although
many of these students returned to India at the end of their studies, the few
who remained became permanent members of the Indian small 'colonies in
Scotland.

The period between the two World Wars did not witness a noticeable

increase in the size of the Indian Colonies in Scotland. Except for some soldiers and seamen who fought on the British side in World War One and then
stayed in Scotland, the Indian Colonies remained almost static. This state of
affairs continued into the 1920s. According to Maan (1992 : 102) '. . . There
is no evidence of any settled Asian communities, outwith the *Laskar* [sea-
man] colonies in any of the cities before the mid 1920s'. Maan (1992 : 124)
further adds that this situation did not change until the end of the World War
Two. In the years immediately after World War Two, an increase in the number of Indian residents was noticeable. The newcomers mainly arrived in
Glasgow which became the centre of Indians in Scotland by this time. Most
of these Indians have been able to earn their living: some of them worked in
factories; a few worked as bus conductors in the major cities; but the
majority of the Indians were not able to find jobs. Therefore, they worked as
pedlars, or self-employed mobile door-to-door salesmen. The pedlars
mainly operated in Glasgow and in its surroundings; some of them also
worked in Edinburgh, Dundee and even in Aberdeen.

While the number of Indians in Scotland continued increasing and
reached a couple of hundred individuals by 1947, the 14th August of this
year witnessed a very important historical event: the independence of India
from Britain's colonial rule which simultaneously led to the formal separation of British India into the independent states of India and Pakistan. This
event not only altered the political relationships between India and Britain,
it also split the formerly Indian residents in Scotland and in Britain into two
groups: the Pakistanis and the Indians (the latter was further divided into
Hindu and Sikh groups). From this time onwards every one of the Pakistani,
Hindu and Sikh populations in Scotland and in the U.K. started emerging as
independent communities with their own social, religious and political institutions. Before entering into the details of the Pakistan population in
Scotland – the subject of the present research – it is essential to give some
details about the rapid increase of immigration to Britain from India and
Pakistan during the 1950s and 1960s.

The rapid increase of immigrants to Scotland and to Britain had been
generally influenced by both 'push factors' at home and by 'pull factors in
Great Britain. On the one hand, the mass migration and swapping of the
Muslim and Hindu populations between the newly independent states of
India and Pakistan caused many social and economic problems in both
countries. These problems forced many uprooted Indians and Pakistanis to
leave their new (but alien to them) countries to go to other places, particularly to Britain where they were allowed to migrate to without many restrictions. On the other hand, the relative economic boom of 1950s in Britain
created more jobs and opportunities for the recruitment of migrant labourers. The early migrants from the Indian sub-continent facilitated the migration of their kin and friends from India and Pakistan to Scotland by sending

them air tickets and providing them ad hoc accommodation in Scotland. According to Maan (1992:162) the total number of Indian and Pakistani residents in Scotland by 1960 reached about 4,000 individuals.

However, one of the most crucial phases in the history of migration from the Indian sub-continent, and indeed from the rest of the New Commonwealth countries to Scotland and to Britain, was between April 1961 and June 1962. The 1962 Immigration Act practically put an end to the unrestricted migration of people from the New Commonwealth countries to Britain. But since the introduction of this Act was seriously considered by the government in 1961 and was strongly expected to come into effect in 1962, large numbers of Pakistanis and Indians rushed to migrate to Britain before missing the opportunity. Thus unprecedently large numbers of people from India, Pakistan (including East Pakistan which is now Bangladesh) and from the rest of the New Commonwealth countries migrated to Britain during this short period.

Although the migration of Indians, Pakistanis and others from the New Commonwealth countries had practically stopped, dependants of the already settled migrants were still allowed to migrate to Britain. As a result, the flow of migration from Pakistan and India to Scotland and Britain continued on a relatively high-scale level throughout the 1960s. This process in turn led to what Jeffrey (1976) calls 'chain-migration': the continuous process of sponsoring kin and relatives to migrate to Britain by those Pakistani/Indian migrants who had already settled in the country. The process of 'chain-migration' appears to be an important factor in the gradual development of many Pakistani/Indian communities of kin and co-villagers in England and Scotland.

The majority of the 1960s migrants settled in England. Nevertheless, a considerable number of these migrants settled in Scotland as well. According to Maan (1992 : 168) by 1970 the total number of Indian and Pakistani migrants in Scotland (including children born in Scotland) reached about 16,000 individuals. The bulk of these migrants settled in Glasgow and Edinburgh.

While 'chain-migration' of people from the Indian sub-continent to Scotland continued throughout the 1960s and 1970s, 1972 marks an other important phase in the history of Indian/Pakistani migration to Britain. On 4th August 1972 the then Ugandan government ordered all Asian residents of Uganda to leave the country within three months. These Asians subsequently migrated to other countries, mainly to Canada and to the USA. A proportion of these 'African Asians' were given a special permission by Mr. Edward Heath's government to migrate and settle in Britain. Many of these Asian refugees migrated to England, but some of them settled in Scotland too. The exact number of the 'African Asians' in Scotland is not known. Nevertheless, according to leaders of the Indo-Pakistani community in

Edinburgh, this category of the Asian migrants accounts for about 10 percent of all Asians in Scotland (see also SEMRU 1987:II:24; Nye 1992:8-9). But, the 'African Pakistanis' in Edinburgh estimate that their number in Edinburgh is about 120 individuals.

Apart from the 'African Asians' who have significantly and suddenly added to the size of Indian and Pakistani populations in Scotland in the early 1970s, recent patterns of migration from England to the country continue to increase this size. The number of Pakistanis, Indians and Bangladeshis who 'migrated' from south of the border into Scotland appears to have increased in the late 1980s up to now. It is difficult to estimate the number of Pakistanis, particularly, who have 'migrated' from England to Edinburgh in the past few years. But the appearance of many 'new' Pakistanis who have come to Edinburgh from English cities is very noticeable. I have met a few dozens of these Pakistanis in Edinburgh recently. When I asked about their reasons for coming to Edinburgh, most of the 'newcomers' told me: 'No Racism in Scotland', 'Less crowdedness' of Scottish cities and 'friendly people'. But it seemed to me that the main factors behind this internal migration were either the establishment of new businesses (mainly through kinship/friendship connections), new family connections (through marriage) or both.

With this brief historical background of migration from the Indian subcontinent to Scotland, the total number of Indians in the country is estimated 10,050 persons, Bangladeshis 1,134 persons and Pakistanis 21,192 persons (1991 Census for Scotland, part I, vol.I:88). It is the detailed numerical description of Scotland's Pakistani population that generally concerns the present research, and to which I turn next.

The Pakistani Population of Scotland

Before focusing on the details of Pakistani residents in the Lothian region and Edinburgh, it is important to mention that significant numbers of people belonging to other ethnic groups also live and work in Scotland. According to the 1991 Census for Scotland (part I, vol.I:88). The total number of these ethnic groups is estimated to be about 62,634 persons, which forms 1.3 percent of the total Scottish population. The various ethnic groups in Scotland and their estimated numbers are presented in Table 2.

Table 2 indicates that the largest ethnic minority group in Scotland are Pakistanis which form 0.4 percent of the total population, or about one third (33.8 percent) of the total ethnic minority population. While the second largest ethnic minority group in Scotland are the Chinese, forming 0.2 percent of the total population and 16.7 percent of the total Scottish ethnic population, the Indians are in the third place: 0.2 percent of the total Scottish population, and 16 percent of the total ethnic population in Scotland.

Table 2 - 1991 Census: Resident Ethnic Population - Scotland

Ethnic Group	Number	% of total population	% of population in 'Other Groups'
All groups	4,998,567	100.0	n/a
White	4,935,933	98.7	n/a
Other Groups	62,634	1.3	100.0
Black African	2,773	0.06	4.42
Black Other	2,646	0.05	4.22
Black Caribbean	934	0.02	1.49
Black Total	6,353	0.1	10.1
Pakistani	21,192	0.4	33.8
Chinese	10,476	0.2	16.7
Indian	10,050	0.2	16.0
Other - (Non-Asian)	8,825	0.2	14.0
Other – Asian	4,604	0.09	7.4
Bangladeshi	1,134	0.02	1.8

Source: I have devised this table based on 'raw' data in Table 6 of 1991 Census for Scotland, part I, vol. I : p. 88

Bangladeshis are among the smallest of Asian ethnic groups in Scotland who form 0.02 percent of the total Scottish population and 1.8 percent of the overall Scottish ethnic population. The general categories 'Other-Asians' and 'Other-non-Asians' form 0.09 percent, 7.4 percent of the total Scottish population respectively; each of the two categories forms 7.4 percent and 14.0 percent of all ethnic minority groups in Scotland, respectively. Unlike the situation all over Britain, where black people are the largest ethnic minority group, this category forms only 0.1 percent of the total Scottish population and 10.1 percent of all ethnic minority groups in Scotland.

Scotland's Pakistani population is scattered throughout the country. However, as Table 3 shows the larger proportions of Pakistanis in Scotland are concentrated in regions that have large urban and commercial centres, such as Glasgow and Edinburgh. According to the 1991 Census, Scotland's Pakistani population is distributed in various Scottish regions as follows:

Table 3 shows that the largest proportion or 69 percent of Pakistani residents in Scotland live in the Strathclyde region. The majority of these Pakistanis live in the city of Glasgow. The second largest proportion or 15.4 percent of Scotland's Pakistani population live in the Lothian region. The overwhelming majority of Pakistanis in Lothian live in the city of Edinburgh. However, the estimated 3,270 figure of the 1991 Census for

Table 3 - 1991 Census: The Distribution of the Pakistani Population in the Various Regions of Scotland

Region	Number of Persons	%
Strathclyde	14,627	69.0
Lothian	3,270	15.4
Tayside	1,300	6.1
Fife	784	3.7
Central Region	681	3.3
Grampian	238	1.1
Highland	101	0.5
Dumfries and Galloway	83	0.4
Western Isles and Islands	55	0.3
Borders	30	0.1
Shetland Islands	15	0.07
Orkney Islands	8	0.04
Total	21,192	100

Source: I have devised this Table which is based on 'raw' data in the 1991 Census for Scotland, Part I, vol : I : pp. 80 - 100 and p. 14

Lothian's Pakistani population is probably an underestimate. Leaders of Edinburgh's Pakistan Community estimate that the total number of Pakistanis in Lothian region is between 5,500 to 6,500 persons.

This discrepancy between the above-mentioned official figure and the estimate of the community's leaders may be due to the recently increasing 'internal migration' of Pakistanis from England to Scotland. It appears, as I mentioned, that more British Pakistanis have migrated to Edinburgh in the past three years – after the 1991 Census was conducted. It is equally possible that some Pakistanis included themselves in the 'Asian-Other' category of the official forms of the Census; or a combination of both the two reasons might have led to the discrepancy between the official and the unofficial estimates. Thus, the unofficial estimate of the Pakistani population in the Lothian region between - 5,500-6,500 persons - seems to be more reliable than the official figure of 3,270 persons.

The Edinburgh Picture

The overwhelming majority of the Pakistani population of the Lothian region live in the city of Edinburgh. Leaders of Edinburgh's Pakistani community estimate that over 6,000 Scottish Pakistanis live in Edinburgh. Unlike some English cities such as Bradford, Middlesborough, the Midlands and certain parts of London, Edinburgh's Pakistani population is generally scattered throughout the city. Nevertheless, I have found that more Pakistani families live in Leith, Wester Hailes, Tollcross, and the New Town, than in other parts of Edinburgh. Despite this relative geographical scatteredness of the Pakistan families in the city, most of them frequently interact with one another via the mosque(s)/community centres, social and cultural gatherings and through family visits. It should be added that because of their experiences and fear of racial harassment many Pakistani families in Edinburgh tend to like living close to other Pakistani families. In fact, clustering of Pakistani families in some parts of the city such as Leith and Tollcross is increasingly noticeable.

According to the 1991 Census for Scotland, the ratio between males and females of the Pakistani residents of the Lothian region is almost equal: the number of Pakistani men in the region is slightly more (1,663 persons) than Pakistani women (1,607 persons). This situation was very different in the 1970s. In the early 1970s the number of Pakistani men in Edinburgh (and in Scotland) was almost double of that of women. This shows that significant number of Pakistani men married in Pakistan and brought their brides to Scotland. The 1991 Census also reveals that more than a half (1,711 persons) of the Pakistani population in the region are born in Scotland. This further indicates that the majority of the Pakistani population in the region belong to the sociological category of 'second generation'. Despite the official underestimate of the total Scottish-born Pakistani population in the region, these results can be extrapolated to the total (actual number) population: it is, at least, a sample of about half of the unofficially estimated number of all Pakistanis in the Lothian region.

Edinburgh's Pakistani population generally tend to be self-employed. Many of them work in grocery shops, restaurants, hotels, bakeries, post offices and in wholesale cash and carry business establishments, etc. These private businesses of Edinburgh's Pakistani residents are normally shared by families and even by extended families. In many cases all or most members of a Pakistani family work together and they all share the income. The collective work of members of the same family in a grocery shop, for example, makes it difficult to define 'employment' and 'unemployment' of Pakistani population in the city. As I will discuss in the next section, a growing number of young graduates who cannot find other jobs assist their families in the running of their private businesses. While such young graduates are apparently self-employed they, in fact, only help their parents because they have no other work to do.

Most Pakistanis in Edinburgh own their private businesses. This is supported by the results of the questionnaire of the present study: parents of all the 60 boys who said that their parents ran a private business also said that they own them (see Chapter IV). However, it is inappropriate to generalise the results of such a small sample to the total population of about 6,000 persons. In fact I observed that many of Edinburgh's Pakistani residents worked for other Pakistanis; still some others did not have any work to do. Due to the lack of data about their employment status and about their level of income, it is impossible to estimate what proportions of Edinburgh's Pakistanis were in upper, middle and lower socio-economic classes (so is the definition and criteria for such categorisation). But my impression is that only a small proportion of them are '*Ameer Log*': or very rich; the majority of Edinburgh's Pakistanis appear to have economically comfortable living conditions. But there are other Pakistanis in Edinburgh who rely on their daily wages and even on Government social security benefits.

As will be mentioned in Chapter II, Edinburgh's Pakistani residents continue to live in what I call a 'modified' joint/extended families, which have adapted themselves to the post migration environment in Scotland (see Chapter II, Section I). According to the survey of the Scottish Ethnic Minority Research Unit (SEMRU 1987, Vol III : 28), the average size of Pakistani households in Edinburgh was 4.41. This figure was a little higher in the sample of 60 boys of the present study - the average household size of the families to which these boys belonged was 5.4.

The overwhelming majority - more than 90 percent - of Edinburgh's Pakistani residents come from the Faisalabad district, in the Punjab province. The rest - about 10 percent come from other places in Pakistan such as: Gujranwala, Sialkot, Rawalpindi, Attakh, Lahore, NWFP (North West Frontier Province) and Kashmir. It is mainly because of the common point of origin of the overwhelming majority of Edinburgh's Pakistani population that they belong to a common *Biraderi*, kinship group or caste - the *Arain* (see Chapter II). The majority of Edinburgh's Pakistanis have a rural background in Pakistan.

As I will describe in detail in Chapter III, the overwhelming majority (about 96 percent) of Edinburgh's Pakistanis are *Sunni* Muslims; a small minority of about 2 percent are *Shiite* Muslims; and probably a little more than 1 percent *Ahmadis* (or *Bahaies*); very few Pakistani Christians live in Edinburgh. All of Edinburgh's Pakistanis speak Urdu which is the official language of Pakistan. However, those from the Punjab province speak Punjabi (their mother tongue) as well.

After this brief historical and present demographic background of Edinburgh's Pakistani residents, I now, turn to the reaction of the wider Scottish society and its social institutions to the presence of these people in Scotland.

II: Exclusion

The Past

The previous pages indicated that the migration of people from the Indian sub-continent to Scotland and to Great Britain is closely linked to the British Colonial rule of the Indian sub-continent. The British political and economic domination of the Indian sub-continent that lasted for one hundred and ninety years (1757–1947) had a strong Scottish connection. Scottish military officers, soldiers, administrators, traders and missionaries had been actively involved in the long British rule of the sub-continent before its partition into India and Pakistan and later into Bangladesh (see Fryer 1984; Miles and Cage 1985; Visram 1986; Muirhead 1986; Cain 1986; Dunlop 1988; Armstrong 1989; Miles and Dunlop 1989; Nye 1992, Maan 1992). Due to this connection, Scots (whether in the then British India and/or later in Scotland) first encountered people from the Indian sub-continent as colonial subjects, servants, seamen, destitute wage-labourers and even as beggars on the streets of major Scottish cities.

Although direct encounters of most Scots with a relatively larger number of people from British India, the largest colony of the British Empire, did not occur until after World War Two, ideas about the inferiority of Indian culture and values as compared to those of the Europeans already existed in Scotland. Similar and even more negative ideas about the culture and values of Britain's black colonial subjects in Africa and in the Caribbean were commonplace among many Scots. The cultures and people of the Indian sub-continent, Africa and the Afro-Caribbean were considered as backward, primitive and even barbaric (see Fryer 1993:63–72). Such ideas and stereotypes were not only confined to the culture of imperial Britain's black and brown subjects, but they also included the character and temperament of these people. According to Fryer (1993:68), Curzon Viceroy of India between 1898–1905, described Indians as 'less than school-children', and in Lord Milnor's opinion the idea of extending self-government to India was 'a hopeless absurdity' as non-white people did not possess 'the gift of maintaining peace and order for themselves'. Fryer further adds that the supposed racial superiority of 'whites' over non-whites was used as the main justification for the British colonial rule over India. In explaining why Indians should be excluded from high ranks of the Indian Civil Service, a resolution of the Governor General in Council in 1904 explicitly said that only white British had this ability: 'partly by heredity, the habits of mind and the vigour of character. . .' (quoted in Fryer 1993:69). This clearly shows that the Indians were considered biologically an inferior race.

More importantly, these racial ideas and stereotypes about the inborn inferiority of Indians were expressed and spread through the writings of senior British/Scottish colonial administrators and missionaries in the country. For example Lord Thomas Macaulay, a senior Scottish colonial administrator in India in the 19th century, described the character and temperament of Bengali Indians in this way:

> His mind bears a singular analogy to his body. It is weak even to help-lessness for purposes of manly resistance, but its suppleness and its tact move the children of sterner climes to admiration, not unmingled with contempt. . . larger promises, smooth excuses, elaborate tissues of circumstantial falsehood, chicanery, perjury, forgery, are the weapons, offensive and defensive, of the people of the lower Ganges. (Quoted in Armstrong 1989:22)

This description of some particular individuals that Lord Macauley, most probably encountered as his servants may be true. But generalising these description to 'the people of the lower Ganges' is very much in line with the 'scientific racism' of the 19th century that attributed different behavioural characteristics to people of different skin-colours.

Apart from these writings, racialised ideas about the racial inferiority of the black and brown people and their cultures were transmitted to the ordinary Scottish citizens through the returning soldiers of Scottish regiments who served in India.

> Scottish army regiments were stationed throughout the British Empire and soldiers returning to Scotland would discuss with their families and friends the people they had encountered while abroad. Their accounts were often shot through with the racist attitudes which justified and explained the presence of the British army in Africa and India. (Armstrong 1989: 24)

It is very likely that the above mentioned ordinary soldiers belonged to the Scottish working class. Thus, the returning soldier had been a direct medium of transmitting negative ideas about Britain's black and brown Indian and African subjects to those sections of the Scottish population who could not read and write; or to those who did not have access to writings that described 'coloured' people as biologically and racially inferior to 'white' Europeans.

Missionaries and the church also played an important role in the spread and development of negative ideas and stereotypes about the values, morality, and character of the black and brown people of India and Africa during the 18th and 19th centuries. Churchmen probably added a further charge to the inferiority of these people to impress on their audience that their faith was the 'right' one so that to justify the work of Christian missionaries as 'civilising'. According to Armstrong (1989 : 24) 'The sermons given by ministers and priests in Scotland during the colonial period often contained references to the work of missionaries and referred to the characteristics of the people whom the missionaries were working to 'civilise'. In addition, the church also played an indirect but very important role in publicising ideas about the inferiority of the cultures of British colonial subjects through the school. Due to the church's strong influence and important role in the Scottish educational system particularly during the 18th and 19th centuries, text books of geography and history contained explicit references to the superiority of 'white' British culture and values over the cultures and values of 'coloured' Asians and Africans. According to Armstrong (1989 : 24) 'the size and power of the British Empire were facts drummed into the heads of every school pupil in the country and the racism inherent in conventional views of the Empire and its people was part of a child's education'. Moreover, according to Fryer (1993:77-81) hundreds of children's books even until the 1960s contained racist tales and stories about 'coloured' people.

Thus, it can be strongly asserted that the tales of returning Scottish soldiers, writings of senior civil administrators, preachings of the church, lessons in the schools, and children's books greatly contributed to the development of negative and racialised stereotypes about the Indians long before they came to Scotland. Not unexpectedly the first direct encounters of Scots with Indians in Scotland did not alter the stereotypes and negative images of the former about the latter. Instead, since the Indians in Scotland were destitute wage-labourers, disempowered servants, and even beggars with unfamiliar habits and facial features, the already existing stereotypes about them were further confirmed. This is clearly evident in the descriptions of the early Indian migrants by individuals and institutions in Scotland. For example, Salter (1873 : 236) described these Indians in Scotland as '. . . as manageable as children...' ; Hammerton (1893 : 138) as '. . . weak creatures'; a medical officer's report in Glasgow (1929) as '. . . have little regard for cleanliness. . .'; and further added to these generalised descriptions of these Indian immigrants in Scotland was a complaint of being a '. . . menace to the social and industrial amenities of the community' *(The Motherwell Times* 11/2/1921)

The above mentioned institutions, institutional practices, and the expressions of personal racialised opinions further contributed to the strengthening of negative mental attitudes and racial prejudice towards the Indians in Scotland. What is more crucial to the present discussion is that these generalised negative stereotypes and attitudes did not remain in minds, but were translated into exclusionary actions and practices against the Indians. Existing documented evidence shows that the early Indian residents in

Edinburgh during the 1920s were largely excluded from the social and cultural life of the city. For example, according to Dunlop and Miles (1989 : 30) 'From the correspondence columns of *The Edinburgh Evening News* it is clear that several dancing halls had operated a "Colour Ban" ever since they had opened while others had recently introduced one. . .'. Dunlop and Miles further add that the more liberal-minded owners of the dancing halls and restaurants in Edinburgh allowed 'Asiatics and Africans' only to 'partake of refreshments but not dancing'. The reason for these 'Colour Bans' was the objections of visitors to the presence of coloured people in the dancing halls.

This evidence clearly points to two important points. First, the evidence unambiguously shows that the Indian and African customers were banned from the dancing halls and restaurants because their skin-colour was black or brown. Thus, due to their colour, the Indians were excluded from social-ising with indigenous population. Secondly, the documented evidence indi-cates that it was the visitors who objected to dancing with 'coloured' people not individual owners of dancing halls and restaurants. This means that the public pressure on the owners of dancing halls and restaurants must have come from sufficiently large numbers of the public to force them to exclude 'coloured' people from social and cultural entertainment. This second point is further supported by the following incidents in 1927. When the Edinburgh Indian Society collectively protested against the city dancing halls/restau-rants' 'Colour Ban' the MP for Argyllshire, Mr. MacQuisten, replied to the Society as follows:

> In my opinion you should be very grateful to these proprietors of the dance halls for what they have done. I am sure that all Indian fathers and mothers will be only too glad to have their sons excluded from dance-halls – places where they are liable to make undesirable acquaintances. (*Edinburgh Evening News* 3 June 1927)

Though diplomatic and polite (and inherently patronising), Mr MacQuisten's statement clearly backed the prevailing exclusionary prac-tices against the Indian residents in Edinburgh. This indicates that exclusion of coloured people from the social and cultural life of the Scottish society had political support.

What has been said so far describes the development of racialised nega-tive stereotypes about people from the Indian subcontinent and outlined some examples of the resultant racial discrimination and exclusionary prac-tices against them in the more or less immediate *past*. In the next section I will examine the extent and the various dimensions of racial discrimination and exclusionary practices against Britain/Scotland's ethnic minority popu-lation (with special focus on the Pakistani population) *at the present*.

The Present

Despite the discrediting of views and theories about the biological and cultural superiority of white people over non-whites and about the disharmonious effects of their presence in European countries (see the works of Miles; Husbands; Cashmor; Hall); despite the increasing strength of the anti-racism movement in Scotland and in Britain (such as, the Anti-Nazi League, the Anti-Nazi Action, Scottish Anti-Racist Movement, National Anti-Racist Movement in Education, Lothian Black Forum etc.) and its campaign for equating racism with other disreputable 'isms' i.e. Sexism, Anti-Semitism, Ageism and even Bodyism; and despite successive government legislation outlawing many forms of racial discrimination (see the 1965, 1968 and the 1976 Race Relations Acts) racial discrimination and exclusionary practices against members of ethnic minority groups continue to be a feature of Scottish/British society.

In the following discussion, I intend to discuss the exclusion of and discrimination against Britain's 'coloured' citizens, particularly Pakistanis in Scotland, in various spheres of social life. I will focus mainly on racial discrimination in *employment, housing, sports/entertainment,* and in the general *social and political* life of the wider British/Scottish society. I will also discuss the nature and the extent of racial *harassment and violence* that are experienced by Pakistanis in Scotland and in Edinburgh.

Employment

Despite the passage of 23 years since the introduction of the 1976 Race Relations Act that penalises racial discrimination in employment, there is much documented evidence, showing that Britain's 'coloured' citizens have been and are consistently discriminated against, at present, in employment. Apart from evidence in the 1960s and 1970s, new research in the past decade including those in the early 1990 indicate that the unemployment rates for 'coloured' people in Scotland and in the U.K. are many times higher as compared to those of the indigenous 'white' population. More importantly, this evidence further indicates that Britain's Pakistani population have the highest unemployment rate among members other ethnic minority groups. The CRE report 'Race Through The Nineties' (1992:10) gives the unemployment rates for the various ethnic groups and the 'white' population of Britain as follows: White: 8 percent; West Indians: 15 percent; Indians: 12 percent; and Pakistani/Bangladeshi 25 percent.

The above figures show that the unemployment rate of Britain's

Pakistani population is more than three times higher than that for the indige-
nous white population. These conclusions about the unemployment rate for
Britain's Pakistani population is consistently confirmed by other studies: the
Department of Employment's survey, 'Ethnic Origins and the Labour
Market' (*Employment Gazette* 1991:67) reveals that Britain's
Pakistani/Bangladeshi population had the highest unemployment rate –
25 percent – as compared with other ethnic groups in Britai. (see also
Brown 1984, 1985 ; McCrudden, Smith and Brown 1991).

Not surprisingly, the situation is not very different in Scotland. A report
of the Scottish Office's research unit, 'Ethnic Minorities in Scotland'
(1991:79) shows that the unemployment rate for Pakistanis in Scotland was
almost as high as it was in the UK as a whole : 24 percent. This report
strongly confirms the conclusion drawn by SEMRU (Scottish Ethnic
Minority Research Unit):

> Unemployment rates were a third higher for ethnic minorities men; for
> women the difference was even higher. Among those particularly affect-
> ed by high unemployment levels were Pakistanis. . .'(SEMRU 1991:2)

Most of these studies attribute the discriminatory practices of 'white'
employers' against 'coloured' people to the employers' racial prejudice:
direct racial discrimination. But it is important to mention that discrimination against members of ethnic minority groups in employment may be
indirect and not resulting from racial prejudice of employers. For exampl, it
is possible that the very high unemployment rate among ethnic minority
groups in Britain may be partly a result of certain institutional practices,
procedures, and 'working cultures' that unconsciously place members of
these groups in disadvantaged positions. The potential employer may not
have any racial prejudice against members of ethnic groups. He/she may
feel that Asians or Afro-Caribbeans may not 'get on', 'fit in' or 'get along'
with the rest of his/her workforce. In this case the employer does not directly discriminate against the Asian or Afro-Caribbean because of the latter's
colour/race; but the potential employers' practices have exclusionary consequences for members of ethnic minority groups. Similarly, some recruitment may be made through word of mouth rather than public advertisement.
This practice is also very likely to prevent members of ethnic minority
groups from knowing about the vacancies, and therefore be excluded from
the list of candidates.

Whatever the actual reasons for the high rate of unemployment of
Pakistanis – direct racial discrimination or unintentional institutional practices – in Scotland and in the U.K., some young Pakistani unemployed graduates told me that they were directly discriminated against in the labour
market because of their race/colour. Three unemployed young Pakistani

graduates, all of whom were born in Britain, told me in 1992 that: 'We have been looking for jobs in this country for the past year. Because of our Pakistani origins we have very little chance to find jobs in this country.'

When I asked the young men why they had little chance to find jobs in the country, they all said in one voice, 'because of racial discrimination'. Then later I found that one of them, an electrical engineer, found a job in Pakistan, and the other, an accountant, was waiting to get a job in Pakistan as well. The third one, a graduate in Physics, had still not found a job after one and a half years of 'filling out countless applications', as he put it. Then this young man opened a shop with his uncle's financial help. He told me about his new status as shopkeeper :

> This is not my choice; I have been searching for jobs for the past one and a half years. But I was unsuccessful. I was convinced that it would be a long time before I will get a job in this country or in Pakistan. Now, I am a shopkeeper - a job that I most hated – but this was the only choice that I was left with.

A few older self-employed Pakistani residents who graduated as lawyers and engineers told me similar stories. One of them said that 'the people in this country think that we (Pakistanis in Scotland) have chosen to be shop-keepers. The fact is that we are denied other jobs, even if we have the best qualifications.'

Although this generalisation did not seem to apply to all highly qualified self-employed Pakistanis in Edinburgh; but many of them could not have found the jobs that they were trained for. As a result many of the educated young Pakistanis, as the above mentioned cases indicate, tend to join their parents' business as self-employed persons. This conclusion is supported by an important study by the Commission of Racial Equality. The CRE study, 'Ethnic Minorities and the Graduate Labour Market' (1990a) connects self-employment of Pakistanis in Scotland and in Britain with discriminatory practices against them in the graduate labour market. The study concludes that there is a serious lack of opportunities for Asian young graduates, forcing them into self-employment. More recent research by Professor Jones and McVoy of Liverpool's John Moore's University further confirms this, as reported in *The Independent on Sunday* (12.6.1994): '. . . One in four of Asian (Pakistani) shopkeepers had a university degree . . . It is not an opportunistic streak but a lack of other opportunities that has driven one in five to 'seek salvation in self-employment'. This evidence indicates close relationships between discrimination against Pakistanis in the Scottish/British Labour Market and their self-employment. This has played a central role in making Britain/Scotland's Pakistani community a 'community of shop-keepers'!

Housing

Recent research about the housing of ethnic minority groups in Britain generally indicates that members of these groups live in better housing conditions than they did in the 1950s. Philips (1987) in his study 'Searching for a Decent Home : Ethnic Minority Progress in the Post War Housing Market' reports a significant improvement in the quality and standards of the ethnic minority housing during the past four decades. This, according to the study, is particularly true in the case of Asian ethnic groups – Indians, Chinese and Pakistanis. As a result of the general upward mobility of the socio-economic statuses of these ethnic groups, they have been able to live in better housing.

However, Philips' study adds that improvement in the housing conditions of Britain's ethnic minorities does not mean equality of treatment. The study shows established patterns of inequality and discrimination in housing against ethnic minorities:

> In the 1980s, then, the NCWP [New Commonwealth and West Pakistan] minorities still live in significantly worse quality housing and in poorer, less popular areas than the white British population. This holds both across and within tenures. Indeed, the high level of owner occupation among Asians (72 percent as against 59 percent of the general population) provides no guarantee of good housing ... The prevailing trend in many cities over the last two decades has been one of growing residential segregation between NCWP minorities and whites, with the former becoming increasingly over-represented in the poorest areas. This is particularly true of the Asian population, whosepotential for residential mixing has been reduced by their relative absence from council housing. As analyses of local authority data have shown, however segregation within the public sector itself is all too prevalent and inequality prevails. (Philips 1987 : 108)

The above findings are generally supported by subsequent studies. These studies, further, reveal various degrees of exclusionary practices and discrimination against ethnic minorities in the allocation of local authority housing, in owner-occupied housing, in renting private housing and even by housing associations (see Smith 1989; CRE 1990b, 1990c; 1990d, CRE 1991; Ginsburg 1992; Skillington 1996).

Apart from the above mentioned empirical evidence about discrimination in housing against members of ethnic minority population on wider British levels, there is abundant evidence about the existence of patterns of such discrimination in Scotland. An important Scottish study *Race and Housing in Glasgow* by Dalton and Daghlian (1989) found that members of ethnic minorities in Glasgow are living disproportionately in below-standard housing. Their quality of housing both in terms of basic amenities and location was not only inferior to that of Glasgow's white population, but was much below the accepted standard of housing. More importantly, the study reveals that this has happened in areas where locally based housing associations operated since early 1970s. These findings are further confirmed by various other studies in Scotland. For example McEwan and Varity's study (1989) found that members of ethnic minorities in Edinburgh were unlawfully discriminated against, in the allocation of local authority housing. The study reveals that Indians, Pakistanis and Bangladeshis were allocated houses in Edinburgh's most unpopular areas. A more recent survey that was conducted for 'Scottish Homes', the National Housing Agency in Scotland, further confirms the inequality in housing for Scottish ethnic minorities:

> Housing for ethnic minorities in Scotland is below the average quality for the rest of the population. . . Residents in ethnic minority households are almost four times more likely to live in over-crowded conditions than residents in households headed by white persons and are also more likely to lack basic amenities . . . (Reported in *The Scotsman*: 15.12.1993)

All these studies generally report inequality in housing for members of ethnic minorities in Scotland and in the U.K. in terms of basic amenities, location and numbers of persons per room or over-crowdedness. What is crucial to the present argument - the connection between exclusion and the making of a 'closed community' - is the disproportionate allocation of housing to ethnic minorities in certain unpopular and poor areas of cities in Scotland and England. This discriminatory practice, as Philips (1987 : 108) suggested earlier, has resulted in the '. . . growing residential segregation between the NCWP minorities and whites, with the former becoming increasingly over-represented in the poorest areas.'

Thus, alongside 'chain-migration' as a factor in the development of ethnic enclaves and ghettos in some British cities, the disproportionate allocation of housing to members of ethnic minorities in certain areas of cities is another important factor in this process. Although, as it will be discussed in Chapter IV, members of Edinburgh's ethnic minorities, particularly Pakistanis, are residentially scattered throughout the city. But the continuous disproportionate allocation of housing to ethnic minorities in certain areas of the city may gradually exclude them geographically and ecologically from the rest of the city. In fact I have observed that in the past four years more 'new-comer' and relatively poorer Pakistanis (mainly internal migrants from England) lived close to each other in Wester Hailes, Leith, and in some other poorer areas of Edinburgh. This might be the beginning of the making of a geographically 'closed' ghettoised Pakistani community in Edinburgh, as has already happened in Bradford, in parts of London and in other English cities.

Sports and Social/Cultural Entertainments

As far as exclusion in sports and social/cultural entertainments is concerned, it more directly affects the British-born young Pakistanis. The major spheres of this form of exclusion manifests itself in discrimination against, and intimidation of, young Pakistanis in public places such as sports halls, dancing halls and in other social clubs. Despite the fact that discriminatory practices and racial intimidation commonly take place in this area, it is the least researched by the government and other independent researchers. It is probably this reason that very little data is available about discrimination against members of ethnic minorities in sports and in places of social/cultural entertainment. Cases of racial discrimination in sports are occasionally reported by the press. But it appears that the press take an interest only in those cases of racial discrimination that are serious or are widely complained about. For example, as a result of intolerable discrimination against Pakistani football players in Ealing, Southall, in 1993 the local Councillor Mr. Khabra was requested to help the players with the issue. Mr. Khabra told *The Independent on Sunday* (5.12.1993) that: 'Football clubs in this country are more racist than in any other country. . . Football is one area in which it [racism] has not been properly tackled.' The Councillor further added that Asian players are frequently harassed and intimidated by white football players and fans in stadiums: 'Asian kids go to Wembley and are intimidated by the fans. You feel yourself isolated in the crowd. You cannot share your excitement because those around you are racist.' Mr. Khabra's comments, in the above quote, seem to suggest that he himself experienced intimidation and harassment in stadiums.

The nature of racial intimidation often gets worse when Pakistani players play against English or Scottish players. Apart from examples of such intimidation in ordinary or less important matches between Scottish/English and Pakistani teams, in 1992 during a cricket test match between Pakistan and England at Headingley in Leeds, English fans threw the head of a pig among the Pakistani supporters of the Pakistan team. This event deeply offended some of the young Edinburgh Pakistanis who had travelled to England to watch the game.

Many young Pakistani sportsmen in Edinburgh told me numerous stories about their experiences of racial discrimination and verbal abuse when they played cricket and football with boys from the indigenous population or played near to them in a public space. The Pakistani boys said that they experienced calling of 'racial names and abuse' when they played football or cricket with white boys in the same team or in separate teams but in the same ground. One of Edinburgh's Pakistan boys described his experience of playing football with Scottish boys as follows:

I liked playing football since I was five years old. I played a lot with other Pakistani boys in Huddersfield. When our family moved to Edinburgh I wanted to join our college team. But they told me they already had more than enough people in the team. Then some other boys in the college told me that I can play in their own team. I couldn't wait, and started playing with them the next day. In the beginning, I really enjoyed playing with them. The team played very well, and I was more than an average player among the boys. I played for the team many times and we often won matches. Only, sometimes, one or two boys in the team called me 'racial names'; I ignored them. But, after a few months more boys called me names; they shouted at me when I made small mistakes. When we went for a drink after a game they did not speak to me; except one or two boys who spoke to me, others ignored me. I felt unwanted, so I had to leave the team after eight months. Now, I play with Pakistani and Arab boys. But Pakistani boys are not good at playing football. We are going to join some Iranian boys and make a new team. The Iranians are very good in football.

The above description is a clear example of an effective process of the exclusion of Pakistanis, particularly the second generation, from sports and entertainments in the wider society. As I will show in the next section, this description provides an answer to Mr. Norman Tebbit's famous complaint to the *Los Angeles Times* (March 1990) that the second generation Pakistani youngster in Britain 'Fails the cricket test'. Mr. Tebbit meant that the second generation Pakistanis, in Britain, despite being British citizens, support the Pakistani cricket team against England's. Mr. Tebbit's observation is obviously correct. But the reason that young Pakistanis support Pakistan against England, is in part because England has excluded them from participation in its sports. As a result, Pakistani youngsters formed their own cricket and football teams and clubs that further add to the 'closedness' of the Pakistan communities in Britain. The British-born youngsters in their Edinburgh Pakistani cricket team are proud of Pakistani cricket; these boys' heroes are not Ian Botham but Imran Khan, Naser Hussain and Wasim Akram!

The exclusionary practices and discrimination against young Scottish Pakistanis in dancing halls and night clubs has yielded a very similar social response from them. This has led to the creation and development of *Bhangra* - a semi-institutionalised Pakistani/Indian equivalent of the Western disco. In order to keep a degree of balance among the various sections of this part of the chapter I will discuss *Bhangra* in the last part of this chapter.

Political and Social Institutional Life of British Society

Apart from exclusionary practices and discrimination against British Pakistani citizens in the areas of employment, housing, and in sports and social/cultural entertainment, they feel largely excluded from the political and social institutional life of British society. Although this form of exclusion appears to be connected to the other spheres of exclusion, it has a subjective nature: a feeling of being a non-citizen.

At this level most Pakistanis in Edinburgh identify with Islam and consider themselves as part of the larger 'Muslim Community' in Britain. The exclusion of Islam from the Blasphemy Law, the government's refused to give Muslim schools grant-aided status, and the absence of Muslim representation in the British Parliament (only recently Mohammad Sarwar was elected as a Labour MP) are the major issues that Edinburgh's Pakistani population often cite as examples of exclusionary practices against them on broader political/societal levels.

Many Pakistanis/Muslims in Edinburgh believe that because they are not represented in British political life, their voice is not heard and their cultural and social needs as a religious community are ignored. One Pakistani intellectual in Edinburgh told me that 'We as Muslims are clearly discriminated against. Look at the Blasphemy Law; insulting Christianity is blasphemous and against the law of the land. But insulting Islam is Freedom of Speech'. The intellectual was referring to the publication of Salman Rushdie's *Satanic Verses* and its social and political aftermath. Then he added that 'We are treated as less than full citizens of this country. There are more than one million [*sic*] Muslims in Britain, and yet we don't have even one MP in the Parliament.' (This remark was made before the election of Mohammad Sarwar). Obviously, the absence of Muslim MPs in the British Parliament is not easily explained. Nor is it an adequate indicator of political participation or non-participation. But the lack of any representation, until recently, or any other mechanism for the expression of their views, in part, makes British Pakistanis feel politically excluded from mainstream society. These feelings appear to be more strongly shared by the religiously orientated academics, and educated Pakistanis in Scotland. The ideas about their political exclusion are easily taken up by the young British-born

Pakistanis who link the political exclusion of Muslims with discrimination in employment and in the general social institutional life in the society. A young well educated Pakistani who worked for an insurance company told me:

> We British Muslims are seen as aliens. Our way to important political and administrative positions is blocked. First, we are denied jobs, and when we get jobs we are not promoted to higher positions. I know many Pakistanis whose promotions to senior positions were deliberately blocked. There is not a single MP, judge nor even a single Pakistan police officer in Scotland. [In fact there is one Asian police officer in Scotland]. I am born and brought up in this country, but how can I feel British if I am not given a chance to have a say about the problems that concern us all – whites and non-whites – in this country?

This sense of exclusion from the political and institutional life of the society was felt by many young and educated Pakistanis both in Edinburgh and in Glasgow. Such view is almost identical to what Cook (1993 : 142) observed about all 'coloured' youths in Britain : 'Regardless of their legal rights and place of birth, black British citizens often find themselves regarded as alien, formally within, but informally without citizenship'.

The general feeling of social and political alienation among Edinburgh's Pakistanis, appear to have increased in the aftermath of the Rushdie affair. It created a new political consciousness among them — a need to further strengthen their sense of community on both micro and macro levels and to defend themselves against exclusion and discrimination. I will discuss the social response of Edinburgh's Pakistani population to their sense of exclusion from the political life of the wider society (particularly in relation to their attitudes towards 'the Muslim Parliament') in the next part of the chapter. First it is important to look at idea that the sense of insecurity and alienation of Pakistanis is further strengthened by their experiences of racial harassment and violence in Britain.

Racial Harassment

Racial harassment and violence against members of ethnic minority groups in Britain is not a new phenomenon. 'Coloured' migrants from Africa, the Caribbean, and Asia have experienced racial harassment and violence since their arrival in Scotland, England and Wales. The existing documented evidence indicates that these migrants were subject of racial attacks in London, Cardiff, Liverpool, Hull and Glasgow as early as the 1920s (see Skillington et al 1992 and Maan 1992). Some of these attacks on Indian migrants resulted in death and serious injuries (see Maan 1992 : 111–113).

The 1940s witnessed a series of racial attacks on Asian and Afro-Caribbean migrants. The most serious and wide spread of these attacks took place in Liverpool in 1948; in Birmingham in 1949; and in Dentford in 1949. Violence against 'coloured' migrants became even more widespread in the late 1950s. Asian, African and Afro-Caribbean migrants were targets of systematic attacks by white youths throughout Britain. In the 1960s Pakistani migrants in Britain particularly became a focus of racial violence. The widespread and systematic attacks mainly by white skinheads on Pakistanis turned into a slogan 'Paki-Bashing' in this period. Mr. Enoch Powell's, MP, famous 'Rivers of Blood' speech in 1969 further escalated the level of violence against coloured migrants in Britain throughout the 1970s. At this time, Bangladeshi and Pakistani migrants were again the main target of racial violence; the scale of the violence which is reported in the 'Blood On Street Report' (1978) indicates that these attacks were almost commonplace in the major English cities. The 1980s witnessed a quantitatively significant rise in racial violence and assaults on members of 'coloured' ethnic minorities throughout Britain. According to the Runnymede Trust's 'Report on Race and Immigration' (1991), the total number of racial incidents in England and Wales during 1988, 1989 and 1990 were: 4383, 5044, and 6359, respectively. The figures for Scotland during the same three years were: 299, 376, and 636, respectively. These figures show a dramatic increase in the incidents of violence against members of Britain's ethnic minority groups. The upward trend in racial attacks in Britain is generally confirmed by other studies that were conducted in Leicester (see Chambers Community Consultants 1989) and in Sheffield (see Racial Harassment Project 1989) (see also for further data on this topic the Metropolitan Police Report 1990).

The above figures are considered an underestimate of the actual incidence of racial incidents both by the Home Office and by independent self-report studies. A survey by Victim Support (1991) 'Racial Attacks in Camden, Southwark, and Newham,' which was sponsored by the Home Office estimated that the number of incidents that were recorded by the police in England and Wales - between 3,000 to 6,000 - represented only 2 to 5 percent of the actual number of incidents in 1991.

What is more directly relevant to the present discussion is that most of the above findings indicate that Britain's Bangladeshi and Pakistani populations are disproportionately victims of racial attacks and harassment as compared to other ethnic minorities. A Home Office inquiry 'Racial Attacks' (1981) showed that Asians (Pakistanis/Bangladeshis) were 50 times more likely to be attacked, and Afro-Caribbeans more than 36 times more likely to be attacked, than the indigenous white population of Britain (see Haralambos 1987 : 394 for very similar conclusions). Moreover, Mayhew et al (1989) concludes that racism contributed to Pakistanis and Bangladeshis being victims of crime more than members of other minority groups.

Contrary to the common belief that 'it does not happen here', and 'racism is an English disease', much Scottish research indicates that racial harassment and violence against ethnic minority groups in Scotland is as evident as it is anywhere else in Britain. The Scottish studies show that the predominantly Pakistani population of Scotland is frequently subjected to racial harassment and violence. These studies reveal that the incidents of racial harassment and violence in Scotland range from (racial) name-calling, abusive phone-calls, NF slogans daubed on doors and walls, throwing excrement through letter-boxes and windows, to breaking windows, damaging/scratching cars and physical attacks some of which have resulted in serious injuries and even deaths. A study by the Scottish Ethnic Research Unit of Glasgow University revealed that of the Indian and Pakistani residents who were interviewed in Glasgow:

> . . . over 80 percent had experienced racist abuse and around 20 percent had been subjected to physical attacks; in addition 50 percent had suffered damage to their property in racist attacks and 79 percent of those interviewed said that they had experienced racist and abusive language more than once or regularly. (quoted in Armstrong 1989 : 11)

Despite the fact that there has been little systematic research on racial violence in Scotland, the above findings are generally confirmed by other studies. A study by Stirling University whose conclusions were reported in 'The Scotsman' (6.1.1990) found that 'half of the members of ethnic groups in the Strathclyde region, predominantly Pakistanis, had been physically attacked; and more than half of them experienced attacks on their houses.' Moreover, the Scottish Research reveals that Scotland's Pakistani population have a much higher rate of criminal victimisation than the population in general in the country (see SEMRU 1991). This report (1991 : 5) reveals that Pakistanis and Chinese were much more likely (15 percent) to experience verbal abuse in their work than were Indians or whites (both 8 percent). The same report further adds that Scotland's Pakistani population were more likely to be victim of 'vehicle crime' than any other ethnic group.

My own observation about the nature and extent of racial harassment and violence is generally in line with the findings of these Scottish studies. In fact in recent years some of the most serious incidents of violence have taken place in Edinburgh: in 1987 a Pakistani shopkeeper in Canonmills, Edinburgh, was stabbed to death by a member of the indigenous population and the incident was generally recognised as racially motivated. The deceased's two young children and wife have since been living in fear without a head of the household. In 1989 a young Somali refugee was stabbed by a group of white youngsters in central Edinburgh. The Somali victim later died from his injuries in hospital. This incident was also widely recognised as racially motivated. The acquittal of one of the attackers and the conviction of the other to 21 months' imprisonment was strongly criticised as too lenient and was followed by a large demonstration in the city. In 1991 two Pakistani youngsters were attacked by a group of white boys near the Meadows in Edinburgh; they were beaten up and one of them was seriously injured and hospitalised. In 1992, 15 graves in a Muslim/Pakistani graveyard in Leith, Edinburgh were destroyed. This incident was considered by the Pakistani community as an expression of racial prejudice against the Pakistani community as a whole. The incident was reported to the police, but as a community leader put it: 'Nothing happened; the police are not bothered about us as living people; our dead and their graves are a non-issue for them.'

There seems to be much truth in what the community leader said: the Pilrig mosque was many times a target of violent attacks, particularly when it was full of worshippers for congregational prayers. Once in 1990 during *Taravih* - special congregational prayers that are offered at night in *Ramadan* - the back door of the mosque was forcefully hit by what seemed to be a large hammer or a large stone for about two or three minutes. As a result the collective worship had to be discontinued. When some of the worshippers and I went to see what happened there was no one near the large metallic door. However, I noticed two freshly written large letters, NF (National Front) - these letters were written beside other NF slogans that were erased, but could still be seen. Such incidents have been repeated. A few months after this incident an Edinburgh police officer (introduced as Mr. Brown), was invited to a celebration in the Pilrig Mosque/community centre. Members of the community complained to the police officer about the recent incidents and about several burglaries of Pakistani houses. The police officer told the audience 'not to keep money or other valuables in their houses or pockets'!

Most important, the British born young Pakistanis in Edinburgh due to their more direct interaction with the wider society (in school, play-grounds, streets, etc.) are exposed to more racial harassment and violence. As I will discuss in Chapter IV in detail, in a sample of 60 boys in Edinburgh 91.66 percent said that they have been 'treated badly because of their race/colour'. These young boys who, unlike their parents, are born and brought up in Britain said that they are told 'Go back to your country' by white boys. This standard exclusionary statement and other racial verbal abuses (see Chapter IV) make these boys, who have not seen any other country but Britain, think seriously about their social belonging and identity. Theirs and their parents' experiences of exclusionary practices and discrimination against them in employment, housing, sports, and cultural entertainment, in political and social institutional life and their experiences of racial harassment have made them question their 'Britishness'; the British-born Pakistanis who constitute more than half of the Pakistani communities search for a social identity and for a social and psychological belong ing - they search for social and psychological security. It appears that the more they experience exclusion and discrimination in the wider society, the more inwardly and boldly they draw the social and cultural boundaries of the Pakistani community – a small-scale 'closed' society within the wider British society, where they find or hope to find a sense of belonging and identity.

III: The Making of a 'Closed' Community

The Concept of Community

The concept of community is one of the most problematic sociological terms, subject to much controversy and disagreement among sociologists for more than a hundred years. Among the prominent sociologists of the 19th century who directly discussed the concept (and the question of community) was the German sociologist Ferdinand Tonnies. Tonnies' pioneering work *Gemeinschaft and Gesellschaft* (1887) laid down the foundations for the subsequent theorising and research about the study of community. In the English-speaking world *Gemeinschaft* was equated with community and Gesellschaft with society or association.

Tonnies' *Gemeinschaft* or community was culturally homogeneous; it had a clear-cut moral and social code whose values were largely internalised by members; family, kinship and religion played an important role in the maintenance of the moral and social order of the community which was often based in a bounded geographical area. Thus, Tonnies' *Gemeinschaft* comprised of three central elements: blood, place (land) and mind that may be equated with the more commonly used sociological concepts of kinship, neighbourhood and friendship. As far as *Gesellschaft* or society is concerned, it was for Tonnies all what was not *Gemeinschaft*; it was mainly characterised by heterogeneity of culture, impersonality of social relationships and by a high degree of the physical and social mobility of the individual members of the *Gesellschaft*.

For subsequent theorising and research the concept and the question of community were of central sociological concern. A group of American sociologists at the university of Chicago were particularly interested in the question of community. Known as the Chicago School, the theoretical works and empirical research of the prominent Chicagoans such as Park (1915), Park and Burgess (1921), Wirth (1938) and Shaw and Mackay (1942) focused on the social organisation (or disorganisation) of the city in the aftermath of capitalist industrialisation, large-scale migration and urbanisation. For the Chicagoans the community question was an empirical question; they were concerned with the 'loss' (or 'decline') of community that, in their view, was responsible for the increased social problems of American cities. Research by later sociologists within the Chicago school tradition produced substantial empirical evidence about the 'Community Loss' thesis (see Bender 1978 for a comprehensive review of this evidence).

The question of community continued to be a matter of much interest for sociologists within and outside the Chicago school tradition. However the works of the Chicagoans have been sharply criticised by the sociologists of community (or community studies) in the 1960s, the 1970s and later. These sociologists strongly challenged the 'community loss' thesis particularly. They argue that community had not been lost; instead, it had been trans- formed in the aftermath of capitalist industrialisation. These sociologists backed their argument by empirical evidence showing the existence of social circles or social networks, ethnic enclaves, etc. where social relation- ships are conducted in a relatively stable way. Although these sociologists accept that social networks, ethnic enclaves, etc. in large cities have been relatively 'liberated' from bounded geographical areas, they continue func- tioning as communities. (see Webber 1963, 1968; Laumaan 1973; Tilly 1973 : Fischer 1977, 1982).

However, despite extensive sociological theorising and research since Tonnies' pioneering work in 1887, the concept of community remains as vague as ever, and sociologists have failed to reach an agreement about a satisfactory definition of community. George Hillary (1955) in his survey of the definitions of community found that the notion was defined in 94 dif- ferent ways (this number has since reached 100 (see Hillary 1983). Hillary's examination revealed that sixty nine of the total 94 definitions agree that community is fundamentally characterised by social interaction, geograph- ical area and some common social bonds among members; seventy of these definitions agree on the presence of a geographical area and social interac- tion as necessary elements of community; but a larger number of these def- initions (73) agree on social interaction and social bonds as the fundamen- tal elements of community (see for further details Bell and Newby 1971; Popline 1972; Leighton 1988).

Recent sociologists of community studies appear to recognise that with the increasing mobility and large scale urbanisation in most western soci- eties geographical area is hardly a necessary element of community. (see Williams 1973; Mingione 1974; Bell and Newby 1976; Cuneo 1978; Janovitz and Street 1978; Leighton, 1988). Many of these theorists and researchers favour the 'social network' approach to the study of communi- ty. As mentioned earlier, according to the 'social network' approach, mod- ern (or post-modern) urban structures continue to include communities in terms of kinship networks, leisure groups, ethnic enclaves, etc. For the proponents of this approach social interaction and common social bonds continue to tie modern urbanites to each other in what are, sometimes, called 'urban villages' that may or may not be situated in bounded geographical areas. According to the 'social network' approach, links between various social networks often extend beyond urban centres to other overlapping networks on regional and even on national levels. (see Mitchell 1969; Wellman and Leighton 1979; Duffee 1980; Cook 1982; Cook *et al* 1983; Leighton 1988).

The 'social network' approach that places a central emphasis on social interaction and common social bonds as necessary elements of community seems to be more applicable to the present study of an ethnic community – the Pakistani community in Edinburgh. However, it seems to me important to add a '*sense of belonging*' to *social interactions* and to *common social bonds* as necessary elements in the study of Edinburgh's Pakistani community. As I will describe in the following pages, the need for a sense of belonging in Edinburgh's Pakistani community mainly arises as a response to the social, cultural and political exclusion of members of the community in the wider Scottish society. Described and defined by these three constituent elements, the Pakistani community in Edinburgh and in Scotland/Britain can be generally studied on national, local and kinship levels.

National Level

Common language, religion, cultural values and customs, and country of origin are the most important common social bonds among Britain's Pakistani population. However, these objective common characteristics become more important in creating a social/political 'conscience collective' among Britain's Pakistani population when they are used as criteria for drawing ethnic/cultural boundaries in a wider inter-ethnic context. Both the official and unofficial definition of Britain's Pakistani population as 'The Pakistani Community in Britain' play an important role in the creation of the social identity of this cultural/ethnic entity and in the identity of the individuals who form it. Definitions the wider society (whether neutral or loaded such as 'Pakistani' or 'Paki' respectively) become part and parcel of the identities of individuals and of the collectivity, wherever they may be in Britain. It is at this broad level that all, or at least, most Pakistanis in Britain see themselves as members of the Broader 'Pakistani Community of Britain', whether they are in Edinburgh, London or elsewhere in Britain.

Identification of the British Pakistani population with the broader Pakistani community becomes more expressive when they confront issues that concern all Pakistanis in the country, i.e. racial discrimination, the state of Blasphemy Law and the Muslim schools. As I will discuss in the next section, the publication of Salman Rushdie's *Satanic Verses* and the collective reaction to it, created an unprecedentedly strong feeling of community among Britain's Pakistani population on the national level. Collective protests and demonstrations against the publication of *Satanic Verses* not only mobilised Britain's Pakistani Muslims but expressed their strong sense of community to the outer world. This also functioned as a channel for communicating their sense of community and social solidarity among themselves.

At this broad national level a direct social interaction may not exist among all or most Pakistanis in Britain. But as mentioned earlier, most Pakistanis in Britain express a general sense of belonging to what is known as 'The Pakistani Community in Britain'. This sense of belonging, sometimes goes beyond ethnic boundaries to include all Muslims in Britain. However, it often finds more profound expressions on geographically and administratively defined local levels.

Local Level

The Edinburgh Pakistani community is an example of what I mean by the existence of Pakistani communities on local levels in Britain. Edinburgh's relatively small Pakistani population not only shares pre-existing common bonds (religion, culture, tradition language and country of origin) but they have developed their own social institutions within the social, geographical and administrative boundaries of the city of Edinburgh. Their regular participation in these social institutions i.e. the Mosque/Community Centre, local Pakistani associations, kinship networks, etc., has facilitated a relatively higher degree of social interaction among Edinburgh's Pakistani population. Due to this higher degree of social interaction among Edinburgh's Pakistanis, most of them know each other face-to-face (or at least know about each other's presence in Edinburgh).

Despite the existence of some feuds, economic rivalries and political or ideological differences among groups and/or individuals and the existence of more than one caste, association and mosque, Edinburgh's Pakistani population perceive themselves as members of one community in the city. This sense of belonging to a community in Edinburgh is clearly expressed in their collective responses to racial violence, representation of the Pakistani population in local, national even on international levels. The definition of community in terms of its constituent elements – common social bonds, social interaction and a sense of belonging appear to apply to Edinburgh's Pakistani community on this intermediate level. It is a level between the national and kinship levels both from theoretical and empirical points of view.

Kinship Level

As I will mention in Chapter II in detail, Edinburgh's Pakistani population belongs to various *Biraderis* or kinship/friendship groups. Members of an (effective) *Biraderi* not only share common bonds of religion, language, customs, country of origin and a common ancestor, but they also have complex reciprocal relationships among themselves. They exhibit a higher level of face-to-face social interaction; individuals have a strong sense of belonging to and strongly identify with the group.

However, the scope of the *Biraderi* is narrow. Not all the important social, religious and cultural needs of members could be fulfilled within it. *Biraderi* could hardly afford to have its own mosque, political organisation and to represent Edinburgh's Pakistani population on national and interna-tional levels (although members of one particular *Biraderi* may have more dominance in a mosque, or in Pakistani political organisations).

Because of the need of Edinburgh's Pakistani population for *inter-Biraderi* close co-operation in the development of collective social institutions, the meaning of community is more applicable to all those who participate in these social institutions. In this sense the meaning of community is more precisely applicable to the Pilrig Mosque/Community Centre. Although dominated by members of the *Arain* Kinship Group, the Pilrig Mosque/Community Centre represents a level of community that lies between the 'kinship' and 'local' levels: on the one hand, the social and organisational scope of the Mosque/Community Centre, is large enough and is designed to cater for the social, cultural, religious, educational, political and welfare needs of all Pakistanis in this area, regardless of their kinship loyalties and affiliations. (Indeed, it is attended by many individuals who belong to various other Pakistani kinship groups.) On the other hand, members have such close social similarities and share such a lot of common ground that this facilitates their social (face-to-face) interaction on a regular basis: the overwhelming majority of the members come from the Punjab province; all of them follow the *Barelvi* school of *Sunni* Islam; and almost all are members of 'The Pakistan Association, Edinburgh and the East of Scotland' (P.A.E.E.S.).

Shared beliefs and social similarities are further translated into action through regular congregational worship, celebration of religious/cultural festivals and other social events in the Pilrig mosque/community centre. This all has resulted in a significant level of a form of social and moral cohesion among members that Emile Durkheim (1984) called 'social solidarity'. Durkheim in his mature work *The Division of Labour in Society*, distinguished between 'mechanical' and 'organic' solidarity. He argued that mechanical solidarity which was based on common beliefs, consensus of moral values and on other social similarities among members was the dominant feature of relatively simple small scale societies. This form of social solidarity, according to Durkheim, transformed into 'Organic Solidarity' in modern complex industrialised societies. 'Organic Solidarity' was based on dissimilarities, social division of labour and interdependence among autonomous individuals and social units in society.

Durkheim's classification seems to apply to the social organisation of Edinburgh's Pakistani community. Because of close social similarities particularity among members of the Pilrig Mosque/Community Centre, its social order is based on what is very similar to Durkheim's 'Mechanical solidarity'. Kinship ties, institutionalised reciprocal relationships and shared religious beliefs and collective worship have not only created social cohesion and solidarity among members; these factors had also led to the development of strong 'conscience collective ' and a high degree of value consensus among them. It is a form of social solidarity that has created a sense of belonging among members. Thus, the Pilrig Mosque/Community Centre is a community within which members have common social bonds, regular social interaction and a strong sense of social and psychological belonging. This definition more precisely applies to the Pilrig Mosque/Community Centre, both theoretically and empirically.

The Pilrig Mosque/Community Centre that is participated by the majority of Edinburgh's Pakistani population is the main focus and the subject of the present study. Thus, the phrase 'Edinburgh's Pakistani community' is more often used to refer to this social, cultural and religious entity in the present study. Nevertheless, since the P.A.E.E.S. formally represents all Pakistanis in the area the phrase is equally used on a local level to refer to the whole Pakistani population of Edinburgh. Sometimes the term 'community' is used to refer to all Pakistanis in Britain. These various usages, however are specified by their related contexts and frames of analyses in the present study.

Edinburgh's Pakistani Community: A 'Closed' Community

Through most of this chapter I have tried to trace the history of large scale migration of people from the Indian sub-continent to Britain and to Scotland. The main focus of discussion has been the dialectics of relationships between the 'host' society and the South Asian migrants: a relationship between the British imperial rulers and colonial subjects; between industry owner(s) and contractual wage labourers; and between a dominant 'white' majority and a subordinate ethnic 'black' (in its political sense) minority community. More importantly this form of power relationship between the larger 'host' society and the migrant ethnic minorities, in

Britain (Pakistanis in the present context) has been accompanied by large scale exclusion of the latter from the social cultural, and political life of the wider society. It has been argued that this historical process of exclusionary practices against Britain's Pakistani population has resulted in a sense of alienation among them – a sense of being second-class citizens. The argument has been strongly supported by empirical data. As will be shown in Chapter IV, this sense of alienation and second class citizenship is particularly strong among the British-born second generation Pakistanis who are more directly affected by exclusionary practices and racial discrimination than their parents.

The sense of exclusion and alienation of British Pakistanis from the wider society has important social and cultural consequence: the emergence of an increasingly 'closed' Pakistani community in Britain and in Scotland – a community whose members search for social and cultural belonging and identity. This defensive reaction has played a crucial part in the historical development of the social institutions of Pakistan communities in Edinburgh and probably throughout Britain - these social institutions are more conservative and inward-looking than those in Pakistan. For example the institution of family in Edinburgh is much more conservative in socialising the British-born Pakistani children to religious and traditional Pakistani cultural values than a comparable family in a Pakistani city. As I will discuss in detail in Chapters II and III Pakistani parents in Edinburgh not only extends the socialisation of their British-born children beyond the family to the mosque-school, but 'discipline' during this socialisation process is much stricter and more conservative than it is in Pakistan. Boys and girls in the mosque-school are taught separately; they are required to wear hats and scarves, respectively; corporal punishment is the main form of discipline and the young boys and girls are taught the more traditional versions of the Islamic belief system and rituals.

Parents' concern about the socialisation of their British-born children to more traditional and strict forms of Pakistani values is not simply that their children may adopt and identify with the culture of the wider society at the expense of their Muslim/Pakistani culture and identity. Parents are more concerned about their British-born children's loss of any identity - British or Pakistani – should they fully adopt Western culture and try to identify with it. Parents argue that this is because their 'Westernised' children will never be accepted as full citizens of the British society. This concern was explained by a father of three young boys in the mosque school who strongly defended the traditional and strict form of his children's socialisation both in the family and in the mosque-school:

> If we don't do this our children will learn from the *Gorahs*, Whites, [see the loaded meanings of *Gorah* in Chapter IV], the *Gorah* way of life and they will behave like the *Gorahs*. But the problem is that the *Gorahs* will

not accept them as British; they will still call them 'Pakis'. So our children will not know where they belong to. If we want our children to be
good Muslims and Pakistanis we have got to teach them our religion and
our way of life - the way it is in the mosque now; we have got to tell the
children that our way of life is different and better than the *Gorahs*' way
of life; don't mix up the two; otherwise you will be lost.

Similarly, this emphasis on the retaining and even promotion of conservative Islamic/Pakistani values is further apparent in the general social atmosphere, rituals of collective worship and in the preaching of the mosque. As
will be discussed in Chapter III all these are aimed at the creation and
strengthening of a moral and social order that is distinctly different from
that of the wider society. Again it is a moral and social order whose values
are more conservative and traditional than those of the country of origin of
this migrant community. A Pakistani student who came to Edinburgh for his
one-year postgraduate studies was surprised by the traditionalism of wedding ceremonies in Edinburgh. The Pakistani student who accompanied me
to a wedding in Portobello Town Hall told me at the end of the ceremony:
'I am really surprised. This wedding was much more old-fashioned (traditional) than weddings anywhere in Lahore, Faisalabad or Islamabad.'
Indeed, all the Pakistani wedding ceremonies that I have observed in
Edinburgh have been more traditional than the wedding ceremonies that I
have attended in Lahore, Pakistan: in two of the three weddings the bride
wore a European wedding dress and the groom a short three piece suite with
a tie; men and women mixed with each other in the large hall of Lahore's
Hilton Hotel and took dinner together. But in all the wedding ceremonies in
Edinburgh both the bride and groom wore traditional Pakistani
dresses/clothes and men and women sat in separate parts of the hall and the
whole social atmosphere was more conservative than at a wedding in
Pakistan.

Likewise, men and women are separated not only during the collective
worship in the mosque but in all other social and cultural occasions. This
separation of men and women among Edinburgh's Pakistanis becomes particularly relevant to the present discussion when it is compared to male-
female relationships in Pakistan: men and women in Pakistani universities
sit side by side in the same lecture hall; they work as colleagues in the same
office; and men and women mix with each other in social and cultural gatherings. A woman even became Prime Minister of Pakistan twice during the
last eight years. When I asked a group of the community leaders about this
contrast a majority of them defended the preservation of traditional
Islamic/Pakistani values including a separation between unrelated men and
women. One of the leaders said:

This place is not Pakistan. Here we are *Pardis* [strangers]; we need something to hang on to. Look at the Black people in London; they followed the English habits and way of life and tried to be like the English. Their children are more Anglicised than the English are, but the English still don't accept them; they don't know who they are and where they belong to; many young Black boys and girls live without their parents in misery, but the English wouldn't give a damn, because they are black. We must stick to our religion and to our way of life more than the people in Pakistan. If we lose our religion and our own way of life then we will not know who we are and where we belong to; and we all know that the British will never accept us.

This sense of insecurity was shared by many people in the community. Most of Edinburgh's Pakistanis who have experienced discrimination and feel insecure find security in community – a Pakistani community to which they could socially and culturally belong; as the above passage implies the more traditional and the more Pakistani their community the more secure many of its members feel.

This sense of alienation, insecurity and a need for cultural belonging of the first generation Pakistanis in Edinburgh is also widely shared by their British-born children. Most of these youngsters identify themselves with Pakistan (see Chapter IV for details). However, these second-generation Pakistanis by and large, differ from their parents who seek belonging and identity in a simple return to conservative religious and traditional Pakistani cultural values. Instead most of the second generation young Pakistanis in Edinburgh appear to interpret these values in a relatively secular and modern context. They reproduce a culture that is modern but, at the same time, markedly Pakistani so that they could identify with it. Although not widely approved of by the first-generation Pakistanis, the 'Pakistani Youth Culture' that is emerging as a direct response to exclusion is also vigorously contributing to the making of a 'closed' Pakistani community, in Edinburgh and in Scotland. *Bhangra* is a case in point. *Bhangra* is a Pakistan/Indian version of Western disco that is periodically organised in Glasgow or Edinburgh by young Pakistanis and Sikhs. Because Bhangra is still not socially approved by the first generation Pakistanis, it takes place between 4-10 pm so that young Pakistan boys and girls can find acceptable pretexts for their late afternoon or early evening absence from their homes.

The large *Bhangra* dancing hall is furnished with all the requirements and facilities of a Western disco hall e.g., special coloured lights, disco music, and a bar which is full of alcoholic and non-alcoholic drinks, etc. Almost everything in the *Bhangra* dancing hall is Western, except the attendants, barmen/women, guards and the music. The music is an interesting combination of Western disco music and of original Pakistani/Asian music; both

Western and Asian musical instruments are used for a disco dancing session. The dancers are young Pakistani, Indian and Bangladeshi men and women. The dance is lively but more Asian than Western.

The whole institution of the *Bhangra* and its related processes are clearly an expression of Indian/Pakistan culture in a Western setting; it is an expression of a cultural identity as the Pakistan co-organiser of *Bhangra* put it:

> I am sure you know that Asian boys and girls in white discos have problems. People laugh at them and harass them there. So we thought why no tour own Asian disco; here is no fear of harassment by white boys. Now, we tell them that we don't need your discos anymore; now all Asian boys and girls come to *Bhangra*; it is our culture and we are proud of it.

Despite the first-generation Pakistanis' disapproval of *Bhangra*, it is very likely to become a popular and legitimate cultural institution of Edinburgh's Pakistani community. But it will be a cultural institution that will further contribute to the making of a more self-sufficient 'closed' Pakistani community. It will fill the existing cultural and artistic gap in present social and institutional arrangements of the Pakistani community. In fact, video recorded *Bhangra* music and dance alongside Indian/Pakistani movies, particularly Pakistani dramas (from Pakistan National Television) are a major social and cultural entertainment for Pakistani families in Edinburgh. Now the Pakistani video shops are an accepted part of the Pakistani business enterprise in Edinburgh.

Apart from the normative and cultural 'closedness' of the Pakistani community in Edinburgh, it is increasingly becoming an economically 'closed' community of self-employed businessmen, shopkeepers, restaurateurs, entrepreneurs etc. As it was shown in the previous section because of a large scale exclusionary practices and discrimination against Pakistanis in employment, many of them have been forced into self-employment. Through family and *Biraderi* connections more and more Pakistanis are being employed by kin and friends. In some cases a Pakistani restaurant-owner or a Pakistani owner of a large department store normally employs other jobless Pakistanis on a part-time basis. In other cases they provide financial help, advice and social support to kin and friends to open small corner shops for themselves. Thus, the Pakistani community in Edinburgh has more than ever become a community of self-employed shopkeepers, restaurant-owners, businessmen, and their Pakistani employees. The relative economic success and expansion of many Pakistani businesses has resulted in the development of a complex infrastructure of Pakistani economic and financial establishments in Edinburgh and Glasgow. Pakistani banks, financial brokerage firms, mortgage companies, estate and travel agencies, have resulted in economic interdependence and a relative economic self-sufficiency within the community. This phenomenon appears to be gradually drawing the economic boundaries of a Pakistani 'closed' community.

As far as communication in economic social, cultural, and political issues among members of Edinburgh's Pakistani community and among the rest of Britain's Pakistanis is concerned, the Pakistani population in Edinburgh and elsewhere in Britain is effectively informed about economic, social, cultural, political and other issues that concern them through a highly professional Pakistani press. This includes daily, weekly and monthly newspapers and magazines, most of which are published in Urdu, or both in Urdu and English. *Awaz* (Voice), *Akhbar-i-watan* (The News of Homeland) and *Jang* (*the file - Jang*, a Persian word, is often incorrectly translated by some Pakistanis as war) are among the widely read and the popular Urdu newspaper among Edinburgh's Pakistanis. The daily *Jang*, particularly, is the most popular Urdu paper in Edinburgh. I have hardly seen any Pakistani home in Edinburgh that did not receive the *Jang* every day. The *Jang* reports news of major events in Britain, Pakistan and in the world; news of events within the Pakistani community in Britain such as cultural, religious and social gatherings, conferences, incidents of racial violence, etc. are regularly reported in this daily newspaper; commercial advertisements, matrimonial, obituaries, and advertisements about Asian/Pakistani cultural and artistic events are also reported in the *Jang*. The daily *Jang* is also supplemented by a colour 'magazine' that normally includes photos of Pakistani film-stars, sportsmen and of Pakistani social and political personalities in Britain and in Pakistan.

The *Jang*'s apparent ideological openness and political neutrality and its coverage of a wide range of issues have made it a very influential and popular paper among Pakistanis in Edinburgh. I have found that for most of Edinburgh's Pakistanis the *Jang* is a most comprehensive and reliable substitute for reading the British daily press. This is mainly because many Pakistanis believe that the British press neglect reporting news that relates to Pakistanis in Britain, and to the Muslim world; some even think that the British press is biased against Pakistanis and Muslims.

Hence, it is not surprising that the *Jang* has become a major window of Edinburgh's Pakistani community to the world; it plays an important role in the making of a 'closed' Pakistani community, on local and national levels in Britain and in Scotland.

The sense of alienation, insecurity and of non-citizenship of Britain's Pakistani population who are predominantly (about 99%) Muslims has been further strengthened after the publication of Salman Rushdie's *Satanic Verses*. Britain's Pakistanis who have consistently experienced exclusion, discrimination and rejection considered the negative description of prophet

Mohammed (P.B.U.H.) as 'Mahound' (false prophet), the Prophet's wives as 'whores' and Prophet Abraham as 'Bastard' (Rushdie 1989:.95,101,381-82) as a conspiracy against their religion and as a most direct insult to their social identity. It was because of their long accumulated feelings of being rejected and of being looked down on that the reaction of British Pakistanis to *Satanic Verses* was so intense; it was even more intense than the reaction of people in Pakistan itself, or in Saudi Arabia and many other Islamic countries (see Appignanesi and Maitland 1989). Werbner who has done extensive research among Britain's Pakistanis for about the past two decades and who has followed the various phases of the Rushdie affair shares this view:

> The Rushdie affair, the confrontation between the Muslim community and the British nation state, . . . revealed deeply felt emotions which might otherwise have remained, perhaps, obscured and unrecognised, even to the people themselves: a sense of stigma and discrimination, of being rejected, of having one's innermost identity and faith derided and disregarded by the wider society.(Werbner 1991 : 344)

Indeed the massive and angry protest of Britain's Muslims, the overwhelming majority of whom are Pakistanis, was much more than a protest against a blasphemous book; it was mainly a protest against racial discrimination, exclusion and against the disregard and unequal treatment of the protesters' religion and an insult to their cultural and religious identity by the wider society. It was mainly because of this reason that the protest against the *Satanic Verses* united the extremist, the secular (cultural Muslims) and even the atheists among Britain's Muslims. Unfortunately, it was the extremists who led the protest and responded to the situation in extreme ways. One example of this is the establishment of 'the Muslim parliament of Great Britain', as an extreme response to political exclusion in the aftermath of the Rushdie affair. An official document of the 'Muslim Parliament' says:

> In the face of hostility and prejudice from non-Muslims, and a lack of protection and understanding from the political system, *British Muslims turned inwards to themselves for support* and outwards to the global Muslim community for protection from Rushdie's insult and abuse. This had the effect of a resurgence of Muslim consciousness and identity . . . (Emphasis added) (The Muslim Parliament of Great Britain 1992: 2)

The above passage most clearly indicates the connection between a strong sense of alienation, non-citizenship and a sense of insecurity and the making of 'closed' Muslim/Pakistani community. The 'Muslim Parliament', which is led and dominated by Pakistani Muslims, has the support of only a relatively small fraction of the larger Muslim/Pakistani population of Britain; but this may be just a matter of time. For example, among

Edinburgh's Pakistani population only an insignificant minority actively support the 'Muslim Parliament'; but there are members of the community who have a 'wait and see' attitude towards the 'Parliament'. Despite the fact that the majority of Edinburgh's Muslims and Pakistani do not support the 'Parliament', a leader of the community showed concern about its attraction to ordinary Pakistanis in Glasgow and Edinburgh: 'The problem is that many Pakistanis say that their voice is not heard and that they are let down; they say if you [the dominant society and the state] don't look after us we ought to look after ourselves'.

'Looking after ourselves' in terms of the establishment of an autonomous Muslim legislative body alongside the British parliament is very unlikely to be tolerated by the wider society, and supported by most members of the Pakistani community in Edinburgh and in Britain. But it appears that there is a general tendency among Pakistanis in Edinburgh to establish a more effective political institution than the 'Pakistan Association for Edinburgh and the East of Scotland' (P.A.E.E.S). The general tendency among members of Edinburgh's Pakistani community about the transformation of the P.A.E.E.S. into an effective political institution is very likely to subject it to pressure from the ordinary members of the community. They want to express their grievances to the wider society more effectively. In this case the P.A.E.E.S. - the least inward-looking of the community's social institution - has to interact more closely with the other institutions of the community that are comparatively more inward-looking. Hence the P.A.E.E.S. would form the 'political wall' in the making of 'closed' Pakistani community.

However, this is not to say that the P.A.E.E.S. is likely to become religiously conservative or dominated by religious extremists within the community. Instead, it is more likely to be led by more secular or liberal British-born Pakistanis, who place stronger emphasis on their 'Pakistaniness' than on religious doctrines and values (see Chapter IV). As the British-born Pakistanis succeed their fathers as leaders of the community, in the next two to three decades, the Pakistani community and its social institutions are very likely to undergo a social and cultural change - they are likely to be more distinctively Pakistani but less religiously conservative; more modern and in a sense 'Westernised'; but paradoxically more 'closed' to Westerners who have excluded them from integration to the wider society. However, much of this may not happen, should inclusion replace exclusion.

In this chapter I have analysed the relationship between exclusion of Edinburgh's Pakistani population from the social, cultural and political life of the wider society and the consequent development of the increasingly inward-looking Pakistani social institutions that constitute the 'closed' Pakistani community in Edinburgh. Now, I turn to the analysis of the social organisation of this community, and the way its social institutions operates as agencies of social control.

2 The Family and the *Biraderi*

Introduction

This chapter is divided into two main parts – the family and the *Biraderi*, or the social network of kinship/friendship relationships. In the first part of the chapter a general account of the institution of the Pakistani (Punjabi) family in its original setting in the Punjab, Pakistan, will be given. Then the state of the Pakistani family and its adaptation to the new social and cultural environment in Edinburgh will be briefly discussed. The discussion will then focus on a detailed examination of the socialisation of the British-born children of Pakistani parents, and on parental authority, as two major mechanisms of social control in the Pakistani family, in Edinburgh.

In the second part of the chapter the institution of the *Biraderi* that links families and individuals in a kinship/friendship framework is discussed. In this part, first, the meaning, forms and structure of the *Biraderi* in Edinburgh will be described. Then *Lina Dina* (taking and giving) or a form of institutionalised reciprocity and the way it creates mutual obligations, interdependence and communitarianism among members of the ('effective') *Biraderi* will be analysed in detail. Finally, the discussion will focus on the analysis of *Izzet* and *Bizati* (honour and dishonour) that operate as powerful mechanisms of social control within the communitarian structure of the *Biraderi* among Edinburgh's Pakistanis.

I: The Family

The Structure and Functions of the Punjabi Family in Pakistan

The traditional Punjabi family, in its natural setting in Pakistan, is a joint/extended patriarchal social unit where two or more generations of close relatives who are affiliated by blood relationship live together under one roof or in a cluster of adjacent houses. They usually share property, land, business and often work together. They pool their income together and spend from their common purse.

This form of the family in the rural areas of the Punjab (where the majority of the province's population live) would, normally, consist of a father and mother, their unmarried sons and daughters, and their married sons with their spouses and sibling. The structure of this form of household could be illustrated as follows:

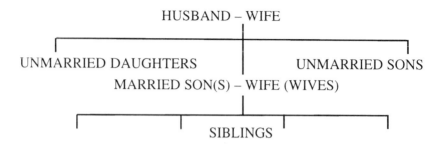

Diagram 1 – The Structure of the Extended Punjabi Family in Pakistan

This structure could also include one or both parental ancestors and a widowed daughter. It could also take the form of a 'stem family' where parents live with one of their married sons (often the youngest), but their other married sons live in separate households, while often sharing their common property. Or in case of the death of the father or both parents, unmarried brothers and sisters, usually live with the wife and children of their older brother who shoulders the responsibility of their education and arrangements for their marriages (see Anwar 1979,1986; Eglar 1960; Henley 1979; Kennedy 1957; Shaw 1988).

Brothers in the joint/extended family who often live in one house or in an adjacent extension share land, business, factory, animals and other kinds of property that they, mainly, inherit from their father. According to the Punjabi customary law, the father's property is passed on along the male line (see Eglar 1960; Maron 1957; Shaw 1988). According to Islamic Law (which has official support in Pakistan), daughter should inherit her father's property, but in practice inheritance goes only to the sons of the deceased. This continued passing on of property (particularly land and house) within the same family over generations seems to be one of the main contributors for keeping the joint/extended family together. In this way the adult male sand other members of the family may work on their shared land, in a fac-tory or in a governmental office, but they all share their incomes.

There is a clear-cut division of labour between the male and the female in the joint family; men and women have their separate areas of responsibilities in the functioning of the joint familial unit. Men's world of activity is, mainly, outside the house. They normally start their day with morning prayer (preceded by the Islamic ablution), that is performed before sunrise in any season of the year. Then, after an early breakfast, men leave home for the family's agricultural farm, or some may go to their business or work in a nearby factory, if there is one. As predominantly farmers, men in the rural Punjab, spend their day in cultivating plants, irrigating the land, harvesting and sowing the crops, selling the products and maintaining the irrigation system.

It is also in the domain of men to attend meetings of the local village and 'Mosque committees' concerning local problems. They are responsible for all contacts with government authorities in matters such as public education, health, taxes and land revenues, judicial cases etc., In sum, men are the Punjabi family's public spokespersons.

Women's activities and responsibilities, on the other hand, are mainly domestic within the physical and social scope of the *Gher* (house). They cook food; bake *Nan* or *Chapati* (two forms of home-baked bread); wash dishes and clothes; clean and take care of the house; they make clothes for the family members, spin, weave, and milk buffaloes. An important duty of women is bringing up children of the family (not only their own). Women in the Punjabi family in Pakistan play a very important role in the basic moral and religious education of the family's children. The joint family as a whole places much emphasis on women's role in the 'proper' socialisation of its children so that they grow up *Neik*, good and pious, people and to preserve their family's *Izzet* (honour) and reputation. Children in the Punjabi family are treated as if they belonged to the whole joint/extended family rather to their own parents. Grandmothers and paternal aunts also play an important role in bringing up the 'children of the family'. Nevertheless, as Kennedy (1957) reports, children have most affectionate relationships with their parents, particularly, with their mothers.

However, despite the Punjabi women's predominant involvement in domestic activities, they are not completely cut off from the outer world. They visit relatives, actively participate in the celebration of social events and in other social activities within the *Biraderi* (network of kinship/friendship relationships). They also go to *Mela*, fairs, or visit saints' tomb in other women's company. Besides this, according to my observation, in the rural Punjab women who belonged to the working class often worked outside the house. They co-operated with men in harvesting and planting the crops and took food to them in the farm. Interestingly, it appeared that women who belonged to middle and lower middle classes rarely worked outside the house. Some of them wore *Pardah* (veil) and their outlook seem to be conservative. However, in Punjabi cities and towns women's work outside the home, particularly in the medical, nursing and teaching professions, was considered as an indicator of modernity and of their higher social status. This appeared to apply to all women, regardless of their social class.

The woman's role as a housewife (or potential housewife) in the rural Punjab does not mean that they are totally dependent persons without an important place in the family. It is recognised that if man is the bread-winner, and the 'public spokesmen' of the family, the woman is considered as an educator of its children, and is a manageress of the *Gher* (house). More important, a woman in the Punjabi culture is recognised as an important guardian of the family's *Izzet*, prestige and honour - that is a dearly achieved social asset in Punjabi society. The author of *A Punjabi Village* writes:

> In this society a woman's co-operation, especially of the *'Chaudhrani'*, the *'Chaudhari's'* mother or his wife is crucial in building up and sustaining the prestige of the man. For women control all provisions and the money. (Eglar 1960:30)

Indeed, the *Chaudhari* (head of the extended family, who is often a landlord), to a greater extent depends on the co-operation of his wife, mother, or of another mature woman, in the maintenance and building of the family's *Izzet* (honour). But in the final analysis, it is the man in Punjabi culture who empowers the woman to 'control provisions and money'. The Punjabi family, remains a strongly patriarchal system where man is the 'taken-for-granted' head. This situation places women in a relatively weak position to express their disagreements with men. Nevertheless the Punjabi family is not as conflict-free a social unit as it may appear.

Next to gender/sex as a basis of division of labour comes age as the basis of the exercise of authority among members of the joint/extended Punjabi family in Pakistan. Respect and obedience to older members in the family is followed as a norm. While being a general norm applicable to all older people in the family, obedience and respect are very clearly observed in the father-child relationships. The children learn that when their parents, particularly the father, talks they must carefully listen to him. What he says is, usually, believed and taken for granted. They rarely make objections or show opposition to what their parents, particularly to what the father, says. Even if such comments are made, they are indirect or conveyed through mother or grandmother. Abusive language and 'impolite' behaviour in the presence of both parents is a taboo. As the children reach adolescence the father-son(s) relationships enter a very different stage. At this stage sons, particularly, the oldest one is expected to behave as a responsible adult. This is because he is going to be the head of the family.

Daughters, on the other hand, are expected to be even more obedient than their brothers. Their obedience to parental authority is considered as an important virtue that is strongly echoed in the general Punjabi culture. Young girls' disobedience to their parents and to other older members of the family endanger their chances of marriage. This is mainly because girls' behaviour, particularly those of marriageable age, is often a subject of scrutiny and gossip among kin and neighbours.

As mentioned earlier the hierarchical structure of social relationships (and of authority) in the Punjabi family is not restricted to the parent-child relationships, but also apply to the relationships among the other members of the joint/extended family. For example, grandparents, uncles, elder brothers and sisters, fathers and mothers-in-law are dealt with respect and obedience. While these relationships are mainly organised on the basis of age, there are also complex rules for ascertaining the relationships of a particular member to elderly persons in the family. For example, while the daughter-in-law is supposed to be respectful and obedient to both parents-in-law, the mother-in-law often exercises a direct authority over her. The mother-in-law has an important role in the economic and social control of the family, often having to 're-socialise' her son's new bride as the 'alien new-comer' to the particular sub-culture of the in-laws' family. But the mother-in-law and daughter-in-law's relationships and those among daughters-in-law themselves often contain the seeds of conflict within the joint extended family. This sometimes leads to the break up of the joint/extended family.

With this general background of the structure and functions of the Punjabi family in its natural setting in Pakistan, it is now appropriate to discuss its structure and functions after migration to Scotland.

The Pakistani Family in Edinburgh

The Pakistani family in Edinburgh and in Britain, in general, is a continuation of the extended family in Pakistan in many ways. However, some of the necessary adaptations of the Scottish Pakistani family to the new environment after migration may mislead the casual observer. For example, some recent research has produced figures which suggest that the extended Punjabi family was radically declining after migration. A survey conducted by SEMRU (Scottish Ethnic Minority Research Unit), in the Lothian and Edinburgh District (1987:28) concludes that in Pakistani households, in the area, '31.1% had three or more adults as well as children - i.e. an extended family structure'. Similarly, research by the Scottish Office, 'Ethnic Minorities in Scotland' (1991:34), shows that only 26% of the Pakistani households in Glasgow, Edinburgh, Dundee, and Aberdeen had extended household structure. Very similarly in the present study, 26.6% of the 60 boys in the Pilrig sample said that one or more of their close relatives (grandparents, aunts, cousins, married sisters, etc.) lived with them in their house. This research either explicitly shows, or at least implies that around three-fourths of the Pakistani population in Scotland live in a 'Nuclear' form of household (a social unit that consists of a married man, and woman with their children).

But are the apparently nuclear Pakistani families in Scotland actually nuclear? A superficial distinction between the nuclear and the joint/extended households in Scotland can be misleading. In fact, I have found that many Pakistani families in Edinburgh that may appear to be nuclear are, in essence, branches of a joint family in Pakistan or in other British cities.

Although the scarcity or high prices of large houses in Scotland has made it difficult for members of most joint/extended Pakistani families to share one residential compound, they continue to live as joint social and economic units. These joint families effectively perform the social economic and emotional functions of a joint Pakistani family that were described earlier.

In some cases an apparently nuclear family in Edinburgh was exactly an extension of a joint family in Pakistan. One brother with his wife and children worked in Scotland, while sending money to his other brothers or/and parents in Pakistan and sharing land and other property with them. He still consults his joint/extended family in making decisions, takes trips to Pakistan for major, ceremonies and his sentiments and loyalty remain with members of the joint/extended family. My research shows that the pattern of visiting relatives in Pakistan and sending them (particularly aged parents) return tickets to Britain is a common practice in the Edinburgh Pakistani community. Furthermore, the relatively common practice of the burial of the dead, and the arrangement of marriages of young men with their kin in Pakistan, keep ties among relatives in Scotland and Pakistan quite strong.

Thus, it could be safely asserted that Edinburgh's Pakistani population continues to have a type of joint family that fits their new circumstances after migration. That is to say, that the traditional joint/extended traditional Punjabi family, in Pakistan, has been or is being replaced by a 'modified' joint/extended family after migration. This 'modified' system while preserving, to a great extent, the structure and most of the functions of the traditional family in Pakistan may not necessarily have a common residence. As the present study is mainly concerned with the Pakistani family in Edinburgh as an agency of social control, the following discussion will focus on the socialisation of the British-born Pakistani children and on 'parental authority' as two major mechanisms of social control within this social institution.

Socialisation: A Process of Social Bonding

Since the Pakistani household in Britain is only a modified form of the joint/extended household in the Punjab, socialisation continues to be one of its major functions in the post-migration situation. Indeed, this is the case in Britain and in Edinburgh. For Edinburgh's Pakistani population, the roles of their families to socialise children to their own values, norms, and beliefs in a Western culture are of even more crucial importance than they are in Pakistan. For most of Edinburgh's Pakistani families, the socialisation of their British-born children starts from their birth. Thus soon after her birth (in hospital) the baby is given a bath and her head is shaved, so that the 'dirty' hair is completely removed. Then *Azan* (call for prayer) is whispered, first in her right ear, then in the left. The *Azan* which consists of thirteen sentences in Arabic has the following meaning: '*Allah* is great' (four times), 'I bear witness that there is no God apart from *Allah*' (two times), 'I bear witness that Mohammad is *Allah*'s messenger' (two times), 'Rush to prayer' (two times), 'Rush to success' (two times), 'There is no God apart from *Allah*'(one time).

This seems to be the most commonly practised ritual among Edinburgh's Pakistanis. I did not find a single case where parents did not do the *Azan* in the ears of their new-born baby: 'if you do not do *Azan* in the baby's ears, then what is the difference between us and the *gorahs*, [the whites]?', said Mrs. M.I. Many of Edinburgh's Pakistani residents believe that the baby understands the meaning of the *Azan* through metaphysical means. Therefore it is considered necessary to whisper the *Azan* in the baby's ears telling her that she is born to a Muslim family and that she is expected to be a Muslim.

News of the birth of the baby is soon conveyed to kin and friends by sending them *Ladoos* (a kind of colourful rounded sweets). Just as in Pakistan, relatives come to see the baby, giving her clothes and money ranging from £5 to £30, the amount depending on the degree of closeness of relation between the donor and the baby. It is a common practice in Pakistan to celebrate the baby's birth by sacrificing a sheep or a goat (two for a boy, and one or none for a girl!). This is called *Aqiqa*. But very few Pakistani families in Edinburgh perform *Aqiqa*. Instead most of these families in Edinburgh send money to relatives in Pakistan to perform *Aqiqa*; or they themselves do it when they next visit Pakistan.

The Pakistani baby in Edinburgh is often surrounded by her close relatives. Besides parents, brothers and sisters, the new-born baby enjoys the care and affection of cousins, uncles and aunts, who may live nearby. She is seldom taken to nursery school as the mother, usually a housewife, is always around. An unmarried sister or an aunt will normally look after the child when the mother is busy with her housework. Mother and unmarried elder sisters play a major role in transmitting the Islamic Pakistani values to the child. When asked, 'From whom did you first learn the fundamentals of Islam?' most boys in the Pilrig 'Mosque-school' in Edinburgh answered that they learned them from their mothers and/or sisters. Some boys mentioned both parents. The Pakistani child at this stage of socialisation is usually strongly attached to parents particularly to his/her mother. And it is at this period (pre-school 5 or 6 years) that the Pakistani child who lives in a very insulated atmosphere picks up the basics of Islamic beliefs and the fundamental Islamic values at home; he/she is socialised to the Pakistani habits and ways of life.

During this period, the only other children with whom these young British-born Pakistanis interact are their kin and other Pakistani children that they meet during family visits or in some other social gatherings. They normally play with and make friends with these boys and girls. Thus, the British-born young children of Pakistani parents in their first 5 or 6 years are brought up in a very insulated Pakistani social and cultural atmosphere - a world that is very different from the world outside; but a world that they have to talk to, listen to and work in. Thus, in order to be able to interact with the wider society these boys are also socialised to its norms and values in the local formal Scottish educational institutions. In fact as these children enter the local Scottish schools they interact more directly with the wider society and learn about its moral and social values through their class-mates, teachers and through the contents of their lessons. It is at this stage that the British-born Pakistani boys in Edinburgh hear about movies, discos, and going out with friends.

It is during the school years that most Pakistani parents impose certain restrictions about the whereabouts of their young children (see Chapter IV about Parental Supervision). Normally, parents strongly advise their chil-dren to be at home, in their work-place (shop/store, etc.), or in the mosque-school after they return from the local school. The occasional failure of some of these children to follow their parents' advice sometimes results in conflict between parents and their children. Some parents told me that going out to movies and discos and socialising with young boys and girls from the indigenous population corrupts their children. But many other parents had other reasons for the restrictive socialisation of their British-born children. A father of two teenage boys told me that:

> To me there is nothing wrong in going out to a movie or even to go out with friends to a disco. When I was young I was used to go to discos on the weekends. But I remember that I was verbally abused and even attacked there. The reason that I discourage my sons from going out to discos and pubs is to avoid trouble.

Another father of three teenage boys and a girl told me of a slightly differ-ent reason for the restrictive supervision and strict socialisation of their British-born children:

> I wouldn't mind if my children learn the British way of life and feel as British. This is their country; they will live here for the rest of their life. But what worries us is that they will not be accepted as British. Then they will be confused about who they are. This is why we bring up our chil-dren as much Pakistani as we can. We have to teach our children the Muslim and Pakistani way of life at home and in the Mosque. We should be able to convince them that the British will always see them as Pakistanis; so they should remain Pakistanis and be proud of being Pakistanis; otherwise, they will be nothing.

These passages clearly indicate that the over-emphasis of many Pakistani parents on the strict socialisation of their British-born children to Islamic/Pakistani values is mainly a reaction to their experiences of exclusion in the wider society. Many parents believe that their British-born children will not be accepted as full members of the British Society and so need to develop social and psychological belonging to Islam and Pakistan. Thus the socialisation process of these boys goes beyond the family into the mosque-school.

The mosque-school that is attended by the British-born Pakistani boys (and also girls in separate class) five days a week is basically a continuation of the Islamic/Pakistani socialisation process of these children that has started within their families. I will discuss the social organisation, the content of *Sabaq* (Islamic lessons), and discipline in the Mosque-school in Chapter III in greater detail. But it is important to mention here that despite several deficiencies of the Mosque-school in creating a suitable atmosphere for teaching and explaining Islamic morality, it provides a congenial environment for the socialisation of these children to Islamic beliefs and rituals. That is to say, that the boys in the Mosque-school are taught the practical procedures of making ablution, making *Azan* (the call for prayer) and the congregational prayers on Fridays, funerals and on Islamic festivals (*Eid-ul-Fiter* and *Eid-ul-Ozha*). Moreover the boys are taught reading of the *Quran* and memorising parts of it that are necessary for praying. This process of socialisation to Islamic rituals enables the young Pakistanis to participate in the community's collective religious/cultural activities. In other words, this socialisation to Islamic beliefs and rituals bonds the British-born Pakistani youngsters to their community's conventional order(see Chapter III for further details).

Some parents do not find the socialisation process of their children - at home and in the Mosque-school - sufficient to bond their children to the community's conventional morality because of what they see as the encroachment of Western culture. This has led them to think about another strategy for the socialisation of their children to Islamic values: a growing number of parents send their children to Pakistan when they approach adolescence. These adolescent young boys (and also girls) go to school and live with members of their extended family in Pakistan for a few years. When the parents are sure that their children are mature enough to resist influences of the Western culture, they call them back to live and work with them in Scotland. Sometimes, the marriages of these boys are also arranged by their parents in Pakistan and they return with their wives. Six of my students in the Mosque-school have left for Pakistan and four others are due to leave. The intended impact of this new strategy can be seen on some of the boys who returned to Britain: 'Pakistan is a better place; people are nice there; houses are bigger than here and people don't call names', I.H. and A.H., two teenage brothers said. But N.S. who is now in his early 20's and who had been to Pakistan for the same purpose, has mixed feelings; 'Some things are good in Pakistan and some here. In Pakistan if you don't have money, people don't talk to you, but here whether you are poor or rich you are the same. But here is too much freedom which is no good'. Accepting Islamic restrictions and considering certain Western values as 'no good' is probably the result of N.S.'s socialisation in Pakistan. Despite his mixed feelings, N.S. seems to prefer the Pakistani way of life. He regularly prays, reads the *Quran* and behaves as a conventional Pakistani young man.

What has been said so far indicates that the Pakistani family in Edinburgh is the major and relatively powerful agency of socialisation of the British born Pakistani children. Because of their fear of the influence of Western values over their children in a social and cultural environment where they feel excluded and insecure, parents do not stop at socialising their children to Islamic/Pakistani values in the home. The process extends to the Mosque-school and even to Pakistan so that the British-born Pakistani children are adequately bonded to the conventional morality of the Edinburgh's Pakistani community. In order to further back up the basic socialisation process, and to ensure obedience to Pakistani/Islamic norms and values, parents are socially and economically in a privileged position to exercise authority over their British-born children.

Parental Authority and Social Control

As has been mentioned, age-based authority remains an important feature of the Punjabi family both in Pakistan and in Edinburgh. Young members learn at home, in the Mosque-school and in the community, in general, to obey and respect individuals who are older than them, within the joint family, the *Biraderi* and even in the larger community. Within the family context, this pattern of respect and obedience to elders, particularly to parents, is not only followed as a ritual echoed in the general culture, but is considered as a fundamental basis of the social organisation and stability of the joint familial unit. Parents (especially fathers) are especially in a strong position to exercise authority over their children. Parents' authority in this context is generally used to back up the basic socialisation process. It is used as the 'legitimate' right of parents to enforce obedience to the norms and values to which the British-born young Pakistanis are socialised. When symptoms of disobedience to parents are felt, children are reminded that disobedience to parents means disobedience to *Allah* which is a big sin. The holy *Quran*, with regard to obedience, kindness and deference to parents advises Muslims in this way:

And be kind to the parents. When one or both of them attain old age in your life, do not say to them a harsh word nor scold them, but address them in terms of honour. And out of kindness, lower the wing of humility and say, 'my Lord bestow on them mercy just as they cherished me in childhood'.

Many Pakistani youngsters who are taught the meaning of the above *Quranic* advice at home and in the Mosque-school, would refrain from disobeying their parents because it is disobedience to *Allah,* which is a punishable sin in the other world. However, if the young boys particularly those who are adult, continue to disobey their parents and challenge their parents' authority, *Allah*'s punishment goes beyond the meaning of mere sin that is punishable in the other world. Parents are empowered to apply part of *Allah*'s punishment in this world as well. Prophet Mohammed (PBUH)says: '*Allah* Almighty may pardon all sins as He pleases, except *Auqooq* of parents. He rather hastens (to punish) its doer in his life before death." (Abu Bakrah in Al-Baihaqi).

The Arabic term *Auqooq*, as a noun, stands for the continued form of disobedience that is deeply annoying and intolerable to the parents. The right of parents (the father in practice) to exercise *Auqooq* has serious social and economic consequences for the 'disobedient' throughout his/her life. The *Aaqq* (the person against whom *Auqooq* is exercised) cannot, according to Islamic Law, inherit his/her father's property; he/she is socially boycotted within the family; and the label becomes a permanent stigma for the 'disobedient' within the *Biraderi* and in the community.

Surprisingly the Arabic word *Auqooq* was unknown to many Pakistani residents in Edinburgh. Nevertheless, they fully understood the fact that parents have the power to deprive their siblings from inheritance. Thus parents not only could use *Auqooq* as a threat but sometimes they actually practise it against their disobedient sons. Take the example of N.R., a young man who comes from an economically comfortable family. His father Mr. G.R. is a religious and honourable man who runs a small business in Edinburgh. Mr. G.R. seems to be exercising relatively strict control over the family members, particularly over his young sons, all of whom have educational qualifications. N.R. the oldest among Mr. G.R.'s sons had an affair with a Sikh girl without the knowledge of his family members. His relations with the girl finally reached a stage where he decided to marry her. The young man asked for his father's permission to get married to the Sikh girl. But his father categorically refused to allow that to happen. Despite this the young man married the Sikh girl privately. When the family and his father learnt about this, they threw him out of the home; N.R. was told that he had nothing to do with the family's property and was prevented from visiting the family. His younger brother says that since that time they have not had any relations with him, and we do not know what he does nor where he lives.

Although this severe reaction of parents to the disobedience of their sons rarely takes place, the threat of the exercise of *Auqooq* always exists. The youngsters in the community are generally aware of this power of their parents; they recognise the religio-economic basis of parents' authority within the family.

Related to the religio-economic basis of parental authority is Pakistani parents' crucial role in the arrangement of their young sons' and daughters' marriages. Parents negotiate the whole process of this arrangement. The wishes and likes of young men and women are expressed to the other party in the arrangement of marriages through parents. And it is also parents who shoulder the (often) huge expenses of the wedding ceremonies/rituals of their young sons and daughters. Hence, as young men and women depend culturally and economically on the vital help of their parents in getting married, their parents are in a strong position to exercise authority over them.

Furthermore, to go beyond the religio-socio-economic sources of parental authority, there is another independent economic source for parental authority in the Punjabi family in Edinburgh. Parents' continued control over the family's property makes its other members, particularly young sons and daughters, economically dependent on them. This is especially the case when the parents are rich (not necessarily in the upper class strata). Parents, generally, pay for the education of their sons and daughters, and for the expenditure on their marriages, and parents provide the luxuries at home i.e. videos, cars and other modern conveniences. Also, young boys and girls can spend money from the family's common 'purse' only with their parents' permission. Thus, because of their control over the family's property, parents have an economic source from where they get the power to exercise authority over their sons and daughters.

It should be mentioned that the government's social security/unemployment benefits have, to some extent, reduced the economic dependency of some Pakistani boys on their families. Some of Edinburgh's Pakistani residents say that a growing number of Pakistani youngsters in Edinburgh claim these benefits. They say that it is not that these youngsters actually 'need' money. But they do so to be less dependent on their parents and, therefore, relatively freer from their control. They complain that the social security/unemployment benefits have given the Pakistani youngsters in Edinburgh a choice to disobey parental authority and to live away from them. The choice to be independent from their family's economic support has enabled some boys to rebel against parental authority they live in youth hostels whose rent is paid by the Social Security Department.

However, the overwhelming majority of Edinburgh's Pakistani youngsters seem to have little choice but to accept their parents' authority which has strong, religious, cultural and economic bases. Even in those cases where Pakistani boys 'ran away' from home and lived independently, they eventually returned to their parents' home. It seemed that they found it difficult to live comfortably without the social and psychological support of their families. Thus, it can be asserted that few of Edinburgh's Pakistani boys could afford to rebel against their parents' authority.

II: The Biraderi : A Social Network of Kinship/Friendship

The Concept and Forms of the Biraderi

The Punjabi family, both in Pakistan and in Britain, is closely linked to the institution of *Biraderi*. Just as the Punjabi family is the basic social unit of relationship among parents, their siblings and some other close kin, i.e. grand-parents and grand-children, the Biraderi provides a basic framework of social relationships among families and individuals in a broader context of kinship/friendship. Social relationships between various families and individual kin and friends in the Punjabi culture are normally organised within the social framework of the *Biraderi*. It is this social framework of kinship/friendship that further lays down the rules of social interaction among members and specifies patterns of social behaviour. For instance, it spells out who will marry whom, with whom to exchange gifts, to whom to do favours, and with whom to compete.

The term *Biraderi* is derived from *baradr*, the Persian word for brother. Thus, *Biraderi* literally means brotherhood. Anthropologists and sociologists who have closely studied Punjabi communities both in Pakistan and in Britain have defined the *Biraderi* in the following ways: according to Anwar (1985 : 62) 'The *Biraderi* includes all the men who can trace a common ancestor, no matter how remote. It refers to the whole patrilineage and any individual member of it'. Similarly Shaw (1988 : 53) defines the *Biraderi* in terms of kinship relationship among its members: 'A *Biraderi* is a large kinship group whose members are from the same caste; usually the *Biraderi* is identified by its caste or sub-caste names.' Wakil (1970 : 5), on the other hand, says that the *Biraderi* '. . . is generally an endogamous group of individuals who consider themselves related to each other through blood or marriage.'

It appears from the above definitions that a *Biraderi* includes only those individuals who are related to each other through the ties of blood and/or marriage. Defining the *Biraderi* in such general terms confuses the concept with caste as the latter also stands for an endogamous group of people who relate to each other through a common ancestral line. However, most students of Punjabi society (including the above-mentioned authors) accept that membership of a *Biraderi* is not necessarily dependent on blood and/or marital links. This may only imply that the *Biraderi* is different from caste.

However, Wakil (1970:5) makes an explicit distinction between two forms of *Biraderi*, one of which is clearly distinguished from caste. According to Wakil (1970: 6) all those people who relate to each other through blood and/or marriage are automatically members of what he calls a 'general' *Biraderi*. In this form of *Biraderi* members have a general sense of belonging to a common extended kinship group or caste; they do not necessarily have face-to-face and reciprocal relationships among themselves. But, whenever some, most or possibly all members of the 'general' *Biraderi,* get involved in *Lina Dina*, taking and giving relationship with each other, they become members of what Wakil calls 'effective' *Biraderi*. Thus, the existence of institutionalised reciprocity, *Lina Dina*, among members is a necessary condition for the existence of an 'effective' *Biraderi*.

As will be discussed later in detail, shared interests and mutual social obligations that result from *Lina Dina* constitute major common ground among members who may not relate to each other through blood and/or marriage. Hence non-kin may become members of an 'effective' *Biraderi*. It is the 'effective' *Biraderi* that is more visibly prevalent in Edinburgh's Pakistani Community.

Caste and The Biraderi in Edinburgh

Edinburgh's Pakistani residents often use the term *Biraderi* in its general sense (social network of kinship relationship) interchangeably with caste. Belonging to a particular caste, or an extended endogamous group whose members relate to each other through a common ancestor, means belonging to the same 'general' *Biraderi* for most of Edinburgh's Pakistanis. In this sense one can only be considered a member of a 'general' *Biraderi* when he/she is related to the rest of the members through blood and/or marriage. It is because of this close connection between caste and *Biraderi* that it is important, first, to give a brief description of the various castes to which Edinburgh's Pakistani population belong.

As mentioned in Chapter I, the total number of Pakistanis who live as British citizens in Edinburgh and in the Lothian are estimated between 5500 to 6500 individuals. Approximately 90 per cent of this Pakistani population come from Faisalabad district of the Punjab province, in Pakistan. The rest of these people (around 10%) come from various other areas in Pakistan such as Lahore, Gujranwala, Rawalpindi, Atthak, Sialkot, the North West Frontier Province and Kashmir. The latter category of Edinburgh's Pakistanis belong to different castes/sub-castes such as *Rajput, Gujar, Jat, Pathan* and *Kashmiri*. But all of the estimated 90 per cent of Edinburgh's Pakistanis who come from Faisalabad belong to the *Arain* (pronounced *Arai*) caste. *Arain* is one of the largest castes in the Punjab province, Pakistan. Most *Arains* originally lived in Jullunder district in the Punjab province of India. After the partition of the former British India in 1947, the *Arains* who were Muslims migrated to the newly created state of Pakistan. Many of these Muslim migrants settled in the Faisalabad district of the Punjab Province, in the predominantly Muslim state of Pakistan. By and large, the *Arains* engaged in vegetable-growing, gardening and in selling their agriculture products in markets. It is because of this occupational background of the *Arains* that they are known as vegetable-growers.

The social position of this vegetable-growing caste in the inter-caste hierarchical structure in the Punjab seems to be somewhere in the lower level of the middle ranking category. According to researchers of the Indo-Pakistani caste systems (see Blunt 1969; Ullah 1957; Eglar 1960; Shaw 1988) the *Arain* caste is neither among the high-ranking *Ashraf* (noble) category of castes such as *Sayed, Qouraishi, Sheikh*, (descendants of Arab rulers) and the *Mughul* and *Pathan* (descendants of *Moghul* and *Afghan* rulers, respectively). Nor it is among the low-ranking *Kami* (artisan) castes/subcastes such as *Mirasi/Nai* (Barber), *Muchi* (shoemaker), *Kumhar* (Potter), *Quasi* (Butcher) and *Tarkan* (carpenters/labourers). The *Arain* caste according to Shaw (1988) is in the lower level of *Zamindar* (landowner) category that includes *Rajput, Jat, Gujar, Dogor* and also *Arain*. Although the *Zamindar* category is generally considered as middle ranking (between the *Ashraf* and *Kami* categories), the more or less exact position of members belonging to a particular caste depends, to a greater extent, on the size of land one possesses. For example, the social position of an *Arain* who possesses much land may be that of a *Zamindar* (landowner). But, the social position of an *Arain* who possesses little land, or no land, may be equated to that of a simple vegetable-grower and peasant. It is probably because of this ambiguity in the social ranking of the *Arain* caste in the inter-caste hierarchy in Pakistan that its social position among Edinburgh's Pakistanis remains controversial and contested. A member of the Edinburgh's Pakistani community who belongs to the *Arain* caste told me that : 'The *Arain* means landowner. We, the *Arains*, have big lands in Pakistan. Many people work for us there. In Britain the *Arain Biraderi* is very strong and rich.' Indeed many of Edinburgh's *Arains* are rich, but their caste is not, necessarily, considered as high-ranking by members of other Punjabi castes in Edinburgh '... all these *Arains* were poor peasants in Pakistan. They grew vegetables and sold them in Bazaar. We don't have time for these people; they belong to a peasant caste', a non-*Arain* Pakistani resident in Edinburgh said.

Whatever the claims of members of Edinburgh's various castes, I reached the conclusion that the social ranking of *Arains* and all other castes is not a static phenomenon - while the collective 'ascribed status' (belonging to a particular caste) remains important, it is the 'achieved status' of families and individuals that plays a more crucial role in ranking them as low, high, or between the two. As will be discussed in the next section an individual/family's social rank and honour were, to a greater extent, evaluated on the basis of their business success (wealth), professional qualifications, number of men in the family/extended family and on their influence and reputation in the community; the 'ascribed' social rank seemed to be only one factor, in this process. Since most of the 'achieved' attributes of families and individuals fluctuated from time to time so were the definitions and redefinition of their social ranking in the community. The attributes and criteria for social status and honour will be discussed later. First, it is important to look at the *Biraderi* as a social institution that provides a social framework for complex reciprocal relationships among its participants and the rest of Edinburgh's Pakistani community.

Lina Dina, Mutual Obligations and Social Bonding

It is relevant to recall Wakil's (1970) important distinction between 'general' and 'effective' *Biraderi* for describing the functioning of this institution in Edinburgh. According to Wakil, people who belong to the same extended kinship group or caste are also automatically members of the same 'general' *Biraderi*. In this case members of a 'general' *Biraderi* do not necessarily have face-to-face and reciprocal relationship among themselves, but they have a general sense of belonging to a common ancestor. Whenever *Lina Dina*, taking and giving relationships and their resultant social obligations among some, most or possibly amongst all members develop, the participants in this complex reciprocity become members of an 'effective' *Biraderi*.

There is an empirical basis for this distinction between the two forms of *Biraderi* as applied to Edinburgh's Pakistani community. Members of Edinburgh's various castes are clearly conscious of belonging to their respective castes or 'general' *Biraderi*s. Although some of Edinburgh's Pakistanis rejected the idea of caste as 'un-Islamic' and some others belittled its importance, for most it had practical implications. An important practical implication of belonging to a 'general' *Biraderi* can be clearly observed in the area of marriage. For example, Mr. S.M. told me that 'I will not allow my two daughters and son to marry outside the *Arain Biraderi*. A few rich Pakistanis wanted to marry my daughter. I refused. I waited until my daughter's marriage was arranged with a boy from our own *Biraderi*, in Glasgow'. When I asked Mr. S.M., 'but the other Pakistanis are also Muslim; they speak the same language and have the same customs as you do; and they are not from a lower caste', Mr. S.M. replied, 'But, they are still different, you know. People from the *Arain Biraderi* are our own people. If my daughter married another person [outside the *Arain* caste], their children will not know which caste they belonged to, and this is not good'.

Mr. S.M.'s views about caste and the practice of endogamy within it were shared by many other Pakistanis, but some had more flexible attitudes towards caste boundaries. Mr. D.R. said:

> I will only prefer my daughter or son to marry someone within my own caste. Nowadays, it is very difficult to find a right partner for one's [marriageable] children in the same caste. I wouldn't mind if my daughter married any Pakistani, even any Muslim.

Mr. D.R. further added that his *Biraderi* was important to him, but like most of Edinburgh's Pakistanis he was pragmatic:

> Nowadays, your loyalties lie where your interests are. Some of my best friends are as close to me as people from my *Biraderi*; we lend money to each other, we do business together, we help each other whenever need be. Basically we trust each other. Actually they are now in our *Biraderi*.

Shared interests and the existence of reciprocal relationships among kin (who belong to the same caste or 'general *Biraderi*') and non-kin constitute 'effective' *Biraderi*. Because of the crucial role of shared interests in the existence and functioning of 'effective' *Biraderi*, its social boundaries are sufficiently flexible for the inclusion of non-kin. There have been several cases among Edinburgh's Pakistanis where (Pakistani) neighbours, partners in business and/or in political/religious ideology, and close friends were accepted into 'effective' *Biraderi*s that were originally based on different castes from those of their 'new' members. It seemed that the strength of shared interests, reciprocal relationships and interdependence among members often kept the 'effective' *Biraderi* functioning. Close and trusting relationships among members of 'effective' *Biraderi* (who are from different castes) have sometimes led to inter-caste marriages in Edinburgh. Thus, 'effective' *Biraderi* in the context of the present study is: *a social institution where members have close and complex reciprocal relationships in a kinship/friendship framework.*

Although the role of belonging to a common kinship remains important in this form of *Biraderi*, it is the reciprocal relationships among members or participants that are crucial. In fact reciprocity is a necessary condition for the existence and functioning of the 'effective' *Biraderi*. But, what is reciprocity in this particular social/cultural context and how does it work?

Reciprocity in the context of the 'effective' *Biraderi* is locally referred to as *Lina Dina*, or taking and giving – the taking and giving of gifts, favours/services and feasts among members of the 'effective' *Biraderi* who are strongly expected to reciprocate. It must be mentioned, though, that giving gifts, doing favours and invitations for meals might take place among any Pakistanis in Edinburgh, at any time without such expectations of return. This may ordinarily happen among friends; or gifts may be given to certain prominent individuals as a sign of respect and appreciation of their knowledge and social/religious status in the community. For example, the gifts that were given to Hafiz Sahib (the *Imam,* or the Muslim priest, of the Mosque) were clearly not intended to be returned; they were a sign of respect for Hafiz Sahib's status as an *Imam*, and a teacher of Islamic teachings in the community. (I was also given gifts by parents of the boys that I taught in the Mosque, without any expectation to reciprocate.)

However, there are certain socially recognised occasions on which taking and giving of gifts have particular symbolic meanings and important social consequences for both the donors and for the recipients. These social occasions are mainly the birth of a baby (mostly a baby boy), arrival of *Haji* (pilgrim) from Mecca, and weddings. On the occasion of the birth of new baby, close kin and friends pay visits to the baby's parents' home to say *Mubarak ho* - Congratulations! When they are shown the new-born baby, then the visitors give money (ranging from £5 to £30), suits for the baby, and other things that may be used for the baby and/or her mother's well-being. Sometimes, money and gifts are given when the baby-boy is circumcised. Similarly on the arrival of the *Haji* from pilgrimage to Mecca, close kin and friends and also distant kin and other people visit him/her to say *Khosh Amadid* - Welcome! But, on this occasion, it is the *Haji* who gives gifts to his/her visitors. The *Haji's* gifts normally include wrist-watches, prayer-mats, prayer-caps, *Tasbih* (prayer beads) and *Abi-Zam Zam* (water of a sacred spring/well in Mecca). The quality and value of these gifts is almost always dependent on the closeness of relationship between the *Haji* and the recipient and also on the existence of reciprocity among them. The recipients of the gifts, on both occasions, are strongly expected to reciprocate what they received when the appropriate occasion arrives.

Alongside these two occasions, the third and the most important and elaborate occasion for taking and giving of gifts, particularly among members of the 'effective' *Biraderi*, is wedding. Weddings among Edinburgh's Pakistanis are considered as the most important and happiest social occasions on which close and distant kin and friends (including those in Pakistan) are invited to attend an often lavish and ceremonial reception which is normally given by the groom's family. At a certain point during the wedding ceremony kin, friends and also some other participants give gifts and money to the bride. The more expensive gifts are given by close kin (i.e,. maternal and paternal uncles and aunts and cousins, etc.) and close friends of the groom and the bride with whom they have a *Lina Dina* relationship in the framework of an 'effective' *Biraderi*. On one wedding occasion in Edinburgh expensive gifts included wrist-watches, a washing machine, a microwave and many Pakistani traditional suits (*shalwar-kamis*). Other friends and kin (mainly women) gave sets of kitchen utensils to the wedding parties (mainly to the bride), whereas others gave them cash ranging from £10 to £50. Then, importantly enough, during the wedding ceremony all the gifts given by kin and friends were publicly displayed. In this public display, the exact quality and value of every gift by individual kin/friends (or by a family) was announced. The groom's mother and sister took a written (or mental) note of every present given by every kin/friend. This is because the quality/value of every gift given by a particular individual conveys specific messages to the recipient(s) and to the various actors involved, in this social process. Therefore, the taking and giving of gifts, on this social occasion, has specific rules that must be cleverly and carefully followed.

First of all, the donors and the recipients, (particularly of expensive gifts) normally have an established relationship of *Lina Dina* among themselves. This is to say that the donor (an individual or the whole family) is someone who returns a gift similar to the one he/she received from the recipient in the past. But, what is even more important as a rule in this context, is that the donor makes sure that his/her gift is not less than or equal to, in value and quality that which was received (see Shaw 1988; Werbner 1990). The donor, according to his/her written or mental records, carefully chooses such a gift that 'acceptably' *exceeds* what he/she received in the past. When I asked Mrs. N.A. why gifts should not be less or equal to what one received in the past, she said that : 'A cheaper gift than what you were given means that you look down on that person [the recipient]. You don't appreciate the gift that you were given.' Although this rarely happens, when it does, bad feelings on the part of the recipient do follow. This further leads to gossip and to the reputation of the donor as *Kanjoos* (miserly) in the community which has serious consequences for his *Izzet* (social honour). Future *Lina Dina* relationship between the two partners are often deemed to be affected. But why can the gift not be 'equal' to that which the donor received in the past? Mrs. N.A. says that: 'This means that I take what you gave me, and that is it – we stop *Lina Dina*'. In fact, I found out that the message that the 'equal' gift sends was not as straightforward as Mrs. N.A. described. The receiving party of the 'equal' gift later, investigates the real intention of its donor. An 'equal' gift would mean stopping *Lina Dina* only when the donor explicitly or implicitly indicates this at a later time. But then, what is the 'appropriate' gift that sends the 'right' message to the recipient(s), and to the other parties involved?

The 'appropriate' gift is only a gift that is 'acceptably' higher in its value/quality from what the present donor received. It is a gift that sends a clear message of the continuation of *Lina Dina* relationship between the recipient(s). This is because the present donor by reciprocating what he/she received, not only meets his/her obligation to the present recipient, but the added value of the gift puts him/her under a renewed obligation to return the gift on an appropriate occasion. Additions to new gifts in future create new obligations and this, in turn, keeps *Lina Dina* continuing indefinitely. In this way Lina Dina is a continuous process that bonds the donor and the recipient (who periodically alternate their roles as donor and recipient) to each other through mutual obligations.

The public display of all the gifts that are given to the bride and groom, and the announcement of who gave what in the wedding ceremony, indicates that the gift-giving is not only an important symbolic communication between the donor and the recipient. More importantly, it is also a communication between the donors themselves and between all the 'active' parties involved, and the rest of the apparently 'passive' community. The communicative function of gift-giving (in a wedding) among the various donors is even more complex and multi-dimensional than that among the donors and the recipient(s) of the gift. In this situation, the various donors, by giving away expensive gifts, not only send messages of respect, and of continuing *Lina Dina*, to the recipient(s). The various donors, by the very acts of their generosity also wage a selfish war against each other – a war of 'gift-fighting', of showing off wealth, and of claims of generosity. The various close kin and friends, particularly, those who have established recent relationship of *Lina Dina* (through marriage and/or close friendship) with the 'effective' *Biraderi* of which the bride's in-laws are members, compete more intensely to 'score points'! Unfortunately, this 'fight of gifts' is one of those fights where 'money speaks' and even fights! Hence, those who have more money and spend it lavishly by giving away expensive gifts are the ultimate winners. While this winning of the 'fight of gifts' enhances the social status of the donor of the expensive gift, it at the same time causes humiliation for those donors who cannot afford to give expensive gifts.

Thus, in order to prevent personal and family humiliation, even the relatively poorer competitors do their best to give away a gift that is at least equal to the gifts of those they compete with. When I asked Mr. A.H., a recently-married young man (but not very rich), about the reasons for spending £260 on a gift for the wedding of his wife's sister, he said 'Well, this is the custom, you know; it is our custom; what else I can say?'. But, Mr. A.H.'s father who was sitting nearby interfered and added in a slightly raised voice that 'He [Mr. A.H.] is now the son-in-law of Z.K. He has to play the game as they [Mr. Z.K. and his *Biraderi*] play it.' The young man's father did not seem happy about his son's expensive gift, but he could not disapprove of it either. This is because both the young donor and his father knew well that in the 'fight of gifts, the young competitor particularly, has to prove that he is not less than anyone else; by giving an expensive gift he sends the message that he is, at least, as equal member as any one else in his new 'effective' *Biraderi*. This kind of competition, in the 'fight of gifts' among kin/friends often leads to open rivalries, jealousies and even to feuds among them. Thus, gift-giving, on this narrower level, has divisive effects.

It may seem ironic then that the competition among donors who are members of the same 'effective' *Biraderi* results in their solidarity and co-operation with the recipient(s) and among themselves on a different level. Competition in gift-giving result in a greater number of expensive gifts for the bride, and this indicates the wealth and solidarity of a particular *Biraderi vis à vis* other *Biraderi*s. It is at this level where the donor and the recipient(s) together send the message of their solidarity to rival *Biraderi*s and to the rest of the Pakistani community in Edinburgh. Through the display of their wealth and solidarity they jointly compete for a superior social standing of their *Biraderi* in the community. They make a claim of leadership. In this way gift-giving becomes a powerful mechanism of symbolic communication, not only among the donors and recipients, and among the various donors themselves, but also among all of the actors involved and the rest of apparently 'passive' community. The communication among members of an 'effective' *Biraderi* and 'others' in the community becomes even sharper when the sphere of *Lina Dina* goes beyond gift-giving to making favours, provision of services, to closer co-operation in business among members of the 'effective' *Biraderi* and to inter-marriages within this close-knit group of kinsmen and friends. Thus, a 'balanced' and 'fair' institutionalised *Lina Dina* (taking and giving of gifts, favours, services, and inter-marriages) strongly bonds the members in the framework of the 'effective' *Biraderi* – a close-knit group of kinsmen and friends who relate to and identify with each other.

The close-knit nature of the 'effective' *Biraderi* is partly a response of Pakistanis in Edinburgh to their sense of social and psychological insecurity in the wider society. The reactive element in the creation (or recreation) of close-knit *Biraderi*s was clearly observable in a speech by a community leader:

> In this country our *Biraderi* is stronger than it was in Pakistan. Here we need the *Biraderi* more than in Pakistan. The *Biraderi* will protect you from racial bullying and harassment; the *Biraderi* will help you if you have trouble with the Police; the *Biraderi* will look after you when you are sick; and who else will bury you in an Islamic way when you die? In the *Biraderi* you are safe'.

The strong emphasis of Edinburgh's Pakistanis on the establishment of close and strong *Biraderi* relationships and the extent of the intensity of the exchange of gifts, favours and services and their related rituals and ceremonies among *Biraderi* members indicates that this social institution is not merely a part of the culture of these migrants that 'migrated' with them to Britain. The close-knit *Biraderi* relationships among members are partly their response to their social, cultural and political exclusion from the wider society and to their sense of insecurity.

The present analysis clearly shows that an individual and a family among Edinburgh's Pakistanis has a strong social bond and a sense of belonging to the 'effective' *Biraderi*. But, this does not negate the fact that the same individual and families also have a sense of belonging to their respective 'general' *Biraderi* and to the wider Pakistani community in Edinburgh. The division of Edinburgh's Pakistani population into various *Biraderi* has led to rivalries and sometimes to irrational competition among them. But the very fact that the different *Biraderi*s compete against each other shows that they share a common culture, rules, and ethos of competition. People often compete with those whom they take seriously. Competition is only a different form of communication.

Thus *Lina Dina* as a powerful mechanism of communication among members of an 'effective' *Biraderi* (on a primary group level) and among members of various *Biraderi*s (on a secondary group level) keeps all/most of close and the relatively distant participants socially bonded to one social and moral order - a social and moral order of a community whose sense of solidarity is further strengthened by its members' experiences of exclusion in the wider British society (see Chapter I Section II); and, hence, of a community that is, in the process of becoming a small-scale society within the wider society (see Chapter I Section III). In sociological terms it is a community where members are socially interdependent and bonded to each other; and it is this type of community that provides a suitable framework for *Izzet*, honour (and dishonour) to operate as an effective mechanism of social control.

Izzet and Social Control

In their ordinary conversations with members of family, kin and friends many of Edinburgh's Pakistanis, particularly, the first generation male, often use a standard *Urdu* sentence: '*Izzet Ki Bat Hi.*' It means that 'It is a matter of honour' (or family honour). When Mr. G.H., a wealthy Pakistani businessman, found out that his 21-year-old son, I.H., regularly attended a casino for gambling, he told his son: 'I don't mind you losing or winning money in the casino; I know that you have great fun there, which is alright. But, the problem is that when people see you in the casino they will tell everybody in the community that, look, G.H.'s son is gambling. This will give me, you and our family a very bad name.' Then Mr. G.H. immediately said '*Izzet Ki Bat Hi*', it is a matter of honour (or family honour). I.H. often won money in the casinos and addictively attended them on weekends. He also understood the meaning and importance of his father's short but powerful Urdu sentence '*Izzet Ki Bat Hi*'. Indeed, it was the power of the meaning of this standard Urdu sentence that stopped him attending casinos in Edinburgh. Instead, he drove many miles to casinos in other Scottish cities/towns. He did so because he believed that in these cities/towns he ran little risk of being seen by other Pakistani acquaintances who would gossip that he is a gambler. According to I.H., initially 'the strategy worked'. But after a period of time he gave up attending casinos altogether: 'It was too much hassle to drive all the way to...'

Similarly, when R.N. failed his first-year university exams, his father, F.N., who is a professional, told him: '... You should not be so lazy. In this community you ought to be either very rich or highly educated. Otherwise you are nothing. If you don't get the degree, this will bring a bad name to all the family'. Then Mr. F.N. completed his advice/warning by the standard Urdu sentence '*Izzet Ki Bat Hi*', it is a matter of (family) honour. Interestingly, failure in the exams of higher educational institutions and dropping out often causes a lasting stigma for the individual concerned that also affects his/her relatives. Many of Edinburgh's Pakistanis not only dropping out from an institution of higher education as an indicator of laziness but, more importantly, as an indicator of lack of intelligence that affects an individual/family's *Izzet* negatively. Thus it may have been due to the anxiety and the pressure of losing *Izzet* that made R.N. work harder and finally get his university degree.

Pakistani parents in Edinburgh, use '*Izzet Ki Bat Hi*' on countless other occasions too. For instance, when parents suspect (or actually find out) that their unmarried sons and daughters may be having pre-marital affairs, or that they (particularly daughters) 'go out' with someone, parents warn them that what they are doing is not a simple personal matter but is a matter of family honour: '*Izzet Ki Bat Hi.*' Similarly, parents use the sentence when their children wear 'unconventional clothes' (e.g., earrings by boys and 'indecent' Western clothes by girls) or go to pubs, discos and drink alcohol. In some cases this sentence is used when one's personal dignity and individuality is threatened/attacked by abusive language or disrespect.

The British-born Pakistanis learn the meaning and importance of the concept *Izzet* at home, in the Mosque-school and in the community at large. When I asked the sample of 60 Pakistani boys in the Pilrig Mosque Community Centre 'How important is the idea of family *Izzet* (honour) to you, personally?' the responses were as follows: about two thirds (63.3%) of the boys said that the idea of family *Izzet* is 'extremely important' to them, and a little less than a third (30%) of them said that it was 'fairly important' to them. Only 5% of these British-born Pakistani boys said that the idea of family *Izzet* is 'not very important' to them, whereas a negligible minority (1.7%) said that it was 'unimportant' to them. These results indicate that *Izzet* (or family *Izzet)* is a well established theme across generations among Edinburgh's Pakistan population.

But now, the question is, what does the concept of *Izzet* exactly mean for an average Pakistani in Edinburgh and what makes people *izzetdar*, honourable? *Izzet* meant various but similar things to Edinburgh's Pakistanis. The words and phrases with which they equated *Izzet* mainly included: 'Honour' (family honour), 'Good Name', 'Good Reputation', 'Respect', 'Social Status', and 'Dignity'. Some members of the community said that the concept meant to them 'piety', 'decency' and control over the behaviour of women in the family/joint-family.

However, the closest synonym to *Izzet* (originally an Arabic word), appeared to be 'honour'. *Izzet* or honour often carried a collectively orientated meaning, i.e. family honour, or the honour of the *Biraderi*. Interestingly, these conceptions of honour are very similar to those of the Mediterranean people in general (see Campbell 1954; Pitt-Rivers 1965, Peristieny 1965; Bailey 1971; Happenstall 1971; Codd 1971; Gilmore 1982; Delaney 1982).

The meaning of *Izzet* as honour, or family honour, is closely linked to its constituent elements. The most important element of *Izzet* for Edinburgh's Pakistanis were: belonging to a higher caste (see pp 74-76 for the hierarchy of castes); a large number of men in the family/extended family (in Britain, Pakistan or elsewhere); social/political influence in Britain and/or in Pakistan; higher professional qualification; reputation of honesty and religiosity; generosity; finally and more importantly wealth and business success. But the existence of even a large number of these elements without others did not necessarily constitute *Izzet*. For example, in one case a person possessed all the above attributes of *Izzet* except wealth. Because he did not have enough money to contribute to the community's charities and to reciprocate invitations and gifts he even lost the social influence that he basically derived from his influential family in Pakistan. People often joked about his old car and his small flat. In other cases, individuals who qualified in all the constituent elements of *Izzet* (including wealth), but lacked generosity were not considered as *Izzetdar* (honourable) in the community. Instead, they had a bad reputation of being *Kanjoos* (miserly). Thus, wealth and generosity must exist alongside the other elements to constitute *Izzet*. In fact, possession of wealth and its spending for public causes compensates for the relative lack of some of the other socially/morally orientated elements of *Izzet*, such as religious observance and belonging to a high caste. One member of the community who commented on the current 'formal' leaders of the community said: 'If you are rich you can buy *Izzet*.' Buying *Izzet*, in this context, meant the contribution of a relatively larger amount of money to building a mosque, to the funeral/burial of kin/friends, contributing to charities and to other public causes. In these ways and by helping and making financial favours to members of the community, the wealthy and 'generous' Pakistanis seemed to have influenced public opinion in their favour. Nevertheless, as mentioned earlier, *Izzet* is much more than mere social influence produced by wealth and generosity. It is the community's evaluation of the claimants of *Izzet* against the complex package of its various intricately interwoven elements. Thus it may be said that *Izzet*, in this context is *an individual/group's perception of its social standing as it is seen and evaluated by the community.*

I will return to the importance of *Izzet* as an agent of social control in Edinburgh's Pakistani community shortly. But, first it is important to know how members of the community communicated the fluctuating degrees of its members' *Izzet*. The central mechanism of evaluating community members and their *Izzet* is gossip. As social anthropological research in other cultures show, gossip plays important role in creating cognitive maps about individuals' social identities and reputations, both in small-scale rural communities and in complex urban social settings (see Campbell 1964; Hotchkiss 1967; Bailey 1971; Pitt-Rivers 1971; Doo 1973; Wilson 1974; Nee and deBary 1974; Merry 1979; 1981):

> Gossip does provide essential information on personal identities, however. It indicates who is trustworthy, who is drug addict, who is a gossip, who one can let into one's house, and who will 'use' the opportunity to 'case' it for a burglary... it can undermine the credibility of leaders and those aspiring to power.(Merry 1981:2)

Despite the fact that the Edinburgh's Pakistani community is geographically scattered in a relatively large city, the high degree of social/cultural connectedness and interdependence among members makes it possible for gossip to operate effectively. Kin/friends often share information and evaluate people's behaviour during their gatherings for the Friday prayer (*Jom'a*), dinner parties, weddings and during the numerous celebrations of cultural/religious events. But, the most important means for the flow of gossip in the community is a product of modern technology: the telephone. Mr. I.H., whose case about attendance at casinos was mentioned earlier, wishes that the British Telecom did not exist at all! '... Even about a small matter, people would phone each other in the evenings. Then everybody would give his own opinion about the damn thing; and they would blow up a small matter' I.R. complained about the malicious nature of gossip in the community.

Malicious or not, people fear gossip because it often involves judgement about their *Izzet* in the community. As mentioned at the beginning of this section, it was the threat of damage to his family *Izzet* that stopped I.R. from attending the casino and induced anxiety in R.N. not to fail again in his exams at university. So, why is *Izzet* so crucially important for Edinburgh's Pakistanis that it operates as a powerful mechanism of social control in the community?

The obvious answer is that *Izzet* is a very precious social asset of a Pakistani individual/family that is very dearly won. Further, and more importantly, a certain degree of *Izzet* is 'required' for membership of an equal standing with the other members of the community – a fellow Muslim and Pakistani. Of course some people may be more *Izzetdar* (honourable), than others. But not having a certain degree of *Izzet* or its complete loss is *Bizati* (honourlessness). *Bizati* is a serious humiliation and disgrace. The *Bizat*, an honourless individual is not necessarily excluded from membership of the community. But his is a membership of the less equal and the less respectable. The *Bizat* is not greeted with full warmth, he/she is spoken to less politely and not listened to attentively. Interestingly, the *Bizat* is often invited to dinner parties, to weddings and to other social gatherings. This dual treatment 'displays' a 'negative example' (see Bailey 1971) of *Bizat* to the rest of the members of the community. However, these negative examples whose 'deviations' are forgivable, are often pressurised to refrain from disreputable activities and to get reintegrated to the community. One young man who broke his engagement which had been arranged by his parents said that:

> Not only my parents, but cousins, uncles, aunts and even my granny would repeat that I have done something very bad and shameful. Every body would tell me that '*Izzet ki bat hi*' [It is a matter of family honour]; and that I should be engaged again with the same girl. Life became so hard for me that I wish I was able to escape from here. Finally, I had to accept what they wanted. Then everybody was again O.K. with me.

This might be an example of what Braithwaite (1989) calls 're-integrative shaming': shaming of the offender, which is followed by re-accepting him into the community. However, in some cases an insensitive and non-compliant *Bizat* may be labelled as *Bisharm Adami* (shameless person). For several and repetitive cases of 'deviance' that inflict irreparable damages on family *Izzet*, the individual concerned is labelled *Bisharm Adami*. It is attributed to the prophet Mohammad (P.B.U.H.) as saying that: 'If you do not have shame, then you are free to do whatever you want to do'.

The *Bisharm Adami* is not only looked down on, but he/she is avoided. He/she is not invited to important dinner parties, weddings, and to other social gatherings. More importantly, he is not trusted as a partner in business, and in other transactions. The prospects of his marriage (if single) and/or of his close marriageable male and female kin, within the community, become bleak. The *Bisharm Adami* is also excluded from taking social and political positions within the community. He/she is not only a less than 'equal' and 'respectable' member, but is an 'outsider' to the community. Precisely because of this reason, it is very difficult to find a *Bisharm Adami*,

in person, within the community. But he/she profoundly exists in the collective 'mind' of the community and in the minds of its individual members
as an extreme example of *Bizati* (honourlessness). People fear to be labelled
as *Bisharm Adami* and the social consequences of this label. It is a fear that
has important implications for social control in the community.

In sum, *Izzet* operates as a mechanism of social control among
Edinburgh's Pakistani community because it qualifies individuals for equal
and respectable membership of the community. Those who lack *Izzet* or lose
it, lose equal and respectable membership of the community; in some cases,
they even may be totally excluded from the community. For most Pakistanis
in Edinburgh the social and psychological cost of losing respectable membership of their community (or exclusion from it) is always too high to pay.

3 The Mosque and the P.A.E.E.S.

Introduction

This chapter is divided into two main parts: the Mosque and the 'Pakistan Association, Edinburgh and the East of Scotland' (P.A.E.E.S.), the two other social institutions that operate as agencies of social control in Edinburgh's Pakistani community. In the first part a general historical account of the institutionalisation of Islamic religious life in Edinburgh, with a particular focus on the Pilrig Mosque, is given. Then the social organisation of the *Sabaq*-class within the Pilrig Mosque and its role in the socialisation of the British-born Pakistani children to Islamic beliefs and rituals is examined in detail. After analysing the social consequences of the *Sabaq*-class for the social bonding of Pakistani children, the discussion focuses on congregational worship and the celebration of religious festivals and the ways that their related sermons and rituals create a sense of community among the participants.

Since most of the institutionalised activities within the Mosque (and in the community) are broadly organised by the 'Pakistan Association, Edinburgh and East of Scotland' (P.A.E.E.S.), this group is discussed in the second part of the chapter, where its formal organisational structure, functions and aims are examined. The bases of social power of the Association, the exercise of authority by its 'Office-Bearers' and its implication for social control in the community are analysed.

I: The Mosque

The Institutionalisation of Islam in Edinburgh

In the early 1950s there were less than ten Muslim families (about 64 adults) in Edinburgh. They did not have an organised religious life. If they prayed, every person did so individually at home or/and at the workplace. There were no arrangements for the weekly *Jom'a* prayer (Friday congregational prayer) or for the two annual prayers of *Eid-ul-Fiter* and of *Eid-ul-Ozha* (the occasions of the end of *Ramadan* and the day of pilgrimage in Mecca respectively). These families gathered for celebration of such important religious occasions at the residences of individual families, mainly at the residence of Haji Ali Mohammad, at 19 Clarence Street.

However, the increasing contacts between these Muslim residents and the overseas Muslim students at Edinburgh University led to a new development: a request to the University authorities to provide a place for *Eid* prayer and another for the arrangement of *Halal* food (mainly meat prepared according to Islamic rituals) for its Muslim students. The permission was granted. The students (and other Muslims) were given free access to use Adam House of Edinburgh University for *Eid* prayer. The authorisation also provided them with a place at the University's premises on Lothian Street, so that their need for *Halal* food could be looked after. This place for *Halal* food later became famous as Khoshi Mohammad Restaurant, named after its owner/manager.

With Adam House as an *adhoc* hall for *Eid* prayers and the Khoshi Mohammad Restaurant as a centre for Muslims' eating and gathering, this state of affairs continued until 1964. By this time, according to the early Muslim migrants, there were more than 70 Muslim families and a larger number of Muslim students in Edinburgh. The need for an organised body to cater for the religious, social and cultural requirements of this new Muslim entity in Edinburgh was strongly felt by its individual members. Consequently, this situation gave birth to the 'Association for Pakistani Residents'. The new-born Association was temporarily based inside the Khoshi Mohammad Restaurant with Haji Ali Mohammad, a prominent social figure, its first chairman. The Association, aware of the urgent need of the growing Muslim population for an organised religious life continued its efforts to find a suitable place for collective worship as a first step in meeting these needs. In 1967-68 the Association, with the combined efforts of the Muslim students in Edinburgh, acquired premises at 12 Roxburgh Street from Edinvar Association on a rental basis; the rent was negligible.

With the appointment of Hafiz Abdul Karim as an *Imam* (Islamic priest) to lead the five daily prayers and more importantly the *Jom'a* prayer on Fridays, 12 Roxburgh St. was established as the first Mosque in Edinburgh. Although the two storey building with a basement was not structurally designed for the requirements of a Mosque, it served the purpose on a 'something is better than nothing' basis, as a founder of the mosque put it. But, in fact the same structure had soon become more than 'something': a Mosque, a Mosque-school, a place for the celebration of social and religious occasions, for the arrangements of Muslim funerals, and finally a meeting place for Edinburgh's Muslim population. With all these functions of the newly established Mosque, a stronger emphasis was placed on its role as the (only) centre of Islamic teachings (particularly for young children) in Edinburgh. By 1970 this place was known as the 'Mosque and Islamic Centre'. As an active social, educational, welfare and religious institution for the increasing Muslim population, the Mosque soon became too small for the *Jom'a* prayer and so it was performed in a big hall at Haji Ali Mohammad's business premises (opposite the Surgeon's Hall).

The early 1970s witnessed a sudden increase in Edinburgh's Muslim population. In 1972-73 Uganda's Idi Amin decided to expel all Asians from the country who, consequently, migrated to different parts of the world, mainly to the USA, Canada and to the U.K. Some of them arrived in Edinburgh. Also, the oil boom of 1973 brought an unprecedented wealth to much of the Middle East. Some young students from these oil-rich nations decided to invest 'oil-money' in higher education in the West European universities. As a result, a large number of Arab (mainly) Muslim students arrived in the U.K and in Edinburgh to acquire higher and professional qualifications.

In the wake of these developments, in 1973 a decision was taken to build a central mosque in Edinburgh. With modest donations from Edinburgh's Pakistani businessmen and other Pakistani residents in the city, the major financial contributions, to this project were made by Saudi Arabian princes and by the Madina Islamic University in Saudi Arabia. Consequently, with the joint Saudi-Pakistani donations, land for the construction of the planned central Mosque was purchased at Minto Street. But an application for the construction of a Mosque on that particular piece of land failed; the city's local authority did not give Edinburgh's Muslim residents permission for the construction of a Mosque. As a result the land was sold at a loss of £10,000.

After this event, the initiative to choose a place for the construction of the central Mosque was mainly in the Arabs' hands. It was emphasised that land for the planned mosque should be situated near Edinburgh University so that the Muslim students could have easy access to it. In 1980 the present site at Potter Row (separated from the Appleton Tower by a narrow street) was purchased. By this time, because of some differences among the Pakistanis and the Arabs over the management of the fund, the two groups split. Consequently, the 12 Roxburgh St. Mosque (or Mosque and Islamic Centre) became a Pakistani-dominated Mosque, whereas the then standing (and the first purpose-built Mosque in Edinburgh) building, on the newly purchased land at Potter Row, an Arab-dominated one. However, the domination was/is never exclusive: some Pakistanis pray and attend meetings and religious festivals in Potter Row and some Arabs pray and attend religious festivals in the Roxburgh Mosque; there are occasions in which all get together.

In 1985, the Pakistani population of the Roxburgh Mosque also had some disagreements over the use of some charity funds. This induced the leading members of the Pakistan Association to convert the Pakistan Community Centre (Zetland Hall, 11 Pilrig Street) into a Mosque and Community Centre by the end of 1985. The Mosque in this complex was named Markazi Jamia Masjid-i-Anwar-i-Madina (Central Grand Mosque of the Lights of Madina). It also houses the offices of the Pakistan Association for Edinburgh and the East of Scotland which represents the majority of the city's Pakistani population.

With this short background of the institutionalisation of religious life in Edinburgh's Muslim community, now all the three Mosques/Islamic Centres (the Mosque and Islamic Centre on 12 Roxburgh Street; The Central Mosque and Islamic Centre at Potter Row and the *Markazi Jamia Masjid-i-Anwar-i-Madina* at 11 Pilrig Street) actively cater for the social, religious, welfare and educational needs of the community. Moreover, there is a fourth *Madrasa* (school of Islamic education) for children at Temple Park called *Madrasa-i-Ta'lim-ul Quran* in Edinburgh. It is very likely that the school will soon function as a Mosque as well. At present, it caters for the religious socialisation of Muslim children in that area.

It has already been mentioned that the overwhelming majority of Edinburgh's Muslim population are *Sunni* Muslims, and therefore all the above mentioned Islamic institutions entirely follow the *Sunni* school. However, a small number of *Shiite* Muslims (the mainstream *Ja'faries*) as well as the followers of *Ismaili*, the *Bahaie* and the *Ahamadi* sects live in Edinburgh. There is almost no interaction between Edinburgh's *Sunni* Muslims and the last three sects, whereas the *Ja'faries* worshipped in the *Sunni* Mosques prior to getting their own Mosque in mid-1989. Since the overwhelming majority of Edinburgh's Muslims follow *Sunni* Islam, and since there are no significant differences in the belief system and the structure of prayers in the three *Sunni* Mosques, I focus only on the Pilrig Mosque which is attended by over 60% of Pakistani Muslims who are permanent residents in Edinburgh.

The Pilrig Mosque/Community Centre

The Pilrig Mosque and community centre is commonly called the Pilrig Mosque. It occupies a corner of a large residential apartment that is situated in a working-class area, on 11 Pilrig Street, Leith, Edinburgh. The corner houses the Mosque (Markazi Jamia Masjid-i-Anwar-i-Madina), the offices of the 'Pakistan Association for Edinburgh and the East of Scotland' and the flat of the *Hafiz Sahib* (Muslim priest who knows all of the Holy *Quran* by heart). The offices of the Association, with a large meeting hall and *Hafiz Sahib*'s flat, are on the first floor; the women's room (for worship and Islamic education), and another small room for worship and the women's *Wozu Khana* (place for ablution and toilets) are situated on the ground floor. In the basement, there are the men's *Wozu Khana*, a big kitchen, a storage room and a large main hall which is the actual Mosque.

With a capacity for more than 300 worshippers at a time, the hall is decorated with framed verses from the holy *Quran*, names of *Allah*, and the prophet and of Islamic *Califs*. The hall is also decorated with the portrait of *Harmain*, the most sacred Mosques in Mecca and Madina where the *Ka'aba* and the tomb of the Prophet Mohammed (P.B.U.H.) are situated, respectively. It is also decorated with framed verses from the holy *Quran*. One of the verses says: 'Those who trust in *Allah*, He almighty finds solutions (for their problems).' Another says: '*Allah* is the greatest guardian and He is the most merciful.'

As in all *Jam'ia* Mosques (where the *Jom'a* Friday prayer is performed) there is a *Mihrab* (a niche in the wall which shows the direction of Mecca). On the left side of the *Mihrab* is *Minber* (a kind of staircase with three steps from where the *Imam* preaches). The *Mihrab* is situated opposite the worshippers who all face the direction of the *Ka'aba*, the holy house in Mecca. Although unique to this Mosque, there is another stage at the other end of the hall. This stage very much resembles the modern Western-style stages in public halls from where speakers deliver their speeches. The community leaders and the chief guest(s) also sit on the stage facing the audience. It is used for non-worshipping socio-religious and cultural occasions where there is more than one speaker to address the audience. In the hall, all the people, whether on the stage or not, sit on the ground which is covered with a comfortable carpet.

Almost all members of this religious community are permanent residents in Edinburgh and predominantly come from the Punjab province (even from the same districts: Faisalabad and Sahiwal). The socio-religious atmosphere in the Pilrig Mosque is very congenial and there is a high degree of face-to-face-relationships among the people. Unlike the Potter Row and Roxburgh Mosques where a predominantly mobile student population who come from different parts of the Muslim world meet and worship for the period of their studies, the Pilrig Mosque is a comparatively permanent socio-religious community. Because it is situated in an area that is relatively far from the centre of the city, non-Pakistani and casual worshippers are rarely seen in the Mosque. Moreover, unlike the Potter Row and (to some extent) Roxburgh Mosques, members of Pilrig Mosque are predominantly followers of the traditionalist version (or sect) of *Sunni* Islam with a typical (Indian) sub-continental character. Its followers simply call this school of thought *Sunni* or *Ahli-s-Sunnah Wal-Jama'ah*. It is sometimes called (especially by rival *Sunni* groups) *Barelvi*. The latter name comes from Ahmed Raza Khan, a *Sunni* Muslim scholar who lived in the late eighteenth and early nineteenth century at Bareilly, in Uttar Pradesh, India. The *Barelvi* or *Ahli-s-Sunnah Waljama'ah* sect in Edinburgh is a populist-traditionalist version of *Sunni* Islam which is less interested in Islamic political activism and militancy. To a significant extent it is infused with *Sufism* (Islamic mysticism) and with ideas about the mystical powers of saints and even of their shrines. The followers of this Islamic sect place strong emphasis on traditional Islamic values and rituals and the socialisation of their British-born sons and daughters to these values.

Sabaq: **Socialisation Toward Islamic Beliefs and Rituals**

The Concept of Sabaq

At the start of my field work I met three young Pakistani boys while walk-ing in the area of Leith Walk near Pilrig Street. I asked them if they were also going to the Pilrig Mosque. They happily answered: 'Yes, we are going there; we are going to our *Sabaq*.' I accompanied the three young boys (interestingly, all the three were brothers aged 10, 11 and 13) and we talked about *Sabaq* until we reached the gate of our common destination, the Pilrig Mosque. Before we entered the Mosque, one of my companions asked two other boys (who were incidentally also brothers): 'Why didn't you come to *Sabaq* yesterday, and the day before?' Although the answer of the two boys - 'That's none of your business' - had its own importance for my 'field notes', I was more curious to find out what *Sabaq* in the interrogative state-ment meant. On a somewhat provisional basis, I learned that *Sabaq* meant the total class of basic Islamic education that is held in the Mosque. But inside the Mosque (where I was also introduced to the boys as another teacher), the concept of *Sabaq* was used to mean something different: one of the boys told me that: 'My *Sabaq* is very easy today!'. He was referring to his own *Quranic* lesson on that day. Then *Hafiz Sahib* ordered a boy in *Urdu* to 'Concentrate on his *Sabaq*'. He also clearly meant the particular *Quranic* lesson. I was confused, about the varying meanings of *Sabaq*.

Over the next few days, I listened curiously and talked to the boys so that the meaning of the concept was clarified. Finally, I was convinced that the concept of *Sabaq* refers to both: a) The whole class of the Mosque-based religious education, and b) to an individual lesson of religious education in the Mosque. I also found out that the second meaning of *Sabaq* was more prevalent and more directly referred to than the first. The boys commonly used the phrase 'Mosque-School' to refer to the class of Islamic education. Thus the terms *Sabaq* and 'Mosque-School' were used interchangeably to refer to the whole class, whereas *Sabaq* in its second usage referred only to a particular lesson of Islamic education in the Pilrig Mosque.

The Social Organisation and Content of the Sabaq Class

About 120 British-born Pakistani boys and girls are registered in the Pilrig Mosque-school. The overwhelming majority of these boys and girls also, normally, attend the local Scottish schools. Unlike the co-educational local schools, girls and boys in the Mosque-school sit in separate classes. Also girls in the Mosque-school are taught by a female teacher, whereas boys are taught by *Hafiz Sahib* and (at one time) by myself.

The total number of boys (the subjects of the present research) in the

Mosque-school is about 87 individuals. They attend the *Sabaq*-class five days in a week. The class is normally held between 2.00 to 4.00 in the afternoons, from Monday to Thursday, inclusively. While Fridays and Sundays are holidays, the Sabaq-class on Saturdays takes place between 11.00 to 1.00 in the mornings.

The class is held in the large hall or the actual Mosque where the *Jom'a* prayer is performed. The boys, whose ages range from six to 21, sit on the floor that is covered with a comfortable light grey carpet. They normally sit near the walls of the hall and put their books and notebooks on the long wooden benches that are in front of them. A bench may be shared by two or three boys. The physical structure of the class looks like a fort with three walls. In place of the missing 'wall', *Hafiz Sahib* sits. It is a place from where he can easily keep a watchful eye on the boys.

Hafiz Sahib has a moderately long beard and is in his late thirties. He always wears traditional Pakistani clothes, the *Shalwar-Kamis*. With his higher and formal education in Islamic theology and broad knowledge of classical Islamic literature, *Hafiz Sahib* speaks Urdu and Punjabi – the two main languages of Edinburgh's Pakistanis – very eloquently. He can also communicate in Arabic and in English.

Apart from his educational qualifications, because he knows the whole *Quran* by heart and because of his personal charisma, *Hafiz Sahib* is a man of influence and is generally respected in the community and by the boys in the Mosque-school. He is not only a teacher in the Mosque-school but, more importantly *Hafiz Sahib* is considered as a spiritual and religious leader. Respecting *Hafiz Sahib* is not only the scholastic duty of the Pilrig boys, it is also their religious duty and therefore an expectation of their parents and of the community.

During the *Sabaq*-class with a brownish wooden stick in his hand (or on his knees), he calls the boys one by one to sit before him. Each boy puts his books (the holy *Quran*, Urdu language text book, etc.) on the bench before *Hafiz Sahib*. He first cites his previous day's *Sabaq* before *Hafiz Sahib* who corrects him if mistakes are made. Then *Hafiz Sahib* gives the boy a new *Sabaq* to be learnt during the class period. Every boy goes through this process individually to learn to read the holy *Quran* in Arabic. The boys learn to recite the *Quran* without understanding the meaning. But learning to read the *Quran* in Arabic has important implications for the social bonding of these boys to the community of believers. Learning to read the *Quran* enables an individual to memorise, at least, some parts of it that are essential for praying. A Muslim can not perform a prayer unless he/she knows certain verses of the *Quran* by heart. Thus, the ability to read and know by heart some parts of the *Quran* makes the Pilrig boys 'communicate' with *Allah* individually, and also collectively alongside the community of the believers.

However, learning to read the *Quran* in Arabic is only one part of the religious socialisation of the British-born Pakistani boys in the Mosque-school. These boys are also taught the fundamentals of Islamic faith - the five pillars of Islam which are:

1 - *Shahadah* : The declaration of faith in Islam which is: 'There is no God but *Allah* , and that Mohammad (P.B.U.H.) is the prophet of *Allah.*' This is also called *Aiman-e-Mojmal* (faith in brief).

2 - *Salah* (or *Namaz*, in Urdu) , : praying five times in 24 hours.

3 - *Sawm* (or *Roza*): fasting from early morning until sunset every day during the month of *Ramadan*.

4 - *Zakah* (or *Zakat*): Islamic welfare contribution to the poor by a well-to-do Muslim every year (the details of how much and who should pay the *Zakah* is beyond the scope of this book).

5 - *Haj*: pilgrimage to Mecca once in a well-to-do Muslim's life.

Every one of the five Pillars of Islam are explained in detail by *Hafiz Sahib;* then the boys are required to learn these details by heart. In some cases the boys are required to learn some of the Arabic scripture related to the five pillars by heart. For example, the Arabic scripture called *Iman-Ul-Mufassal* (faith in detail) should be learned by heart. It says: 'I believe in *Allah*; in his angels; in his books; in his messengers; in the last day [Day of Judgement] and that, indeed, everything good or bad, is decided by *Allah* the Almighty; and in the life after death.' The words 'books' and 'prophets' include belief in the Prophet Jesus and his Book, the Bible, which are a part of this package of Islamic faith.

The *Iman-ul-Mufassal* constitutes the fundamental basis of a Muslim's faith in the supernatural powers the Angels , the Day of Judgement and the Life After Life,(and hence the Hell and Heaven) and, more importantly, in *Allah* the Almighty who decides/decided the fate of all individuals. The young believers are further told that they will be rewarded for their faith and obedience in the teachings of *Allah* (conveyed through Prophet Mohammad), and they will be punished should they reject and/or disobey these teachings. These rewards and punishments may take place in this, or in the other, world or in both.

Obviously, faith in the existence, powers, and sanctions of the supernatural could directly influence and control an individual's behaviour, as Ross (1901); Durkheim (1915), Tocqueville (1945) and Parsons (1937) recognised long ago. The pronouncement of such belief in a particular social context is especially important from the social control point of view: the public acceptance of the *Iman-ul-Mufassal* in a large group of other young believers who know one another face-to-face creates collective sentiments of belonging to a shared moral/religious community. The importance of such belief is described by Emile Durkheim in this way:

They [religious beliefs] are something belonging to the group, and they make its unit. The individuals which compose it feel themselves united to each other by the simple fact that they have a common faith. A society whose members are united by the fact that they think in the same way in regard to the sacred world and its relations with profane world, and by the fact that they translate these common ideas into common practice is what is called a church [or a mosque] Durkheim (1915:44)

Indeed, the pronouncement of *Iman-ul-Mufassal* in the Mosque and its regular translation into collective worship is a process of identification with the community and an implicit moral and social commitment to abide by its rules. Breach of the group's rules would be considered as a betrayal for which the deviant will have to pay in high social and psychological cost - feelings of guilt and the fear of punishment by supernatural powers and by the community itself. The translation of a common faith into a regular common act of collective prayers is not only a part of worship but is also integral to the *Sabaq*-class in the Pilrig Mosque.

In most of the four seasons of a year at least one prayer falls during the class period. So all the boys, particularly those who are above the age of nine, are required to do *Wozu* (ablution) for the prayer. The boys go to the *Wozo Khana*. There they learn practically how to make *Wozu*: they wash their mouths, noses, faces, arms, feet and dry them with special towels provided. Then an older boy makes *Azan* (call for the prayer) which is in standard Arabic words. After that, the boys stand in straight rows, behind the *Imam* to pray in congregation. When the prayer ends, the boys go back to their benches to resume their *Sabaq* (or they leave for home if the prayer time coincides with the end of the class).

This practice is repeated five days a week, during the *Sabaq*-class. Obviously, the practice of learning Islamic praying involves worship and 'communicating' with *Allah* (if the actor intends and believes so). But the real purpose of this practice is learning the manners, rules and rituals of Islamic worship. It is a socialisation that enables the British-born Pakistani boys to participate in the major congregational prayers alongside the adult members of the community. It is a part of the process of the integration of these boys into the mainstream socio-religious community. It is their integration not only as believers, but also as participants in the translation of faith into practice.

Moreover, the Mosque-school is not limited to socialisation to Islamic faith and rituals as the only form of social control in the *Sabaq*-class. In order to ensure that this socialisation process goes smoothly and in order to 'prevent misbehaviour', the Mosque-school also uses direct forms of social control i.e. corporal punishments.

While it is strongly emphasised that during the class, everybody should concentrate only on his *Sabaq*, norms of the Mosque-School are broken from time to time: some boys talk, make noises, use bad language and punch each other, etc. Most of this behaviour is not only considered as diverting the students' attention from their *Sabaq*, but is labelled 'bad' and 'offending' by the standards of the community and the Mosque.

In order to prevent such 'misbehaviour' and meanwhile to maintain an 'orderly' educational atmosphere, several disciplinary measures are taken: first of all, *Hafiz Sahib* keeps watchful eyes on everybody and with a brownish wooden stick in his hand he demonstrates to the students an active presence of surveillance of their behaviour in the class. Staring is the first warning for the misbehaving boy. Most boys, when stared at, automatically respond by quitting indulgence in misbehaviour and refocus on their *Sabaq*. They fully get this symbolic message and know the consequences should they continue to misbehave. While almost every student responds to this first warning, its impact is more momentary on some. When some of the boys repeatedly 'misbehave', then the stick comes into action: the 'misbehaving' boy may receive a few blows on his palms, hips or back. The disciplined boy does not show any disagreement. Instead, he becomes calm and quietly refocuses on his *Sabaq*. But despite this, some boys would repeatedly indulge in 'misbehaviour'. In this case, he is ordered to stand on his feet and read his *Sabaq* until permitted to stop, or he might be asked to sit in isolation from the rest of the boys in the class. While this disciplinary measure might be accompanied by corporal punishment, it is mainly used against the 'misbehaviour' of the relatively older students (normally about 14). The older boys cause problems more frequently than the younger ones. Therefore a group of them is separated from the rest of the class and come to *Sabaq* at a different time.

Another way of controlling misbehaviour inside or outside the Mosque is an exercise of social-psychological pressure that can be called 'shaming'. This non-corporal punishment is more commonly used against those boys who misbehave during the prayer or occasionally against those who hurt one of the students outside the class (provided the victim complains). An example of 'shaming' happened once during the evening prayer when there was loud laughter and noise in the back *Saf* (row). Just when the formal prayer ended, *Hafiz Sahib* asked some of the 'good boys' to point out who was responsible for the laughter during the prayer. The accused boy was ordered to come to the front of the worshippers, i.e. his classmates and some community members. He was questioned with a raised voice 'Why did you laugh and push other boys during the prayer?' The boy was so ashamed in front of all the crowd that he could not say a word to defend himself. He silently admitted his 'misbehaviour'. Then *Hafiz Sahib* told him '*Sharm nahi ien?*', 'aren't you ashamed (of your bad behaviour)?' Then he ordered the boy to stand against the front wall of the hall (in front of the crowd) until the prayer was concluded by *Du'a* (the concluding prayer). The boy had no choice but to stand there. Everybody was watching him while he could not look at anything except the wall. After the prayer, the boy was advised by *Hafiz Sahib* not to repeat what he did, and was encouraged to be a 'good boy'.

Despite the lack of sufficient educational facilities in the Mosque-school and an apparent incompatibility between the voluntary internalisation of Islamic faith/morality and corporal punishment as the two main forms of social control during the *Sabaq*-class, the school appears to be successful in achieving its objectives - the transmission of Islamic faith and morality to the British-born Pakistanis. Most of the Pilrig boys were able to perform prayers, individually and collectively alongside the adult members of the community on Fridays and on other religious occasions. In addition to this, when I asked the question 'How much of the Islamic teachings do you think we should follow in our daily lives , in this country?', the results were as follows: one half of the boys said that we should follow 'all Islamic teach-ings' whereas more than a third of (36.6%) said 'the major Islamic teach-ings'. Only 13.3 percent of the boys said that we should follow. 'only those Islamic teachings that involve rituals and ceremonies', where none of the 60 boys said that ' It is no longer necessary for us to follow Islamic teachings'. These results indicate that only one half of the sixty Pilrig boys are in favour of following all the Islamic teachings, in this country. This strong position was taken mainly by the younger boys (10-13 age-group). The other half had a more flexible position. This, in turn is indicative of the extent to which the *Sabaq*-class has been effective in the social bonding of its British-born Pakistani pupils to the socio-religious order of the Pakistani community in Edinburgh.

Congregational Worship, the Sense of Community and Social Control

a: The Jom'a Prayer: A Weekly Renewal of Commitment to a Shared Morality

Salat or formal (ritualistic) prayer is one of the most important features of Islamic religious life. A Muslim is strongly required to observe *Salat*. The prophet called *Salat* 'the foundation of Islam'. It is also the most common-ly and regularly observed way of worshipping God in Islam - from the daily five times to the weekly *Jom'a* and to the annual *Eid* prayers. While a Muslim is required to pray five times a day (preferably in congregation), the practicalities of life in Britain, it seems, make it difficult for most Muslims to meet this requirement : only a few people attend the Mosques in Edinburgh for their daily prayers performed in congregation.

However, the *Jom'a* (Friday) prayer which cannot be performed except in congregation is taken very seriously by Edinburgh's Muslim population. Many Muslims leave their shops and businesses for the Mosque on Friday afternoons to respond to the order of *Allah* who said: 'When it is called for the prayer of Friday, hurry to the worship of *Allah* and leave business' (*Al-Quran*). Around one o'clock every Friday both sides of Pilrig Street and the area surrounding the Mosque are crowded with the cars of Muslim worshippers. Many of them will have driven from distant parts of the city and the new brands of many cars show that their owners are successful businessmen. The entrance of the Mosque is also often crowded with the incoming men and young boys and some women too (I will mention shortly that women perform this prayer in a separate room within the Mosque). Inside the building, just before entering the main hall in the basement, the ablution place is always very busy with men and boys making *Wozu*: washing hands, mouth, nose, arms, and feet which is a necessary condition for prayer. But some people have already made *Wozu* at home. They take off their shoes and enter the main hall to join the rest of the worshippers who are sitting in *Safs* (rows) on the carpeted floor. This floor is covered with special prayer mats on Fridays.

All the people face the *Mihrab* and the *Minber* (and therefore Mecca) from where the *Imam* delivers his *Khotba* (formal Friday sermon) in Arabic. Older people normally sit or stand in the front *Safs* and the younger ones in the back. Although this is not a rule, it is considered desirable and it is an indication of respect for older people. Women, however, pray in a separate hall on the ground floor. While they are part of the same congregation, the women worshippers follow the rituals and the prayer led by the *Hafiz Sahib* through a loudspeaker in the women's hall. In principle, women can pray in the same hall, but this rarely happens in the Mosques of more traditional *Sunni* Muslims.

The formal prayer which starts at 1.30 p.m.(in all seasons of the year) is always preceded by a sermon in Urdu/Punjabi by *Hafiz Sahib*. At about 12.45 p.m. the young and eloquent but traditional-looking and charismatic *Hafiz Sahib* goes up the *Minber* to preach. The *Hafiz Sahib* carefully selects his sermon subjects: they may coincide with certain events and sacred days in Islamic history such as the *Ashura* (the day of the martyrdom of *Imam* Hussain, a grandson of the prophet), or with current events concerning Muslims in Edinburgh, Britain and occasionally in the Islamic world. For example, the publication of *Satanic Verses*, the Gulf War, and the situation in Bosnia. But normally, the Friday sermon is a weekly message of reminding the faithful of their commitment to Islamic morality - the *Awamir* and *Nawahi* (obligations and prohibitions, respectively). *Awamir* and *Nawahi* are umbrella concepts that cover a very wide range of issues from very private to very public: from drinking, eating and dressing to the virtues of

cleanliness, honesty, modesty and chastity; from social manners and greetings to duties and obligations to parents, kin, neighbours, the needy and to
the state and society.

Aware of the fact that many of his audience may already know about
these issues, *Hafiz Sahib* expands on and relates them to the daily lives of
Muslims in Edinburgh. By mentioning examples from Islamic history, current affairs and humorous tales from Pakistani folklore, the sermon turns
into an interesting and practically orientated lesson on Islamic morality and
values. Special emphasis is often placed on the prohibition of drinking alcohol and of not having pre- and extra-marital relationships. He warns people:
'These are two of the biggest of the seven sins in Islam.' Then, he explains
the 'damaging personal and social consequences' of these 'sins', citing a
saying of the prophet: 'Alcohol is the mother of all evils'; then he explains
that once you are drunk, then you lose self-control; you may verbally abuse
your friends and other people; you may commit indecent assaults and *Zena*,
(adultery) even against close relatives; or you may kill someone', *Hafiz
Sahib* explains. Then he mentions the punishments that await the drinker of
alcohol in the other world. Parents are warned not only to prevent their
young sons and daughters from indulging in drinking and mixing with the
opposite sex, but also to prevent them from going to pubs and discos. 'These
places corrupt the youngsters and lead them to *Zena*.' He cites a verse from
the *Quran*: '...and do not go (even) close to *Zena* [let alone committing it].'
Then he explains how pubs and discos create the atmosphere for vice and
Zena. *Hafiz Sahib* often relates *Zena*, and the high rates of divorce, incidents
of rape, illegitimacy and even AIDS in Britain, to the free mixing of males
and females. Then he draws a sharp line between what he calls 'permissive
values' of Western societies and the values of an Islamic community. A
reactive element (to exclusion and discrimination) becomes clear in the
drawing of 'their' and 'our' values when *Hafiz Sahib* refers to some of the
verbal abusive attacks on the Mosque, the Muslim graveyard and other
racially motivated harassment of some members of the community:

> This is what this society produces: hooligans, vandals and barbarians.
> When people abandon their religion, traditions and respect for older
> people, this is what happens to them. We must learn a lesson from this.
> If you want to be protected from crime and all other evils we must
> return to *Allah* and follow the teaching of Islam strictly and sincerely.
> *Allah* will protect us from the evil acts of hooligans and criminals if we
> close our ranks and create a true Islamic community where there is no
> alcohol, free mixing of women and therefore no indecency, *Zena* and
> violence.

It is important to notice that outside the Mosque, drinking alcohol and extra-marital relationships (among other prohibitions of the same degree of seriousness) are viewed as criteria for the labels of 'good' and 'bad' Muslims in the community. The labels *Sharabi*, drinker (of alcohol) and *Zani* (a person who commits *Zena*) are extremely derogatory and disreputable social stigmas. So is unrestricted mixing between unrelated men and women - these facts point to the existence of important relationships between the Mosque and the community. The audience in the Mosque are careful listeners and recipients of the Mosque's 'moral' lesson and the Mosque is an important source of the community's morality and moral judgements. Hence, it is a major agency of the community's social control.

To return again to the process of the *Jom'a* congregational prayer, the first phase of the ritual ends with *Du'a* or concluding words of prayer to *Allah* for forgiveness of sins and for guidance to the right path while everybody holds their hands up in the air. Then, the *Azan* (call for prayer) is made. After four *Rakats* of individually performed prayer by every worshipper, the *Imam* goes up the *Minber* to deliver the first of the two *Khotbahs* (the formal sermons). It is a reading from an Arabic text which is standard across most of the Muslim world. Its contents include prayers and greetings to the prophet Mohammed (P.B.U.H.), to the four *Califs*, to the descendants, companions and all followers of the prophet. When the first *Khotbah* ends, then the *Imam* sits on the *Minber* for about two minutes, to signify a break between the two *Khotbahs*. Then he stands again and cites the second *Khotbah* in Arabic. Its contents are also as standardised as those of the first one (though in some Muslim Arab countries new *Khotbahs* are prepared every Friday). The contents of the second *Khotbah* include prayer for guidance, granting strength to Muslim rulers for the implementation of Islamic Law. It ends with a verse from the holy *Quran*: '*Allah* commands justice, fairness and giving [their dues] to close relatives ...' (*Al-Quran*).

Although only a few people can understand the meaning of the two *Khotbahs* (which are in Arabic), everybody listens devoutly to them. This is because the two *Khotbahs* are considered as a collective prayer which is read and performed by the *Imam* on behalf of the rest of the worshippers. After the second *Khotbah* another *Azan* is made, then all the people stand in very straight *Safs*, shoulder to shoulder, facing the *Ka'aba*. The *Imam* reads verses from the holy *Quran* with *Tajvid* (a special rhythm of citing the holy *Quran*), while the worshippers silently listen. The worshippers follow the *Hafiz* in *Roko'a* (bowing) and *Sajda* (putting one's head on the ground) and in other rituals that he performs. After the congregational prayer ends, everybody performs six more *Rakats* of prayer individually. The weekly *Jom'a* prayer is much more than a system of signs, rituals and a sermon about Islamic morality that have been described so far; when the *Jom'a* prayer is performed, the worshippers' thoughts are centred upon:

their common beliefs, their common traditions, the memory of their ancestors, the collective idea of which they are an incarnation; in a word, upon social things ... the spark of social being which each individual bears within him necessarily participates in this collective renovation. The individual soul is regenerated, too, by being dipped again in the sources from which its life came; consequently, it feels itself stronger, more fully master of itself, ... (Durkheim 1915:348-49).

Many Muslims would find Durkheim's theological description, in the above passage, not applicable to Islam, but most are likely to agree with his social explanation of holding common faith and its translation into collective action. The Pakistani Muslims who are excluded from the wider society and feel insecure and alienated (see Chapter 1) find spiritual security and strength in their sense of community. The *Jom'a* prayer is constitutive of a collective expression of shared sentiments and a sense of community of deeply held feelings of unity - a unity of praying before one *Allah*; towards one place (the *Ka'aba*); after one spiritual leader, *Hafiz Sahib*, (the *Imam*) and reading or listening to the same set(s) of verses from one book, the holy *Quran* which says: '...You alone we worship; from you alone we seek help. Guide us along the straight path...' (*Al Quran*). The expression of the feelings of communality and unity is clearly present in the contradiction between 'we' and 'us' with 'you alone'..

This expression of shared sentiments and the feelings of unity by the faithful during the *Jom'a* prayer, has important implications for social control: it is the renewal of the existent commitment of the worshippers to their shared sets of moral and religious values. It is the renewal of a commitment to *Allah*, to obey him and at the same time it is a commitment, with each other that they will abide by the norms and values of their 'moral community'. By warm embracing with the *Hafiz Sahib* and among themselves at the end of the worship, the faithful further strengthen this commitment. But, the embraces on the occasion of *Eid-ul-Fiter* are even warmer, a topic to be discussed next.

b: Eid-Ul-Fiter: Sharing of Hardship and Happiness

Apart from the weekly congregational *Jom'a* (Friday) prayer the religious calendar of Edinburgh's Pakistani community includes other important occasions for collective worship and/or celebrations that bring its members together. The most important of these occasions are *Eid-i-Milad-un-Nabi* (the birthday of Prophet Mohammad (P.B.U.H)); *Ashura* (the day of martyrdom of *Imam* Hussain, nephew of the Prophet); *Shabi Ma'raji Nabi* (the night when Prophet Mohammad was taken by *Allah* to *Arsh*, a place in the metaphysical world); *Shabi Barat* (the night when the destinies of everybody are fixed for the next year); the days of passing away of Hazrati-Nizamudin Awleia and Hazrati Imam Ahamd Raza Khan (two saints and spiritual leaders of the *Barelvi* sect); *Eid-ul-Ozha* (the day of pilgrimage to Mecca); and *Eid-ul-Fiter* (the first non-fasting day after the month of *Ramadan*). While there are some differences in the way these events are celebrated (some include formal prayers, while others do not) all of them involve rituals and ceremonies that are very similar. Since it is beyond the limits of this book to discuss all of these religious/cultural occasions, I would focus only on *Eid-ul-Fiter*, the most important of these socio-religious events.

*Eid-ul-Fite*r is preceded by a month of fasting, *Ramadan*. During this month, all adult Muslims must abstain from eating, drinking, smoking and any conjugal relationships from early morning until sunset every day. A Muslim is expected to remain abstemious as *Ramadan* is a month of *Ibadat*, (worship) and it is considered as a 'training' for the faithful to control human passions and desires.

Apart from fasting during the day, Muslims also offer long prayers called *Taravih* in the evening/night. These prayers are generally performed in congregation. In the Pilrig Mosque the whole *Quran* is recited, every year, during *Taravih* over 28 evenings, by *Hafiz Sahib* who knows all of it by heart.

An important and joyful part of a fasting day is *Iftar* (breaking the fast at sunset). After many hours of thirst and hunger from early morning to early evenings people - young, old and children - gather in the Mosque to break their fast together. The collective breaking of the fast together with the food is called *Iftar* in the Pilrig Mosque. It is a fully fledged meal with a lot of soft drinks, sweet dishes, and dates. The *Iftar* is hosted by a different member of the community every evening in turn. As the time of *Iftar* approaches all the people sit around a meal mat in rows. When the first words of *Azan* for the evening prayer (performed just after sunset) are said, everybody starts breaking his fast. This collective breaking of the fast is again conducive to a sense of community. All the more so because of the shared provision of the food. To share in this is to be made to feel a part of this community. 'Eat, eat brother, you spend more energy, you work hard, throughout the day at the University' - I too was 'brought in' by the simple fact of sharing food. But it is more than sharing food. It is the sharing of hardship and suffering throughout the day; sharing of happiness of overcoming hardship (at the time of breakfast); and above all sharing of the belief and determination that has made possible an absolute abstention from eating, drinking, smoking, conjugal relationship, and 'sins'. Thus the importance of fasting, for social control, is more than the control of human passions for the period of a month. Its true importance is found in the sharing it involves. A sharing in faith and proving it by deeds through which the faithful reaffirm their social bond and loyalty to the community and to its moral order.

However, *Ibadat*, worship, does not end at the *Iftar* (breaking the fast). After the *Iftar* the third of the five prayers is performed in congregation. Then some people stay for *Taravih* (performed two hours later), others go home and come later for *Taravih*. While this situation is repeated every evening for the whole month of *Ramadan*, the last 10 days of the month are special; this is because the revelation of the Holy *Quran* is believed to have been completed on one of these nights. This night is called *Lailat-ul-Qader*, in which one's prayers are supposed to be accepted by *Allah*. During these last ten days of *Ramadan* the Mosque is crowded with worshippers in the evenings. It is also during these days that people make preparations for the *Eid*-day: exchange *Eid*-cards with friends and relatives; buy new clothes to wear on the day of *Eid* and get their houses ready for receiving visitors.

When the long awaited *Eid*-day is reached, both sides of Pilrig Street become very crowded with cars, men, women and children, most of whom wear new smart clothes. While many men and young boys are in smart Western clothes, many others wear Pakistani traditional garb, *Shalwar Kamis*. Women and young girls in traditional Pakistani clothes add to the colourfulness of the scene. This scene is an expression of cultural identity lived through the celebration of the *Eid*-day.

As everybody enters the first corridor of the main building they separate into two groups: the men go downstairs to the large hall in the basement, whereas the women go to their own smaller hall on the ground floor. The number of men and women is three or four times larger than the capacity of the Mosque. Therefore, the *Eid* prayer and its related rituals of exchanging *Eid* greetings have to be performed at three separate times: 08.30, 09.30 and 10.30 in the morning. Still each time, the halls of prayer are overcrowded. The *Eid* prayer is preceded by a sermon very different to other sermons. It focuses on issues that are considered of vital importance for the community's unity, moral and social survival.

Hafiz Sahib generally starts his speech by talking about the disciplinary role of fasting in controlling human passions, desires and greed, as an introduction to a more central issue concerning the community. Then he places special emphasis on the most important issues and events of the year. For example, on one occasion, he singled out greed and selfishness of members of the community. He said that events during the past year had shown that greed and vicious economic competition among members of the community had created jealousy and hatred: 'Greed and love of money have diverted people's attention from religion and the community to materialistic competition which has led to jealousy and therefore to disunity in the community. That is a social disaster.' He continued 'Success is not in making money, drinking, dancing with women and in luxury; *Allah* says: ' .. and indeed, those succeeded who remain pure.' He recited a verse from holy

Quran. Hafiz Sahib further added 'You should not buy sin with money; instead spend your money in doing things that are useful for your religion, community and the people.' Finally he reminded the audience to pay *Sadaqat-ul-Fiter* - an obligatory contribution by every individual to the poorer members of the community and to other charitable causes.

On this occasion *Hafiz Sahib* further pointed out that some people occasionally organised drinking and dancing parties, and that he knew about this. He strongly discouraged this behaviour, citing another verse from the holy *Quran* '... and compete with each other in doing good things and in advising piety. Do not co-operate with each other in commission of sin and violence.' He derived from this verse the meaning of collective responsibility to prevent 'immorality' in the community. *Hafiz Sahib*'s speech clearly shows an awareness of the deviations of some of members of the community. He directly told the audience that the community does not 'turn a blind eye' on the breaches of its moral norms and appealed to the audience for the mobilisation of the community to control 'deviance'.

After the congregational *Eid* prayer, all the participants stand up and embrace one another saying *Eid Mubarak* (Happy Eid). Most importantly it is on this occasion that people who have some resentment or hostility towards one another over the past year (in such situations in Pakistani culture, the two parties often avoid talking to each other) will embrace and greet each other. They must forget their resentments or hostility and forgive one another. If the resentment is very deep, then the community leaders and *Hafiz Sahib* reconcile the two parties. They have no choice but to accept 'the goodwill' of the community leaders: if they don't, they will not only be opposing the elders' opinion, but the refusal is also considered sinful because the happiness of *Eid* must be shared. Those who refuse to share the joy and happiness of the day and refuse the 'good will' of the community's leaders will be subject to the community's sanctions. Some of these sanctions are enforced by 'The Pakistan Association for Edinburgh and the East of Scotland', a topic to be discussed next.

II : Pakistan Association, Edinburgh and East of Scotland (P.A.E.E.S)

Organisational Structure, Functions and Aims

The Pakistan Association is an organised response by Edinburgh's Pakistani population to their new social, cultural and individual needs, that have emerged since their migration to Britain. A large part of these needs are of such a nature that the traditional Pakistani social institutions - the family, the *Biraderi*, and the Mosque - cannot cope with effectively. The ineffectiveness of the traditional Pakistani social institutions stems mainly from the fact that they are not designed to deal with the new needs of the population. The Association as a formal organisation with necessary financial and managerial resources responds to these needs through the mobilisation of the Pakistani population and by seeking assistance from certain institutions in the wider society. The new needs of Edinburgh's Pakistani population range from individual problems related to communications with formal and informal institutions of the wider society, arrangements for funerals/burials of the dead and other general welfare services to the religious/cultural socialisation of youngsters, celebration of cultural religious occasions and matters related to collective action against racial discrimination and violence etc. Meeting these needs constitutes the formal manifest aims of the Association. In order to achieve these aims more or less efficiently, the Association has developed a formal (or semi-formal) organisational structure.

But despite problems of legitimacy and popular representation, the Association continues to be an important institution in the life of the community, and an agency of social control. It has earned the recognition of official British institutions as the 'spokesman' of Edinburgh's Pakistani Community. As a bridge between Edinburgh's Pakistani population and the wider society, the Association has acquired a significant amount of prestige both within the Pakistani community and in the wider society. Due to its social influence in the community, and its control over resources to provide for the needs of Edinburgh's Pakistani population, the Association has the power to exercise authority and to act as an agency of social control in the community. With this general background to the P.A.E.E.S., I now turn to the discussion of its formal structure and aims and the way it acts as an agency of social control.

In the course of the past 30 years since its establishment in 1964, the organisational arrangements of the Pakistan Association, Edinburgh East of Scotland (P.A.E.E.S.) has evolved from being a kind of simple 'social club' into a bureaucratic or semi-bureaucratic structure with its own constitution. The constitution elaborates the Association's structural organisation and specifies its functions, aims, and activities. The document (and its various amendments) includes eight key sections. The eight sections are about issues that relate to the Association's objectives (aims), membership, voting system, elections and general meetings, office-bearers and their roles, finance and amendments to the constitution.

Membership in the Association is one of the central issues to the constitution. In theory, all Pakistani residents of Edinburgh, Lothian and Fife, can be members of the P.A.E.E.S., as article no. 1, section III, of the constitution states:

> Membership of the Association will be open to all Pakistanis residing in Edinburgh, Lothian and Fife, including those who are interested in the welfare of Pakistan and Pakistanis.(Constitution of P.A.E.E.S. 1971:1)

The article leaves the Association's doors open to the membership of all Pakistanis regardless of their affiliation to different *Biraderis*, religious sects etc. The ordinary members of the Association pay membership fees. The amount of the fees is not fixed and changes from time to time. The ordinary members are entitled to vote for the position of chairman and members of the executive committee. Members, moreover, are expected to attend the Association's general meetings and to express their opinions about various issues and problems that concern the community. However, the Pakistan Association has not gained the participation of all Pakistani residents in Edinburgh, Lothian and Fife. It is estimated by the leaders of the Association that it has the support of the overwhelming majority of Pakistani residents in this region. This includes 'active' membership and 'passive' support of the Association. Another group of Pakistani residents in Edinburgh have set up a rival cultural/welfare organisation to the Pakistan Association. This Pakistani organisation is known as the 'Pakistan Society'. Leaders of the Pakistan Society and other independent Pakistani residents in Edinburgh accuse the Association of being undemocratic, and dominated and led by a group of Pakistanis who use the organisation for their personal interests. Whatever the truth of this claim, the Pakistan Association is generally considered as the main body that represents Pakistani residents in Edinburgh, Lothian and Fife.

The organisational structure of the Association is formed on modern bureaucratic lines. The central apparatus of the organisational structure of the Association is its Executive Committee – an elected body that is responsible for the overall policy-making and for the running of the Association. According to the amendment of 6th June 1988 of the Association's constitution, the Executive Committee shall comprise 31 members. All members of the Executive Committee are elected in general elections that are held every two years. The hierarchical order of the division of labour (and power) of the Executive Committee is as follows:

a.   Chairman
b.   Senior vice-chairman
c.   Vice-chairman
d.   Secretary
e.   Joint secretary
f.   Treasurer

The above hierarchical order of the Executive Committee has undergone some changes and modifications since the start. In a general meeting of the Association in July 1993 a new post was added to the existing order of the Executive Committee. The new post is named 'Chief Patron'. This position, in theory, is honorary, without 'official' powers. But critics of this decision say that the real purpose behind it is to let the existing leaders continue their control over the Association. Some members of the Association complained that the conditions of the eligibility for the position of 'Chief Patron' apply only to the out-going Chairman of the Association!

The top office-bearers (or leaders) are mainly responsible for general policy-making. As 'official' leaders of the community, these individuals perform many other functions, i.e. mediation in intra-group disputes; heading the community's delegations to conferences; and chairing the celebration of social and cultural occasions of the community. More importantly, the top office-bearers of the Association deal with matters that relate to the community's relationship with the wider Scottish/British society and its formal and informal institutions. These matters include contributing to the policy-making of the Race Relations Council, the Council of Interfaith Relations and the police in the prevention of crime, particularly, racial attacks and harassment, etc. In short the top 'office bearers' of the Pakistan Association act as an official bridge between the Edinburgh's Pakistani community and the institutions of the wider society. It is mainly because of this that, unlike the other three social institutions of the community (the family, the *Biraderi*, and the Mosque), the P.A.E.E.S. is a relatively open and outward looking institution in its interaction with the wider society. Nevertheless it is the other traditional institutions of the community that to a considerable extent influence the policies of the P.A.E.E.S. As a response to the social and cultural needs of Edinburgh's Pakistani community, the P.A.E.E.S. has to translate its members' feelings, emotions and grievances to the wider society. For example in 1989 when Edinburgh's Muslim and Pakistani population protested against Salman Rushdie's *Satanic Verses* the then Chairman told the Edinburgh *Evening News* (12.6.1989) that 'the Muslim community of Scotland feels it has been let down by the community at large'. The Chairman, who did not favour violent demonstrations and Ayatollah Khomeini's *fatwa* against the author Rushdie, added that: 'my message to my Scottish friends is: if you were in my shoes what would you do?' The chairman of the P.A.E.E.S. who demanded the banning of the book implied that he was under pressure from the community in demanding a ban on the book.

As far as the application and practical embodiment of the Association's policies are concerned it is the task of smaller units within the Association that are called 'Committees'. Each committee comprises about 6 individuals headed by one of the 31 members of the Executive Committee. The head of each committee is called 'Convenor'. Some larger committees may be divided in to further smaller units that are called 'Sub-Committees'.

The various committees that currently function within the organisational structure of the Pakistani Association are:

a.   Committee for education
b.   Committee for religious affairs/mosque
c.   Committee for trade
d.   Committee for development (fund-raising, entertainment)
e.   Committee for sports and youth

Convenors of these committees are responsible for the effective running of their respective committees. They are also responsible to report to the executive committee in the Association's monthly meetings. Expenses for the activities of the committees are normally paid from the Association's budget. The main sources of this budget are membership fees, and money collected through donations, gifts and fund-raising.

With all the organisational arrangements that have so far been described the Pakistan Association has targets of achieving some specific aims. According to section II of the Association's constitution these aims are:

a.   To look after the interest of Pakistani community in the area.
b.   To promote good relations amongst Pakistanis and other ethnic communities and amongst the host community.
c.   To maintain mosque and school for religious studies of   Pakistani children.
d.   To celebrate national and international days, including religious days.
e.   To maintain a library consisting of Urdu and religious books
f.   To acquire a piece of land for burials and funerals.
      (Constitution of P.A.E.E.S. 1971:1)

It is difficult to assess the extent of the Association's success in achieving each of the aims/objectives. What is observable is the fact that the

Association has been successful in providing a general organisational framework for the various aspects of the life of Edinburgh's Pakistani residents. The Association has provided its members and other Pakistanis in the area with means and facilities for collective worship, celebration of social/cultural festivals and events, the religious/cultural socialisation of the British-born young Pakistanis and a place for the burial of their dead according to Islamic rituals. This would seem to indicate that the Association has achieved most of its aims to a significant extent.

The Pakistan Association has not only given an organisational structure to the community's life, but it has also given the community a formal recognition on national and international levels. For example, the Pakistan Association has very good relationships with the Scottish Local Authorities, members of the British Parliament, prominent politicians, the Scottish police and various local Scottish/British institutions. All these formal institutions recognise the Pakistan Association as a 'Formal' spokesman of Edinburgh's Pakistani community. Mr. Bader, a leader of the Pakistan Association said:

> The Association is the 'voice' of Pakistanis. It has fought for the rights of its members and non-members alike. It is democratically elected and recognised by the Embassy of Pakistan, all local authorities and relevant agencies. (Bader, 1985:5)

Similarly the Association has gained recognition outside the U.K. For example, in 1983, the late president Zia-Ul-Haq formally invited leaders of the Association to visit Pakistan. Leaders of the Association also formally visited the European Parliament in Brussels in 1984. Moreover the Association also raised funds for the victims of natural disasters in Turkey and Bangladesh, and has actively supported international and humanitarian causes.

Having achieved the status of a 'formal' cultural/religious and welfare organisation and a significant degree of national and internal prestige, the Pakistan Association is clearly in a position to act as an 'official' spokesman of Edinburgh's Pakistani population and as an agency of social control in the community.

Power, Authority and Social Control

Social power and one of its major manifestations, authority, are fundamental aspects of all socially organised groups, or associations. Power and authority both are, in turn, closely linked with social control. Most social and political scientists agree that power plays a vital role in the orderly existence and continuance of all associations. According to Robert Bierstedt (1970 : 351): 'Power stands behind every association and sustains its structure. Without power there is no organisation and without power there is no order.' Certainly the orderly existence and functioning of a football team, a university, a tribe and a state owe a great deal to the existence of power relations in the organisational structure of each of these associations. A university without the existence of power relations among the principal, deans of faculties, heads of various departments, and the rest, will cease to function as an organised social group. Power in this and other similar cases, moves the machine of association and enforces associational norms.

But, despite the vital importance of power to the functioning of associations, it is one of the most difficult sociological problems to fully grasp and analyse. This is mainly because social power, like electrical power, is unseen. Just as we can see only the effects of electrical power – heat, light, sound, etc. – we can see only the manifestations of social power in terms of force, exercise of authority, etc. Nevertheless, social philosophers and sociologists have attempted to define power. For instance, more than three centuries ago, the British philosopher Thomas Hobbes (1958 : 78) defined power as 'Man's present means for any future apparent ends'. Like Hobbes, Weber, the German sociologist, also defined power in dispositional terms;

> In general, we understand by 'power' the chance of a man or a number of men to realise their own will in a social action *even against the resistance of others* who are participating in the action (Emphasis Added) (Weber 1968 : 926)

It is clear from both Hobbes, and Weber's definitions that power has a dispositional meaning. That is to say that power is the *ability* and *capacity* of an individual to impose his/her will on others, or successfully threaten to impose, to achieve certain ends; it is not the *actual* imposition. Bierstedt (1970 : 348) in his *Social Order*, describes the dispositional nature of power more explicitly: 'Power is the ability to employ force, not its actual employment, the ability to apply sanctions, not their actual application . . . it is a stance not action.'

By shedding some light on the meaning and nature of power, it is only vaguely understood that it is a latent energy whose manifestations in terms of force and the exercise of various forms of authority etc. can be seen; not the phenomenon itself. However, it maybe possible to explore that where this mysterious phenomenon, power, comes from and what are its sources and bases. At this point it may be appropriate to return to the description of power relations and its social basis in the Pakistan Association, Edinburgh and the east of Scotland.

As mentioned earlier, the Pakistan Association is basically a collective response of Edinburgh's Pakistan residents to their new needs, after migration to Britain. But to meet the Pakistan residents' individual, social and cultural needs requires resources such as money, skill, property, management etc. The P.A.E.E.S. is the only organised Pakistani group in this area that possesses most of the necessary resources to meet the Pakistani residents' new needs. (The previously mentioned rival 'Pakistani Society' is too small to have any major resources to meet the social and cultural needs of Pakistanis in the area.)

First of all the Association's leaders because of their relatively higher level of education and longer period of residence in Britain are personally able to provide advice/assistance to individual Pakistani residents. The recipients of this kind of advice/assistance are normally those Pakistani residents who due to their poor communication skills in English face difficulties in dealing with official British institutions. The Association's leaders assist such individuals in matters that relate to translation, completion of various application forms, writing official letters, etc. The leaders also provide informal advice to Edinburgh's Pakistani residents about business matters, such as selling and buying of property, banking, and in areas of migration, housing and social security. Moreover, since the Association is recognised both by British official institutions and by Pakistani diplomatic missions in London and Glasgow, its leaders also act as referees for members of the community in matters such as marriage, divorce, visa renewal and the issuing of travel documents etc.

Apart from using the personal skills of its officials to assist individual Pakistanis, the Association has other organised collective resources to meet the residents' new cultural, religious and educational needs. For example the Association has its own budget and property; it controls and administers the Mosque, the Mosque-school, and the various committees for cultural activities that were mentioned in the previous section.

The Association's leaders claim an ability to mobilise social, economic and managerial resources of Edinburgh's Pakistani population to meet their various needs. The ex-chairman of the Association told me: 'We are proud to be able to look after the Pakistani community. We are here to help all Pakistanis in this area. We have the resources.' It may be an exaggeration to claim that the Association has vast economic, social and other resources to meet the Pakistani residents' various needs in Edinburgh. Nevertheless, the fact that the Association has mobilised and controls these resources (however modest they may be) has important social consequences for the consolidation of its position of power in the community. This is not only because the controllers of resources (leaders of the association) may withdraw from assisting, advising and providing other welfare services to individuals in the community. But, mainly, it is because many (if not all)

Pakistani beneficiaries of these resources genuinely feel obliged to the Associations' leaders – they accept their leadership and show deference to them. Thus the Association's control over the various resources to cater for the needs of Edinburgh's Pakistani population constitute a major source of its social power in the community.

The second major source of power of the Association in the community is the prestige and *Izzet* (honour) of its leaders. This source of power seems to be closely linked with the 'official' status of leadership in the Pakistan Association. However, the relationship between the two seem to be complex and have a circular form: while pre-existing personal prestige and family *Izzet* (and their other correlates such as wealth and education etc.) play a determining role in gaining leadership status in the Association, the latter further enhances the leaders' personal prestige and family *Izzet*. It is the combination of both – enhanced prestige/family honour and official leadership status – that constitutes the basis of effective power; it is at this level that associational power manifests its authority in the community. Now, the question is what forms of authority may the Association leaders demonstrate and what are the limits of this authority?

To try to answer these questions, we can draw on Max Weber's (1964) work where he distinguished three forms of authority: a) 'Traditional', b) 'Rational-legal', and c) 'Charismatic' authority. Charismatic authority, according to Weber is a kind of exceptional (or divine) endowment of grace that is imputed by followers to leaders. Contemporary examples of this form of authority may be the authority of Mahatma Ghandi, Martin L. King, and Ayatollah Khomeini. Legal-rational authority, on the other hand, according to Weber is the authority of highly organised groups such as that of the modern state. And finally traditional authority for Weber is the semi-political decisions made by chiefs of tribes in societies where the processes of government are not fully institutionalised.

The nature and form of authority that is exercised by the Pakistan Association resembles what Weber called traditional authority. This is mainly because the Association has strong elements of informal traditional organisation in it. The formal statuses of leadership within the Association are closely connected to informal networks of friendship, kinship and other connections. Thus, the exercise of authority by the Association's leaders resembles that of tribal chiefs, but with a bureaucratic veneer.

The spheres in which the Association's authority is exercised are mainly domestic. Chief examples would be problematic marriages, domestic violence, divorce, or separation etc. Disputes in business and inter-family, inter-*Biraderi* or personal feuds are other spheres where the Association's leaders exercise their authority. In all these spheres the 'traditional' nature of the Association's authority clearly manifests the exercise of authority through the process of informal mediation. The Association's leaders normally mediate between disputing parties to 'narrow down their difference, and reach a settlement that is fair and acceptable to both parties.' the Vice-chairman of the Pakistan Association told me on one occasion. He added 'We use our good will in settling disputes between Pakistanis in this area. We can do little more than using our good will.' But the vice-chairman also said that though he and his other colleagues cannot force the disputing parties to accept the decisions they make, non-compliance to the decision is not without serious social consequences within the community. The most common sanction against non-compliance is what the Vice-chairman described as 'We don't give them lift.' 'Not giving lift' in effect means ignoring someone's presence or importance. But the symbolic meaning of *not giving lift* within the community goes much beyond this; it is equivalent to the non-relevance of the non-compliant in the community. This implies that he will not be listened to in community affairs; he will be regarded as less than a *Sharif Adami* (decent man) and less than equal member of the community. Sanctioning non-compliance in this way in effect is a form of social 'outcasting' that in turn lowers one's *Izzet* in the community. It is at this point that the exercise of authority is linked to the most powerful mechanism of social control in the community – the mechanism of *Izzet* and *Bizati*. The individual who is 'not given lift' (ignored) and not considered as *Sharif Adami* has less *Izzet* in the community. As I mentioned in Chapter II (Section II), *Izzet* is a most dearly achieved social asset of individuals and families in Edinburgh's Pakistani community; it is rare for individuals to risk losing it.

Thus much of the authority of the Association's leaders operates through the community's informal networks of social control. Nevertheless, the Association's exercise of authority is not always confined to mediation that is backed by informal mechanisms of social control. In certain situations, the Association can use its 'formal' authority for controlling non-compliance to its decisions and in cases serious deviations from the community's norms. For example, amendment no. 4 to the Association's constitution (dated 22 May, 1988) states that:

The executive committee will be empowered to terminate membership of any person who in their knowledge is involved in any anti-social activities and whose membership could bring disharmony in the Association.(Constitution of P.A.E.E.S., amendment 1988:1)

The term 'disharmony' and the phrase 'anti-social activities' can be broadly interpreted to include non-compliance to the mediatory decisions by the Association's leader. This remains a theoretical sanction and a threat. The problem in implementing this sanction may have counter-productive results as a leader of the Association explained:

> We are careful in terminating the membership of those members who are involved in activities that are incompatible with the goals of our Association because he can easily turn against the Association. But, this does not mean that we will always tolerate serious anti-social characters in the Association. Our reputation is very important to us.

In fact, throughout my field work I did not observe a single case where a member was expelled from the Association. However, I did observe direct intervention of the Association's leaders to liquidate a situation that was interpreted as 'incompatible' with the community's values: a group of young boys and girls organised a *Bhangra* in Napier College (now university) in Edinburgh. Some of the 'Conformist' boys informed the Association's leaders about the time and place of the *Bhangra*. Three leaders of the Association directly went to the hall where the *Bhangra* was taking place and stopped it. 'When we appeared in the hall where *Bhangra* was, the boys immediately stopped the music, then we asked all the girls and boys to leave the place and go home. Then everybody immediately left the hall', the ex-chairman of the Pakistan Association said. *Bhangra* as a response of young Pakistani girls and boys to cultural exclusion is very likely to become acceptable as time goes by. But what is important in this case is the moral and social authority of the Pakistan Association and its implication for social control in the community.

Thus, it may be concluded that, alongside the family, the *Biraderi* and the mosque, the P.A.E.E.S operates as an important agency of social control in Edinburgh's Pakistani community. The main bases of the power and authority of the P.A.E.E.S lie in its leaders' social influence and *Izzet* in the community, in their Biraderi connections and in the social, economic and managerial resources that they command. These social bases of power enable the elected body of 'Officebearers' in the P.A.E.E.S to exercise authority in the community.

PART TWO: DEVIANCE

Introduction to Part Two

The first part of the book examined the social organisation of Edinburgh's Pakistani community and its various social institutions. The analysis mainly focused on the various social processes, mechanisms, and institutional arrangements that produced and at the same time maintained social order in the community. In other words, the main question to answer was how did individual members relate to each other and were they socially bonded to the community? The answers to this question help to describe social control as the normative aspect of social organisations; these descriptive answers relate to the general theory of the social control. The principal question that is asked in this part of the book is different but closely related to the first question: how strong are the individual members' social bonds to their community? This question explains conformity and deviance; it is related to a theory of crime/deviance.

The particular criminological theory that explains crime and deviance in terms of the strength or weakness of an individual's social bond, and the one which is used as the theoretical framework for the study of deviance among a sample of 60 Pakistani boys in Edinburgh, is commonly referred to as Travis Hirschi's (1969) formulation of Social Control theory. The theory and its applicability as an analytical framework for the present study of deviance are briefly described below.

Unlike mainstream criminology's 'old' question, 'Why do some people break the rules of society?' criminological social control theory asks a more novel and interesting question: 'Why don't we all break the rules of society?': Hirschi (1969 : 34) answers, 'We would if we dared'; Steven Box (1971 : 140) further adds '. . . But many of us dare not because we have loved ones we fear to hurt and physical possessions, and social reputations we fear to lose.' That is, most of us choose not to violate society's rules because we would pay a high social, psychological and material price for our criminal/deviant behaviour. Like Classicist criminologists, the modern social control theorists argue that we are 'rational' and 'calculative' in counting the pros and the cons of criminal/deviant behaviour. Those of us who lose little or nothing by violating society's rules are more likely to become involved in crime and deviance.

For Hirschi, it is our social bond to society that keeps our criminal/deviant impulses in rein. He contends that people who have strong social bonds to the conventional order to society are less likely to break its rules. Conversely, those who have weak or broken social bonds to society's conventional order are more likely to break its rules.

The first most central concepts in Hirschi's statement are *social bond* and *conventional order*. Social bond refers to the complex web of the individual's ties to society and to its social institutions that develop in the process of his/her social interaction. For Hirschi the most important contexts for the development of an individual's social bond to the society are his/her immediate social environment such as the family, the school and peer group. These fundamental social institutions further bond the individual to the wider societal institutions and to the social order. Hirschi suggests that social bond comprises four fundamental elements - Attachment, Commitment, Involvement and Belief (each one of the four elements of social bond will be theoretically and empirically examnined in Chapters V and VI)

The second central concept in Hirschi's social control theory is *conventional order of society*. It refers to those fundamental societal values that are largely shared in society. The idea of conventional order is based on one of social control theory's basic assumptions about the existence of a degree of consensus among members of society on core societal values. The control theorist assumes that certain core societal values, such as safety of the individual and of his/her property, freedom of expression, tolerance, and individuals' welfare, etc. have societal currency. It is because of this assumption underlying social control theory that it is listed among 'normative theories' in criminology. Because of this, it can be asserted that social control theory applies better to culturally homogeneous societies where a higher degree of normative consensus among members exists. Small-scale communities that are culturally homogeneous and with a high degree of normative integration are most appropriate social groups for the empirical 'test' of social control theory.

This last point suggests the rationale for the use of Hirschi's social control theory as a theoretical framework for the present study of deviance in Edinburgh's Pakistani community. As was discussed in the first part of the book, a very high degree of normative integration exists in Edinburgh's Pakistani community: apart from common language, ethnic background and country of origin and customs and traditions, shared Islamic beliefs and values play a central role in the moral and normative integration of Edinburgh's Pakistani community. It is an ethno-religious community whose members share a common moral and social order. At this point it seems appropriate to recall Etzioni's (1969) classification of social organisation into 'coercive', 'utilitarian' and 'normative'. Edinburgh's Pakistani community falls into the latter category. According to Etzioni's view, social control in a 'normative' organisational setting operates mainly through the internalisation of norms; the predominant pattern of compliance in such setting is attitudinal conformity.

Because Hirschi's formulation of social control theory is generally 'tested' through the measurement of attitudes towards conventional institutions, persons, values and beliefs, it can be more prudently examined empirically in the normative organisational setting of Edinburgh's Pakistani community. Moreover, the clarity of the assumptions of social control theory, its empirical adequacy and testability makes it a very suitable theory for empirical 'testing' (see Kornhauser 1978: 250-55). It is not surprising that the social control model has greatly influenced the area of empirical criminological research, particularly in the United States. And yet it is little known to British criminology. The existing body of British criminological research and the most recent Social Sciences Citation Index (S.S.C.I.) indicate that the modern version of social control theory has never been empirically 'tested' in this country. This clearly points to a gap in the existing body of criminological knowledge in the U.K. It is because of all these reasons that Hirschi's formulation of social control theory is selected for an empirical 'test' in the present study.

The results of the empirical 'test' of Hirschi's social control theory in a sample of 60 Pakistani boys in Edinburgh – The Pilrig Boys – are examined in Chapters V and VI of this part of the book. However, before this, Chapter IV describes who the Pilrig Boys are, and who are seen as deviants, and non-deviants among them by the Pakistani community in Edinburgh.

4 The Pilrig Boys and Deviance

Introduction

The sample of 60 Pakistani boys in the present study is referred to as 'The Pilrig Boys' because they all gather for their cultural/religious education six days a week in a Mosque-school that is situated in Pilrig Street, in the Leith area of Edinburgh. This chapter is directly based on empirical data about the Pilrig boys and is divided into two main interrelated parts:

a. Sample characteristics and general preliminary data about the Pilrig boys.
b. Deviance and a typology of the Pilrig boys.

The first part of chapter consists of five closely interrelated sections. In the first I will discuss the age distribution, place of birth and family background of the boys, including their parents' ability to read and write, their level of education and occupations. In the subsequent section an account of the boys' interaction with the wider society mainly through the (local Scottish) school and 'best friends' is given. Also the use of television in the Pakistani home, and the exposure of the Pilrig boys to Western values through this 'window from the outside world' is discussed in detail in this section.

The third section follows on from this to discuss the responses of the Pilrig boys to the wider society's culture and its influence on them. In order to examine the extent of the influence of Western values on these Muslim boys the discussion focuses on the attitudes of these boys to three important issues that are central to the social and moral order of Edinburgh's Pakistani community. They are: 'wearing of Western clothes by Pakistani women'; 'having girlfriends'; and 'arranged marriage'. The main point to be examined in this section is that how different are the opinions of these (second-generation) Pakistani boys about these issues from the dominant values of the Pakistani community.

In the subsequent section the negative aspects of the Pilrig boys' interaction with the wider society - experiences of racial discrimination and harassment - are examined. The scale and forms of the racial discrimination experienced by these boys are analysed in the light of both qualitative and quantitative data. Finally, the cultural and social-psychological responses of the Pilrig boys to their experiences of racial discrimination (and exclusion) by the wider society are analysed in the fifth section of the first part of the chapter. This part of the chapter is completed with an examination of the issue of identification and social belonging - British or Pakistani? It is at this point that the discussion shifts to a slightly different but related issue - deviance.

In the second part of this chapter, deviance (as a sociological category) forms the main theme of discussion. First, the definition of deviance on a theoretical level is critically examined. A more comprehensive definition that takes into account various dimensions of deviance and provides a more solid theoretical framework for the present empirical study of deviance is suggested.

Then, on the basis of the field data of the present study, deviance is operationally redefined in the social and normative context of Edinburgh's Pakistani community. Seven fundamental norms within the social/normative context of the Mosque-school and the wider Pakistani community are identified. The degree of deviance among the Pilrig boys is determined on the basis of the frequency of breaking each of these norms by an individual boy in the sample over a period of two years. This is depicted as lying in a continuum of four degrees of deviance – from the least deviant boys to the most deviant. In the light of the ethnographic data about the boys, certain patterns of behaviour emerged about each of the four categories. Because each of the four patterns of behaviour about the 60 boys had a dominant feature, each category was named by this feature. Thus, the four categories of the Pilrig boys are: the Conformists, the Accommodationists, the Part-time-Conformists, and the Rebels. Finally, because of the close and well established connection between age and crime/delinquency in criminological theory and research, the relationship between age and deviance in the Pilrig sample is examined in the last section of the chapter.

I: The Pilrig Boys

The Boys and their Parents

Place of Birth

The overwhelming majority of the Pilrig boys are British-born. According to the present data 81.66 percent of these boys were born in the United Kingdom, whereas only 18.33 percent of them were born in Pakistan. However most of the latter category were brought by their parents to the UK when they were only 1, 2 or 3 years old.

Table 4 shows that among the British-born boys in the Pilrig sample more than a third (35 percent) were born in Edinburgh; 1.66 percent in Glasgow; and the remaining 45 percent of the boys were born in English cities, mainly, in Huddersfield, Bradford and London.

Table 4 - Place of Birth of the Pilrig Boys

City/Country of Birth	% (Number)
Edinburgh	35.00 (21)
Glasgow	1.66 (1)
English Cities	45.00 (27)
Pakistan	18.33 (11)
Total	100.00 (60)

This indicates that a strict definition of 'second generation' would only apply to the 81.66 percent of the Pilrig boys. While the rest (18.33%) may be called 'child migrants'. But, in the context of the present study, it makes more sense to call the latter category a 'second-generation' as well. This is because the Pakistan-born boys, in the present sample, were brought to the UK at a very early age. Their socialisation in the family, in the school(s), and their experiences in the wider social environment seem hardly different from those of their fellows who were born in the UK.

Age

The Pilrig boys come from a relatively wide range of age groups. The youngest of the boys in the present sample are aged 10, whereas the oldest are 21. According to Table 5, the largest proportion of the boys (41.66 percent), in the present sample, are aged between 10 to 13 years. A minority of 8.33 percent of the boys are aged between 16 to 18 years, whereas, those who are between 19 to 21 years old constitute about a third (31.66 percent) of the Pilrig sample.

It must be mentioned that in Edinburgh's Pakistani community (and among Muslims in general) age is an important criterion on the basis of which a boy's (and also a girl's) social and religious responsibilities are determined. According to *Hafiz Sahib* (the *Imam* of the Pilrig mosque) the age of 14 or 15 is the age of *Bolugh* (puberty). He added that, 'at this age a boy is required to pray, fast and he is fully responsible for his behaviour and

Table 5 - Age Groups of the Pilrig Boys

Age	% (Number)
10-12	41.66 (25)
13-15	18.33 (11)
16-18	8.33 (5)
19-21	31.66 (19)
Total	100.00 (60)

actions'. However, some parents believed that a Pakistani boys reaches *Bolugh* towards the end of his 12th year of age.

Despite the existence of a wide range of age groups in a relatively small-er sample (60 boys), age seems to be a very important sociological variable in explaining deviance and conformity among the Pilrig boys. I will return to this issue later in this chapter. First it is important to look at the family background and social attributes of the Pilrig boys' parents.

Family Structure and Parents

The Pilrig boys appear to come from stable families that are not affected by divorce, separation, illegitimacy and bigamy. Families of only two boys are affected by bereavement. Fifty-six out of the 60 Pilrig boys said that they lived with their real fathers and real mothers. Two of the boys said that because their real parents have recently returned to Pakistan, they lived with their uncles. Only one boy said that he lived with his step-father because his real father died; and another lived only with his mother because his father, a shop owner, was stabbed to death (the incident is widely considered to have been racially motivated).

Although most of the Pilrig boys (and their parents) do not live with their grandparents, uncles and cousins in the same house, they lived close to these relatives or/and are in close and frequent contact with them. In many cases parents of the Pilrig boys shared business/property with their immediate kin. Thus, the Pilrig boys are not deprived of the warmth and social and psychological support that a Pakistani boy may enjoy in an actual extended household in Pakistan. Moreover, the apparently nuclear families of the Pilrig boys are considerably large. As mentioned in Chapter II the average family size in the present sample is 5.4.

Parents' Ability to Read and Write

Despite the fact that parents of many of the Pilrig boys have rural backgrounds in Pakistan, the overwhelming majority of them can read and write, at least in Urdu. As Table 6 indicates, 71 percent of the boys said that their parents were able to read and write; 16.66 percent of them said that only their fathers could read and write, whereas only 6.66 percent of them said

Table 6 - Parents' Ability to Read and Write

Parents	% (Number)
Father & Mother	71.66 (43)
Father only	16.66 (10)
Mother only	3.33 (2)
Neither Parent	8.33 (5)
Total	100.00 (60)

that only their mothers could read and write. A small minority of 8.33 percent of the boys said that both of their parents were illiterate.

The figures in Table 6 indicate that more fathers of the Pilrig boys as compared to their mothers could read and write. This may not be surprising in the patriarchal culture of Pakistani society and of Edinburgh's Pakistani community. But as discussed in Chapter II it is the mothers who mainly shoulder the burden of socialisation and basic education of the Pilrig boys.

Fathers often have little time to spend with their children. However, these data do not show the level of education of the parents of the Pilrig boys and their ability to read and write in English. This issue is examined next.

Parents' Level of Education

The phrase 'level of education' in the present context means the acquisition of formal educational qualifications by the parents of the Pilrig boys in Pakistan (although some parents were educated in the UK).

For the present purpose, it is important to mention that the extent of the use of English language in the primary and secondary schools in Pakistan varies according to the type and social status of these schools. For example, in many prestigious public primary schools in large cities, The English language may be as much used as Urdu, whereas the main medium of education in primary schools in rural areas is, by and large, Urdu. But, the extent to which English Language is used in secondary schools and colleges in

Table 7 - Parents' Level of Education

Level of Education	Father % (Number)	Mother % (Number)
College/University	37.33 (20)	20.75 (11)
Secondary	37.73 (20)	32.07 (17)
Primary	13.20 (7)	18.68 (10)
Informal	11.32 (6)	28.30 (15)
Column Total	100.00 (53)	100.00 (53)

[1]The base number for this set of data is 53. Seven of the respondents were not able to answer the question about their parents' education

rural Pakistan, generally, enables students to write, read and speak in English, more or less, proficiently.

With this brief background, the present empirical data indicate that more than three fourths (75.46%) of fathers and more than a half (52.82%) of mothers of the Pilrig boys can, at least, read and write in English.

According to Table 7, almost two fifths (37.73%) fathers of the Pilrig boys and a little more than one fifth (20.75%) of their mothers have college/university education. Once again, almost two fifths (37.33%) of the boys' fathers have secondary education, whereas about a third (32.07%) of their mothers have this level of education. 13.20 percent of fathers and 18.20 percent of mothers of the Pilrig boys have primary education. As far as informal education (home/Mosque based) is concerned a much larger proportion - 28.30% - of mothers of the Pilrig boys compared with 11.32% of their fathers are informally educated.

Table 7 reveals that more fathers have higher levels of education than mothers, in the Pilrig sample. As I mentioned earlier, it would have been more important if more mothers had higher levels of education, as it is the mothers who play a crucial role in the socialisation and pre-school education of Edinburgh's Pakistani boys and girls. Nevertheless, as all mothers (except the 8.33% shown in Table 6) have at least some education; they still make an important contribution to the process of cultural and religious socialisation of their children.

Parents' Occupation

Edinburgh's Pakistani community is, mainly, a 'business community' whose economic activities by and large concentrate in the private sector. According to Table 8 the majority (56.66 percent) of the Pilrig boys' fathers work in their own shops; one tenth (10%) of them run their whole-sale businesses; 8.33 percent run their own restaurants, bakeries and guest-houses; 6.66 percent work in family-run post-offices, news agencies and as *Imam* in the Mosque. Only one tenth (10%) of fathers in this sample work as engineers and accountants. The rest (8.33 percent) of the fathers, are economically inactive, among whom 5 percent are unemployed and 3.33 percent are retired from work.

Moreover the table shows that the overwhelming majority (73.33%) of the mothers of the Pilrig boys work as (full-time) housewives; 13.33 percent of the mothers help their husbands in the family shops; 6.33 percent do sewing outside home, and another 6.33 percent of the Pilrig boys' mothers work as doctors, teachers and community workers.

The data in Table 8 indicates that only about a fourth of mothers in the Pilrig sample are involved in activities outside the house. But, in fact half of these mothers (those reported to be helping their husbands in their shops)

Table 8 - Parents' Occupation

Occupation - Father	% (Number)	Occupation - Mother	% (Number)
Shopkeeping	56.66 (34)	Housework	74.33 (44)
Business (Wholesale)	10.00 (6)	Helping in the Family Shop	13.33 (8)
Restaurant, Bakery and Guest House	8.33 (5)	Sewing	6.66 (4)
Post Office, News Agency, *Imam* (Muslim Priest)	6.66 (4)	Doctor, Teaching and Community Work	6.66 (4)
Engineering, Accountancy	10.00 (6)	-	-
Unemployed	5.00 (3)	-	-
Retired	3.33 (2)	-	-
Total	100.00 (60)		100.00 (60)

basically work as housewives; they come down to the shop that is often adjacent to their flat, when they have not much to do in the house. Thus, only about one seventh (13.33%) of all mothers in the Pilrig sample are involved in full-time activities outside the house. All the rest (86.33%) of the mothers are housewives.

Establishing relationships between parents' (mainly fathers') type of occupation and their level of monthly or yearly income is a very difficult task, in the present study. First of all some of the respondents were not willing to answer questions about their families' monthly, or annual income. Many others did not know how much income their families had.

Secondly, categorising types of occupations, in the present study, and then placing them in an arbitrary order of 'Low', 'Middle' and 'High' incomes seem to me misleading. For example it would not be correct to assume that an owner of a baking factory, or of a big restaurant, has more income than a shopkeeper. This is because many shop owners in the present sample own one, two or more shops (and other property). Similarly, it would be incorrect to assume that a shop owner has more income than professionals such as doctors, engineers, accountants, or vice versa. Thus, it may be said that parents of the overwhelming majority of the Pilrig boys are self-employed businessmen/shop owners. They are, by and large, well-to-do economically.

The Boys in the Wider Society

The School

Unlike some multi-cultural cities where the younger members of racial/cultural minority groups tend to go in large numbers to specific schools (for certain racial/cultural reasons), the Pilrig boys do not seem to have such tendencies. They attend various schools and colleges that are scattered throughout the city of Edinburgh. According to the present data, the only school that is being attended by a relatively larger number (16.66%) of the Pilrig boys is 'James Gillespies', in central Edinburgh. However, there were no specific reasons for the boys to attend this particular school except for its central location and easy access.

The boys, particularly those at the primary level, are immensely interested in attending their schools. The culturally induced aspirations for acquiring formal education and strong parental encouragement on the one hand, and meeting new friends in a new environment with better educational and recreational facilities, on the other hand, seem to be the major reasons for the boys' enthusiasm for attending Scottish schools. A Pilrig boy in James Gillespie's primary school told me:

> I like my school a lot, because most of my teachers are polite. I have lots of friends at school and wouldn't like to leave that school. We get maths every day except on a Friday, because Friday is our fun-day - no work! We also get a sweet at the end of the day from our teacher.

The content of what this boy said clearly indicates that he is well adjusted to the social and psychological environment of the school. Despite his different ethnic/cultural background, the boy feels that he is one of the boys in the school. This pro-school attitude is shared by most of the Pilrig boys. As another boy said:

> I like my school very much. Our teachers are very kind and polite. They
> only get angry when you get into trouble. Then, they give you punishment
> exercises. We do a few projects every year, and we study-out, sometimes.
> We do a lot of exciting things, like fun-run, sponsor swim and can can. I
> am going to stay in this school until I am about 18 years old, so I get more
> education and I will get paid more.

As the above passage shows, the boy continually refers to himself and his
class fellows as 'we' and 'us'. The boy's interest and participation in his
school's collective educational and recreational activities seem to indicate
his full involvement in the educational process.

As it will be discussed in Chapters V and VI in detail, a large majority of
the Pilrig boys have strong attachments to their local Scottish schools. Most
of them regularly attended their school; they cared much about what their
teachers thought of them; and they liked their schools very much. Moreover,
a large majority of the Pilrig boys had a high level of scholastic performance.

What has been mentioned seems to suggest that the school is the Pilrig
boys' bridge to an active participation in the cultural, social and
(future)occupational life of the wider society. It also provides the boys
opportunities for making new friends outside their own community.

'Best Friends'

As is discussed in Chapter V (section - attachment to peers) the actual
friendship pattern of the Pilrig boys is generally located within their kin-
ship/friendship groups. The closest friend, in the Pilrig sample were, normally, members of the same kin group who were related to each other
through the ties of blood and/or marriage. These friends and also kin called
each other '*Bhaie jan*', brother/older brother, and '*Cazan*' (cousin). It is this
pattern of friendship within kinship that provided an actual framework of
intimacy, mutual trust, and identification for the boys in the Pilrig sample.
Nevertheless, the Pilrig boys did have friendships with non-Pakistani boys
from the indigenous population in Edinburgh. They called many of their
non-Pakistani peers 'best friends'. It seems that the boys used the phrase
'best friends' somewhat indiscriminately for whoever they sat with in the
same class and/or played with in the same playground. It is within this
broader meaning of 'best friendship' that the Pilrig boys' circle of friendship, seemingly, goes beyond the boundaries of kinship and of the Pakistani
community. It was within this context that all the Pilrig boys were asked:
'Think about the best friends that you have. Are they ...?:'(see Table 9)

Table 9 - The Pilrig Boys' 'Best Friends'

Best Friends	% (Number)
All Pakistani/Mostly Pakistani	40.00 (24)
About half Pakistani/half Whites (and others)	43.33 (26)
All Whites/Mostly Whites	16.67 (10)
Total	100.00 (60)

Table 9 shows that while two fifths (40%) of the Pilrig boys said that all or most of their 'best friends' are Pakistani boys, more than two fifths (43.33%) of them said that about half of their best friends are white boys and about half of them Pakistani boys. Only about one sixth (16.67%) of the boys said that all or most of their 'best friends' are white boys.

As the above mentioned data indicate, the apparently widened circles of friendship have given the Pilrig boys an opportunity to interact closely with non-Pakistani boys in the school, in the play ground, during camping tours and in many other events.

Although, as discussed in Chapter Two, experiences of racial discrimination and harassment might have discouraged the Pilrig boys from establishing close ties of friendship with boys from the indigenous population. Nevertheless these boys' contacts and interactions with their non-Pakistani 'best friends' can hardly be without important social consequences. The Pilrig Pakistani boys learn and have to conform to certain manners and values of the student 'sub-culture' within the school. They learn there about 'Rangers' and 'Celtic'; about 'discos' and 'pubs' and about what are the best movies on television and in Edinburgh's cinemas

Television

The typical Pakistani home in Edinburgh is a small world in its own right - a world that represents Pakistan in Edinburgh in some important ways. A quick description of this small world is possible by focussing on the family's sitting room - a room that represents Pakistan physically, socially and psychologically.

Probably, the first things that would attract a guest's attention are a large photograph of a Pakistani political leader, a family photo, a landscape from Pakistan, and verses from the Holy *Quran* (in Arabic script) that normally decorate walls of the sitting room. Sometimes, a framed verse of the holy *Quran* is put on a book-shelf that contains a copy of the Holy *Quran* and a dozen volumes of Islamic and Urdu books. On the ground, modern furniture and sofas are half covered with hand woven Pakistan-made cushions. The daily *Jang*, the popular Urdu newspaper is often on a coffee table in the room.

Most family members, including men, wear the traditional Pakistani clothing, *Shalwar-Kamis.* They warmly and intimately talk, joke and gossip with each other in Urdu/Punjabi. When parents and other adults talk on somewhat serious topics, the children listen to them very politely. Moreover, the smell of hot Pakistani food that is being cooked in the kitchen is often felt. An Urdu/Punjabi song that is often played on the stereo system further add to the Pakistaniness of the social and psychological atmosphere of the sitting room.

But, this small world of a different moral and social order has an open window to the surrounding world - this window is the 'irresistible' television, as a Pakistani parent put it.

In the Pilrig sample, virtually every one of the 60 boys had a colour television set at their homes. Most of the boys said that they also had VCRs. For these boys, watching television is a major indoors recreation. The overwhelming majority of the boys said that if they did not have 'something very important to do', they watched television. I will return to what the boys most often watched on television but, first, it is important to know about the attitudes of parents and the community to this issue. Do parents restrict their children from watching television?

All parents, the Mosque and the local Pakistani newspapers are aware and, to some extent, concerned abut the influence of television over young Pakistanis in Edinburgh, and in the UK. Nevertheless, most parents, the Mosque and the local Pakistani press regard the television as a medium of both 'good' and 'bad' influence over the younger members of the Pakistani community. For example, the weekly *Akhbar-E-Watan* while addressing Pakistani children in the UK, wrote:

> Certain educational and informative programmes of the [British] television are admirable. But the [British] television's corrupting programmes are the enemy of our natural emotional delicacies and are against our high moral values and norms. (translated from *Akhbar-e-Watan*, 19.11.1989)

The weekly newspaper warned parents about the 'corrupting' influences of the British television on their children. The view of *Hafiz Sahib* is in line with that of the weekly *Akhbar-e-Watan*: 'Some programmes of the television are corrupting, but others are good and useful. Parents should not allow their children to watch the corrupting programmes', *Hafiz Sahib* said. All programmes that included violence and semi-naked females were considered 'corrupting'. Some commercial advertisements were also included in this category.

Most parents of the Pilrig boys are in favour of a selective watching of television by their children. Parents tend to discourage their children from watching 'corrupting' TV programmes and films by warning them about the serious consequences of this behaviour in this world and in the life after life. However, only some parents try to impose restrictions on their children to watch television selectively, or not at all. But, these parents do not seem to be very successful, as one parent complained: 'If you do not allow them to watch television they get bored. Then, they do worst things at home or go outside.' This may be the situation in the minority of cases. The most important fact is that most of the boys, particularly the younger ones, accept their parents' moralising message about the 'selective watching' of British TV's four channels. One of the boys in the Mosque school summarised the views of his classmates after a 30-minute discussion about 'watching television' as follows:

> We think that television is a good and bad thing. You learn from some programmes about this country and about the world. It is also great fun. But watching dirty programmes and films is *gunah* [sin]. They are against our religion.

Interestingly, most of the boys had full knowledge of the daily TV programmes. But which of the TV programmes did the boys most often watch? Children's BBC, cartoons, *Home and Away*, *Dr Who*, *Happy Days*, *EastEnders*, *Casualty* and *Neighbours* were among the programmes that the Pilrig boys most often watched. *Neighbours* was the boys' particular favourite. Now, the question is: to what extent are some of the values that are normally portrayed in the stories of Ramsay Street *Neighbours* (i.e. premarital relationship and its expression), compatible with the values of Edinburgh's Pakistani community?

Parents generally do not have a clear-cut answer for this question. Whatever the reason, they prefer to remain quiet about the extent of the exposure of their children to 'Western values'. But the answer of many of the Pilrig boys to the above question is 'It is OK!'. This may indicate the extent of the influence of the wider society over the Pilrig boys – an issue to be examined next.

Influence of the Wider Society

It has been noticed in the previous section that interaction of the Pilrig boys with the wider society through school, friends and television has brought them face to face with British social manners, values and morality. But, certain sets of these values and morality are still considered as 'foreign' in Edinburgh's Pakistani community to which most of these boys have a strong sense of belonging. The present section examines the extent to which the Pilrig boys have been influenced by the values of the wider British society. However, since the English language, particularly the local Edinburgh accent, plays an important role in the interaction of the boys with the wider society, it is important to see, first, how well the Pilrig boys speak the English language.

The English Language

Many theorists and researchers of race relations have argued that learning the language of the host society by members of ethnic groups is the first step in their assimilation to that society (see Gordon 1964; Robinson 1982; Sheu 1983). Although the success of the assimilation process may depend on many other variables, it is common sense that knowing the language of the host society is the major means for members of ethnic groups to communicate with that society; it is their key to a possible participation in the general social and institutional life of the host society.

All the Pilrig boys were able to speak, read and write in English. Nevertheless, those who spoke English correctly and with Edinburgh accents were known in the Mosque-class, as speaking English 'very well'. The boys who spoke English correctly but with a mixture of Scottish and Pakistani accent were considered as speaking 'well'. There were a few boys who communicated in English with a Pakistani accent and thought that they spoke English 'fairly well'. Thus all the Pilrig boys were asked: 'How well do you speak the English language? Do you think that you speak it . . ..:'.

The data in Table 10 indicate that three fourths of the boys spoke English not only correctly but also with a perfect Edinburgh accent. About one fourth (23.33%) of the boys spoke English correctly but with a mixture of Scottish and Pakistani accents. Only a negligible minority (1.67%) said that they communicated merely fairly well in English.

The Pilrig boys took pride in speaking English accurately with an Edinburgh accent. Most of the boys spoke in English among themselves. In

Table 10 - The Pilrig Boys' Ability to Speak English

Ability to speak English	% (Numbers)
Very Well	75.00 (45)
Well	23.33 (14)
Fairly Well	1.67 (1)
Total	100.00 (60)

fact many seemed to speak English more fluently than their mother tongue, Urdu/Punjabi. However, the Pilrig boys were strongly encouraged by their parents to speak in Urdu/Punjabi at home. They were also taught Urdu in the Mosque school. Parents' emphasis on Urdu/Punjabi language was not only because it was an important element of the cultural/ethnic identity of their British- born children. It was also due to the fact that some parents were unable to communicate with their children when they spoke in English, particularly in the local accent!

The data at hand show that while the Pilrig boys spoke Urdu/Punjabi and English, their mastery of the English language, particularly of the local accent, has enabled them to communicate more effectively with the wider Scottish society than their parents do: they generally felt more comfortable speaking in English than in Urdu/Punjabi. Would this mean that these boys have more liberal attitudes, compared with those of their parents, towards some core values of their community?

Attitudes Towards Pakistani Women's Clothes

One of the important social values and a self-evident feature of the cultural identity of Edinburgh's Pakistani community is the clothes of its female members. *Shalwar-Kamis*, loose trousers and a long blouse, with (or without) a *Dupatta*, head scarf, are normally worn by Pakistani women in Edinburgh.

For most Pakistani men and women these traditional clothes of Pakistani women are not merely a strong element in expressing their cultural identity. Also, wearing these clothes is thought to be carrying an implicit message of decency and modesty *vis-à-vis* the 'dangers' of what a Pakistani father of young girls called an 'environment of provocations and seductions'. He added with humour that wearing *Shalwar-Kamis* is like a declaration of 'No s** please; we are Asians!'. Indeed, the more serious meaning of this humour is shared by many men and women in the Pakistani community in Edinburgh. For most of them wearing *Shalwar-Kamis* represents a woman's decency and modesty, and therefore reflects positively on her good reputation and on her family's *Izzet* (honour). In fact, it is the woman's reputation and her family's *Izzet* that matters; any damage to the two have very serious social consequences for both the individual woman and for her family (see Chapter II, Section II).

In contrast, some British-born Pakistani boys (and also girls) see the wearing of *Shalwar-Kamis* by young Pakistani girls as 'a slavish following of culture' as a college student put it. He added that wearing these clothes by Pakistani women is a 'self-inflicted exclusion from the society and this invites racial prejudice'. Interestingly, these young boys say that it is alright for older Pakistani women to wear *Shalwar-Kamis*, but not for young girls. I asked the boys why? 'Young girls have more contact with the people in this country. They go to school, to shopping and other (public) places', one of the boys said, while others agreed with the answer. Another boy added that wearing *Shalwar-Kamis* by Pakistani girls, in this country is 'just unsuitable; they are not attractive to us, if you see what I mean!'

This changing attitude of some young Pakistani boys towards tradition seems to have created a quiet controversy between them and the elders who dominate the community. The situation may indicate simply an inter-generation gap. But for many parents and elders in the community, it is more than this: the influence on their British-born children the values of the surrounding 'Western' culture. Against this background, the Pilrig boys were asked. 'What do you think about Pakistani girls wearing western clothes? Do you think that:..'

Table 11 shows that a significant minority (15%) of the Pilrig boys see nothing wrong with the wearing of Western clothes by Pakistani girls in the UK, whereas more than two fifths (41.67%) of them accept this practice provided it does not go beyond the limits of 'decency'. On the other hand, more than a fourth (26.67%) of the boys say that wearing Western clothes is absolutely wrong, whereas 16.67 percent of them say that they do not have a definite stand on this issue.

When the first and second categories of the responses in the above table are merged, the general picture of the data becomes further clearer: in principle, for more than a half (56.62%) of the Pilrig boys wearing of Western clothes by Pakistani girls, in this country, is acceptable.

Table 11 - The Pilrig Boys' Attitudes towards the Wearing of Western Clothes by Pakistani Girls

Response Category	% (Number)
'There is nothing wrong with it.'	15.00 (9)
'There is nothing wrong with it as long as it is decent.'	41.67 (25)
'It is wrong.'	26.67 (16)
'I do not have an exact idea about it.'	16.67 (10)
Total	100.00 (60)

These data indicate a significant departure from the dominant view in the community that, generally, disapproves of Western clothes for Pakistani girls. But, it seems to be a moderate and reformist departure, as the data clearly indicates. Another dividing issue among some young boys and most parents and elders in Edinburgh's Pakistani community is whether Pakistani boys can have girlfriends.

'Having Girlfriends'

In Edinburgh's Pakistani community, where pre-marital chastity is one of the central values of its moral and normative order, the idea of having a girlfriend is 'foreign' and un-Islamic. Most parents, elders and the religious leaders of the community strongly disapprove of any pre-marital relationships/friendships with women. They argue that having a girlfriend is not only a violation of Islamic rules, but it is a serious threat to the formation of a stable Muslim/Pakistani family and to the functioning of the social organisation of the extended kinship. One elder of the community explained this argument:

First of all having a girlfriend is not allowed in Islam - full stop! Secondly, once one of our boys goes out with a girl, he may marry her without his parents' agreement and that will not work. Even if the boy does not marry his girlfriend, he may continue seeing her after a proper marriage [arranged marriage]. And this will destroy his family life, as simple as that.

But, many Pakistani boys are not totally convinced by this argument. They say that 'having a girlfriend' is a useful and even necessary experience before the formation of a happy and stable family. For these boys it is through the relationship with members of the opposite sex that a boy could choose the 'right' partner of his life. Some of the boys who see no escape from 'arranged marriage' support the idea of 'having girlfriends' simply because, 'we should have some fun before our marriages are arranged', a Pilrig boy and his friends, said.

Parents, in general, are aware of the differences between their attitudes and the attitudes of their British-born children towards pre-marital chastity. Most parents believe that the 'liberal' attitude of their children towards pre-marital chastity is due to the influence of the values of the surrounding society.

But, the question is to what extent is the idea of 'having girlfriends' acceptable to the Pilrig boys? And how widespread is this general idea among them? To try to answer these questions, the Pilrig boys were asked: 'What do you think about Pakistani boys having girlfriends?'

The data in Table 12 reveal that there exists a surprisingly large gap between the apparently dominant morality of the community regarding 'having girlfriends' and the Pilrig boys' attitudes towards this morality: Only 28.33 percent of the boys conform to the community's morality according to which it is wrong for Pakistani boys to have girlfriends. All the rest, 71.67 percent, say that, in general, it is alright to have girlfriends.

Having said this, among the latter category of the boys only 23.33 percent of them radically depart from the community's morality, saying that there is nothing wrong with having girlfriends. A comparatively larger proportion (28.33%) of the boys say that 'having girlfriends' is alright provided the motive behind the idea is 'just friendship' or the 'intention of marriage'. This means that the latter category of the boys is basically loyal to the community's values and morality. They only interpret the 'migrated morality' of the community in accordance to the realities of their altered social circumstances. Similar to this position is the attitude of the 18.33 percent of the boys who say that 'having girlfriends' is alright if the girl is a Pakistani. This category of the boys may or may not be loyal to the community's morality about pre-marital chastity, but they know that a relation-

Table 12 - The Pilrig Boys' Attitude towards the Idea of Having a Girlfriend

Response Category	% (Number)
'It is alright.'	23.33 (14)
'It is alright if the idea is just friendship or intention of marriage'	28.33 (17)
'It is alright if the girl is Pakistani'.	18.33 (11)
'It is alright if the girl is white.'	1.67 (1)
'It is wrong.'	28.33 (17)
Total	100.00 (60)

ship with a Pakistani girl can hardly be without serious social consequences. That is to say that if a girl-boy's relationship is discovered, it will be very difficult for the boy, particularly, to escape an eventual marriage. This is because the reputation of the girl is at stake in this situation.

As a whole, the data at hand indicate that the attitudes of the majority of the Pilrig boys regarding 'having a girlfriend' have departed significantly from the apparently dominant morality and values of their community. Nevertheless this departure is, by and large, moderate and 'reformist' rather than radical and rebellious.

Now the question is: would this departure from the community's values have implications for the institution of 'arranged marriage'?

Arranged Marriage

As mentioned above in Chapter II, arranged marriage (in its various forms) is the normal way of marital union between potential partners among

Edinburgh's Pakistani population. Parents (and close kin), by and large, choose and make arrangements for the marriage of their sons and daughters. Quite often the potential partners are members of the same kinship group or *Biraderi*. This would normally mean that the potential husband and wife have some familiarity with each other before their marriage is arranged. But the familiarity does not necessarily mean that they have made the choice to be future partners. In some cases male and female kin may have a romantic attachment to each other or a desire to marry. In other cases the future partners may have hardly seen each other. In any case, it is mainly parents who play the major role in the choice and the arrangement process of their sons' and daughters' marriages.

Parents and the community's elders generally justify the existence and continuation of the institution of arranged marriage. Most parents argue that the institution of arranged marriage has not merely migrated with them to the UK; it is also and more importantly, a necessary element in the stability and social functioning of the Pakistani family, kinship and the community as a whole.

However, many British-born young Pakistanis openly question the practice of arranged marriage. Some of these boys reject the whole institution of arranged marriage and see it as the cause of unhappiness for some Pakistani families. Others among the young Pakistanis in Edinburgh only disagree with what they called 'too much' interference and the exercise of power (including manipulation) by parents and kin in choosing wives for them. That is to say, these youngsters want to have more say in the choice of their future wives, while basically agreeing with the institution of arranged marriage.

Many parents and elders are, again, quick to blame the influence of 'Western' values and culture for the increasingly changing attitudes of their sons and daughters towards arranged marriage. One elder of the Edinburgh's Pakistani community described this situation as 'A price that we pay for saving the Pound. Which one is more important, our religion and customs or money?'. Then Mr A.G. answered his question himself by saying that religion and customs were 'more important'. Mr A.G. and other elders in the community showed their serious concern about the changing attitudes of a growing number of Pakistani boys and girls in Edinburgh towards arranged marriage. But the important question is how far have these youngsters' attitudes changed towards arranged marriage?

To try to find an answer, the Pilrig boys were asked: 'In which of the following ways would you like to marry?' *See Table 13.*

Table 13 reveals that while 22.03 percent of the Pilrig boys accept their marriages to be totally arranged by their parents, a much larger proportion (37.29) would like to have the right to say 'no' in a marriage that is basically arranged for them by parents. On the other hand, 22.03 percent of the boys would like to choose their future partners by themselves with leaving their parents only the right to say 'no'; and a significant minority (18.64%) of the boys want to marry according to their own choices alone.

The contrast between the boys who, in principle, accept arranged marriages and those who do not, becomes more striking when the sum of the first two response categories is compared with the sum of the last two. About three fifths (59.32%) of the Pilrig boys either totally or conditionally accept their marriages to be arranged by their parents, whereas about two fifths (40.67%) of them would basically like to choose their partners by themselves. That is to say that the majority of the Pilrig boys still accept arranged marriage, in one or another form.

Table 13 - The Pilrig Boys' Attitude towards Arranged Marriage

Response Category	% (Number)
'Your parents' choice as they regard a girl as suitable for you.'	22.03 (13)
'Your parents' choice leaving you the right to say 'no'.'	37.29 (22)
'Your own choice leaving your parents the right to say 'no'.'	22.03 (13)
'Your own choice alone.'	18.64 (11)
Total	100.00 (60)

Nevertheless, the fact that about two fifths of the boys would basically like to marry by their own choice can have important consequences for the institutions of the Pakistani family and for the extended kinship in Edinburgh - a concern that is shared by many Pakistani elders in Edinburgh.

The Climate of Race Relations

The interaction of the Pilrig boys with the wider British society has not always been as smooth as it has been described in the past few pages. The kindness of teachers in the school, the friendliness of classmates and the consequent adoption (to varying extents) of certain 'Western' values by the Pilrig boys represent only one side of their interaction with the wider society. The other relates to these boys' unpleasant experiences from interacting with some members of the wider society on the street, in the playground and in other public places. These unpleasant experiences and unhappy memories of the Pilrig boys are, by and large, caused by the more or less recurring verbal abuse and occasional physical attacks on them. The more or less recurring nature and the apparently racial context of these incidents seem to have created the fear in the minds of the Pilrig boys that they are always the potential targets of verbal abuse and physical attacks by members of the indigenous population. However, unspecific verbal abuse and many physical attacks are not necessarily racially motivated. Incidents of physical attacks, mugging and other forms of street violence against members of the general population are one feature of urban life in Scotland and elsewhere. Thus, in order to specify the context of the verbal abuse and physical attacks that the Pilrig boys say they have suffered, the boys were asked: 'Have you been treated badly because of your race/colour?'

Within this specified context of the question, 91.66 percent of the boys (55 individuals) answer with 'yes', and the rest, 8.33 percent (5 individuals) with 'No'. But what did bad treatment that is due to one's colour/race mean to the Pilrig boys? Many things, the boys say; these mainly include: being called racial names; racial verbal abuse; insulting sign-language; 'spitting on you', 'staring at you as if you were a piece of sh**', 'chasing', 'battering'; 'slagging about' and 'physical attacks'. While many examples of these forms of bad treatment clearly have a racial context, some of them such as chasing, battering and physical attacks may still be general acts of hooliganism and street violence. But many of the victims of these acts in the Pilrig sample said that these acts of violence against them were often preceded by racial verbal abuse. This particularly happened when the Pilrig boys replied to such verbal abuse. Nevertheless, the data at hand reveal that among those Pilrig boys who said that they were treated badly because of their race/colour, only one fifth (11 individuals) of them reported physical violence against them. The rest four fifths (44 individuals) reported calling of racial names and verbal abuse.

These names and verbal abuses included very interesting words, phrases and sentences. The most commonly used words and phrases were: 'Paki' (also spelled/pronounced 'Paki' or 'Pukie'), 'Paki-bastard';'blackie'; and 'blackie bastard'. Other relatively less commonly used words were: 'chocolate', 'lulee', 'pad', 'monkey', 'sambo', 'wog', 'nigger' and 'coon'. Some of the most commonly used sentences included: 'Go back to your country'; 'Go back where you have come from' and 'Go back to your sh**land'.

All of the Pilrig boys said that these words, phrases and sentences were 'very insulting' and 'hurting'. Even words like 'chocolate?' I asked the boys why were these words insulting to them. The boys did not know why such words were insulting, saying only that 'they are just hurting' and 'they are used as insults'. But one older boy added philosophically: 'Any word boys use with bad meaning for long time becomes an insult. And when it is used in that situation [atmosphere of tension], it really hurts, if you understand what I mean.' I understand that the boy probably meant that no word has an inherent good or bad meaning; it is the socially constructed and reconstructed meanings of words and their situational usage that convey 'bad' or 'good' messages. Thus, the meanings of 'Paki' and 'chocolate' can have different meanings in different contexts and situations.

In order to investigate how frequently the Pilrig boys experienced the kind of bad treatment that has been discussed so far (racial verbal abuse and physical attacks etc.), the boys were asked: 'How often have you experienced this kind of treatment?' *See Table 14.*

Table 14 indicates that 10.91 percent of the Pilrig boys said that they experienced (racial) bad treatment almost every day, whereas 23.64 percent of them had such experiences about once or twice a week. Another 10.91 percent of the boys said that they experienced (racial) bad treatment about once or twice a month, whereas 54 percent of them said that they had such experiences only once or twice in several months.

The overall picture of Table 14 indicate that the majority (54%) of the Pilrig boys experienced (racial) bad treatment less frequently; and a significant minority of 45 percent of the boys experienced this kind of treatment relatively more frequently. The kind of climate of race-relations in which the Pilrig boys live, it seems, has had a deep psychological impact on them, both as individuals and as a group. Calling of the 'racialised' names such as 'Paki', 'blackie', 'sambo', 'nigger' etc. and 'go back to your country', has made the boys feel that they are not members of the wider British society; and that despite having been brought up in this country, these boys feel as if they were outsiders in it. This has important consequences for these boys' social identity.

Identification: British or Pakistani?

The Pilrig boys' most common response to the existing climate of race relations is apparently defensive: they respond to their experiences of racial discrimination and harassment through 'walking together', 'going out together', and 'sticking together', as one of the boys put it. Indeed 'sticking together' was one of the most clearly observable patterns of behaviour among the boys. But, the social functions of 'sticking together' goes far beyond a simple defensive mechanism against exclusion and fear of vio-

Table 14 - Frequency of Experiencing (Racial) Bad Treatment

Response Category	% (Number)
'Almost every day'	10.91 (6)
'About once or twice a week'	23.64 (13)
'About once or twice a month'	10.91 (6)
'About once or twice in several months'	54.00 (30)
Total	100.00 (55)

lence which the boys see as essentially 'racial'. 'Sticking together' has important social implications for the sharpening of these boys' sense of ethnicity, cultural belonging and for a more marked separation between 'us' and 'them'. Indeed, this has been happening, as one of the boys told me 'if we are Pakis, they are *Gorahs*. *Gorah* is a name that is used by Pakistanis in Edinburgh (and elsewhere in the UK) for the indigenous British population. The literal meaning of '*Gorah*' in Urdu is simply white. But, in the context of the existing race relations, the meaning of '*Gorah*' is as much loaded and pejorative as that of 'Paki': 'A *Gorah* is always rude to his parents and has no respect for them; he gets drunk; he sleeps around even with men; he does not actually believe in God, he just pretends to....' One of the boys gave this description of a '*Gorah*' and the others endorsed it. This negative description of the indigenous members of the society very much seems to be a reaction to the racial exclusion and intimidation that these boys experience in the wider society (see the previous section). This description points to the drawing of new social boundaries between 'them' and 'us' - between the socially constructed new meanings of the 'Paki' and the '*Gorah*'. This reversing of the meanings of 'us' (as goodies) and 'them' (as baddies) seem to be a constituent component of the 'reactive' element of the Pilrig boys' sense of ethnicity and their identification with it. Thus, it is not surprising that most of these boys not only identify with their ethnic/cultural status in this country, but also take pride in it. It was in this context that all the Pilrig boys were asked: 'How much of the time do you feel proud of being a Pakistani in this country?' *See Table 15*

Table 15 indicates that a large majority (70%) of the Pilrig boys said that they are 'all the time' or 'most of the time' proud as Pakistanis in this country; a minority of 18.33 percent of these boys said that they are 'half of the time' proud as Pakistanis, whereas a smaller minority (11.67%) of them said they are 'only once in a while' or 'never' proud as Pakistanis in this country.

The general picture of Table 15 indicates that the overwhelming majority of the Pilrig boys positively identify with their ethnic/cultural status as Pakistani and take pride in it. But what about these boys' identification with their adopted country, Britain? It must be admitted that one of the failings of the questionnaire that I devised and used as a tool for collecting data for the present study was that it did not include a question about the identification of the Pilrig boys with Britain (i.e., how much of the time do you feel proud of being British?). Nevertheless, the ethnographic data that I have collected, to some extent, makes up for this gap in the present study.

As mentioned previously in this chapter, many of the Pilrig boys take pride in speaking English well, in their educational achievements in Britain, and of their understanding of modern British culture and adopt certain British values and social manners. These boys know that they are the citizens of Great Britain and that it is their adopted country. But, most of these boys are not confident enough to call themselves Scottish/British. In a group discussion on the issue of cultural identity one of the older boys in the Pilrig sample said:

> You know that I am born in Edinburgh; I am brought up here. For me this is my country and I speak the language like any other Scottish person; I am like any other Scottish person. But when I meet people at parties or somewhere, they start talking to me as if I have just come from Pakistan - they are often sarcastic. Sometimes, when I introduce myself as Scottish, people do not believe me; they laugh!

This view of the college student was shared by most boys in the group. However some other boys in the discussion group said that 'we are Pakistani Scots'. Then, two younger boys said that 'our parents are Pakistanis; but we are not, we are Scottish'. But these two boys were ridiculed as one boy told them that 'even if you become Robert Burns, you will still be a Paki!' Then all the boys laughed.

Table 15 - Frequency of Feeling Proud of being a Pakistani in Scotland

Response Category	% (Number)
'All the time/Most of the time'	70.00 (42)
'Half the time'	18.33 (11)
'Only once in a while/never'	11.67 (7)
Total	100.00 (60)

The general ethnographic evidence suggests that exclusion and the non-acceptance of the Pilrig boys as Scottish/British by the wider society seems to be discouraging these boys from identifying themselves with Scotland/Britain. But since cultural belonging and identification fulfil certain social and psychological needs of these boys (and probably of all human beings), they have little choice but to seek them in their ethnic/cultural roots that are vividly represented in the traditional social institutions of Edinburgh's Pakistani community - a community that is in some important ways in the process of becoming a small-scale society within the broader Scottish/British society. Now the question is that to what extent do the Pilrig boys conform to, or deviate from the norms and values of this small-scale society - Edinburgh's Pakistani community. But first it is necessary to see what deviance is.

II: Deviance

The existing literature on deviance indicate that sociologists of deviance have found it difficult to agree on a general definition of deviance (for review of the literature see Gibbons and Jones 1975 and Clinard and Meier 1985). Various factors seem to be responsible for the difficulties in reaching a general definition: on the one hand, deviance is a social phenomenon that is relative to culture and time. That is to say, definitions of various forms of deviance may vary from culture to culture, and from time to another. Therefore, every culture and time would require different definitions of deviance. Moreover, the cultural and normative complexities of most modern societies add to these difficulties. On the other hand, the fluidity and situationality of the meaning of 'acts' in a social world that is interpreted as 'phenomenological' by some sociologists would make it extremely difficult to have a general definition of deviance.

Nevertheless, students of the sociology of deviance and crime have attempted to define deviance in general terms. They have approached the definition of deviance in many different ways. These different ways of defining deviance may be merged into two general approaches: The first approach is of those sociologists and criminologists who have broadly defined deviance in terms of activities that violate the social norms of a particular society. For example one proponent of this approach says that:

> Deviance constitutes only those deviations from norms in a disapproved direction such that the deviation elicits, or is likely to elicit if detected, a negative sanction. (Clinard and Meier 1985:7)

On the other hand, proponents of the second approach contend that deviance is not an innate quality of acts; instead deviance is a behaviour that is labelled so in a particular social-interactive context. For example, according to Becker's widely quoted statement:

> Social groups create deviance by making the rules whose infraction constitute deviance, and by applying those rules to particular people and labelling them as outsiders...Deviance is not a quality of acts that a person commits, but rather a consequence of application by others of rules and sanctions to an 'offender'. The deviant is one to whom that label has been successfully applied; deviant behaviour is what people so label. (Becker 1963:9)

It can be clearly seen in the above definitions of deviance that the first emphasises social norms and the acts that violate the norms; and the second places strong emphasis on the social contexts in which norms (or rules) are created and selectively applied to those who violate them. These differential emphases on elements of a definition, leave both these definitions less than satisfactory. The first definition seems to be too general and vague: it is insensitive to the complexities of the social context where deviance takes place. The second definition is clearly a half definition - a definition of 'Secondary deviance' that does not include 'Primary deviance' (the first involves acts of those rule breakers whose self-concepts are affected through labelling processes by the agencies of social control, whereas the second refers to the acts of rule breakers whose self-concepts have not been affected - see Lemert 1959).

This is not the place to go into further details of the controversy over the definition of deviance. Nevertheless, it is important to say that it is possible to suggest a relatively 'balanced' definition of deviance that accommodates the different emphases and concerns of the proponents of both the 'normative' and of the 'labelling' approaches to the definition of deviance. Before a detailed empirical description of deviance in the context of the present study is given, I suggest the following relatively 'balanced' theoretical definition: *deviance refers to the violation of norms of a particular community/society by its members, at a particular time, whether the 'violators' are publicly labelled as deviants or not, and whether a sanction is applied or not.*

First of all, according to the proposed definition, deviance is a 'meaningful violation' of norms - a violation the meaning and implications of which are understood both by the community and by its violating member. Thus deviance can only take place within the socio-normative context of a particular social group, and by its members alone. Only a member of a Muslim or a Jewish community can commit a deviant act when he/she eats pork; only a Sikh would be seen as deviant when he/she removes his/her body hair. However, this is not to suggest that non-members' violations of the norms of a community are always exempted. Neither is this to suggest that certain norms are not shared by all (or most) social/cultural groups within the wider society. In such cases social norms are very likely to acquire a formal or semi-formal status - the status of official rules or laws. This is an area where serious legal and political controversies between different groups in culturally and normatively complex societies often arise.

Related to the relativity of deviance to culture, is its relativity to time. As many of the cultural norms of social groups/societies change from time to time, so do the definitions of deviance. An act that is considered deviant today may be normal tomorrow, and the other way round. Many people still remember that at certain times in Great Britain, it was considered deviant for women to smoke cigarettes or/and consume alcohol in public. The relativity of deviance to time, moreover, point to its situational aspect as well. That is people's definitions of deviance change depending on particular social situations. For example, nakedness or half-nakedness of participants in certain 'beach parties' is considered normal on an *adhoc* basis - 'moral holidays'!

Finally the proposed definition of deviance clearly and explicitly includes both 'Primary' and 'Secondary' forms of deviance. The social context and the process of labelling behaviour as deviant is an important element of any definition of deviance. And yet, it will be wrong to contend that an unde-tected and/or unsanctioned breach of norms/rules is not deviance. Any account of deviance must also pay attention to rule-breaking that is not labelled/sanctioned.

Hence, the definition suggested above is claimed to be a more 'balanced' and comprehensive definition of deviance on a theoretical level. However, it cannot resolve the more fundamental contextual problems of deviance on an empirical level. But it is important to say that the suggested definition provides a useful theoretical background to the empirical description of deviance within the socio-normative context of the present study.

The Social Context of Deviance in the Pilrig Sample

In his classic work, *The Behaviour of Law*, Donald Black says:

> It [social control] defines and responds to deviant behaviour, specifying what ought to be : what is right or wrong, what is violation, obligation, abnormality or disruption.' (Black 1976: 105)

Indeed, in the present study of social control and deviance in Edinburgh's Pakistani community, it is the social institutions (or agencies of social con-trol) of the community that constitute its normative order. The family, the *Biraderi* (network of kinship/friendship relationship), the Mosque and the formal organisation of the community (P.A.E.E.S) define the conduct norms and standards of behaviour. These agencies of social control also specify what is deviation and how it should be responded to and dealt with.

Drawing on the work of Gibbs (1965,1981) about the definitional attrib-utes of norms, it is these agencies of social control of Edinburgh's Pakistani community that collectively evaluate, and respond to behaviour; and create collective expectations about how people are likely to ,and ought, to behave. The family, the *Biraderi*, the Mosque and the formal organisation of the community specify and evaluate that members of the community ought or ought not to behave in certain ways; they specify what are the 'appropriate' responses - positive or negative - to various types of behaviour; and finally, it is these agencies of social control that make predictions about how mem-bers are expected to behave in different social situations.

However, it must be said that the empirical investigation of the defini-tional attributes (indicators) of norms has been one of the most complex issues in the present study. First of all, the extent of consensus about what is ought to be or ought not to be, the extent of the severity and enforcement of sanctions, and finding out how far members of the community really behaved as they are expected to, needed a down-to-earth investigation

(including taking part in non-malicious gossip!)

Secondly, all social norms did not apply to all age groups in the same way - individuals belonging to different age groups had different degrees of obligations (or none at all) to obey some of the community's norms. For example, smoking cigarettes for boys who were under about 15 years of age was strongly disapproved, whereas the same behaviour was somewhat tolerated for boys who were older.

Thus in the context of the present study of the Pilrig sample, only those conduct norms were selected as criteria for specifying deviance and conformity that were uncontroversially accepted in the community as most fundamental to the moral and social behaviour of the youngsters. All the three definitional attributes of norms - collective evaluation, collective sanction, and collective expectation - consistently materialised in these norms.

These fundamental conduct norms covered two major spheres of the moral and social behaviour of the Pilrig boys: first, behaviour in the Mosque-school and in the Mosque, itself; and second, general moral and social behaviour in the community and the society at large.

A: The most fundamental norms that applied to the behaviour of the Pilrig boys in the Mosque-school were:

1. Maintaining an orderly atmosphere in the Mosque-school and a full concentration on their daily *Sabaq*, (or of the previous day). Talking with one anothr, playing games, making excessive noise or other forms of disruptive behaviour by students in the *Sabaq*-class were against the basic norms of the Mosque-school. Those boys who got involved in such behaviour were disciplined. Disciplining in the Mosque-school included physical and other forms of punishment that were administered by *Hafiz Sahib* (see Chapter III, Section I for details).

2. Complete obedience to the authority of *Hafiz Sahib* in the Mosque-school. Any opposition/challenge to disciplining/punishing by *Hafiz Sahib* was considered a most serious breach of the norms of the Mosque-school. Such behaviour was considered serious misconduct because *Hafiz Sahib* is much more than a teacher - he is a spiritual figure who is highly respected in the community.

3. As most classes in the Mosque-school coincide with at least one congregational prayer in a day, all the boys in the class who were around 9 years of age and above were required to join the prayer. As in all Islamic congregational prayers, the worshippers must silently follow and listen to *Hafiz Sahib* who leads the congregational prayer. Laughter and other forms of disruptive behaviour by some boys during the prayer was considered as a breach of the sanctity of the prayer and of the norms of the Mosque. Boys who were involved in disruptive behaviour during prayer (mainly in the

back rows while every one was facing the *Makka*) were disciplined/pun-
ished (see Chapter III, Section II for details).

B: As far as the norms of general moral and social behaviour in the community and in the wider society are concerned, they are mainly a reflection
of this particular community's morality - a morality that is reproduced by the
community's agencies of social control, especially by the family and the
Mosque (see Chapters II and III). Unlike the norms of the Mosque-school,
the norms of general moral and social behaviour were proscriptions rather
than prescriptions (prohibitions rather than obligations). The most fundamental norms of general moral and social behaviour among young men in
the Edinburgh's Pakistani community are:

    1. Prohibition of drinking alcohol, smoking cigarettes and the use of dan-
gerous and addictive drugs. However, smoking cigarettes for boys who
were over the age of 15 was not very strictly prohibited, whereas the same
behaviour for younger boys was almost as much strictly prohibited as drinking alcohol for all the boys. (see Chapter III, Section I).

    2. Prohibition of 'going out' with girls or 'having girlfriends'. (see Chap-
ter III, Section I for details)

    3. Disapproval of going to discos and *Bhangras*. Occasional attendance
at discos and *Bhangras* was, to some extent, tolerated in the community.
But since attending discos and *Bhangra* was assumed to be associated with
drinking alcohol, and a free mixing with women, it was generally disapproved.

    4. Strong condemnation of involvement in inter-group violence, bullying
and vandalism outside the Mosque. These kind of activities normally took
place between the children of members of two kinship groups or within the
same kinship group as a result of economic competition, feuding and jealousies. Boys who were involved in such behaviour were reported to *Hafiz
Sahib*, either by victims or other boys; and they were disciplined.

    There was a broad consensus among Edinburgh's Pakistanis about the
centrality of these seven norms to the community's moral/social order. Since
all of the above seven norms directly reflected the community's morality,
news of breaking these norms travelled very quickly throughout the community. Members of the community gossiped about boys who violated these
norms; they were disciplined by parents or by *Hafiz Sahib* (though *Hafiz
Sahib* mainly disciplined boys who broke the norms of the Mosque-school).
Those who repeatedly broke these norms were labelled as 'bad boys'.

    As both teacher and a friend of the Pilrig boys I was in a uniquely suit-
able position to know about the extent of involvement of these boys in these
deviant activities. I learnt about them not only through gossip in the community and in the Mosque-school, but also most of the boys who frequent-

ly broke or rebelled against these norms openly talked to me about their 'violations'. In some cases I accompanied these boys to discos/*Bhangras* as participant-observer. The frequency of breaking each of the seven fundamental norms by each of the 60 boys was recorded for a period of one year. Towards the end of the first year of my field work, it was possible to use the frequency of breaking these norms by each of the 60 boys in discriminating between the conformists and the non-conformist (deviant) boys. Hence, these data were used to generate in a continuum from the most conforming to the least conforming to the seven norms. An interesting observation in this regard was that those boys who more frequently broke the norms of the Mosque-school and were disciplined, also broke most of the moral and social norms of the community more frequently. These boys were also labelled as *shararatis* (trouble-makers) by their conformist classmates; they did not have a good reputation in the community.

Furthermore, in order to confirm the validity of my rating of the behaviour of the 60 boys, I requested the *Hafiz Sahib* to rate the boys' behaviour. Interestingly, *Hafiz Sahib*'s (judgmental) rating was very similar to my own rating that was based on the frequency of breaking the selected seven norms. However, *Hafiz Sahib*'s rating discriminated only between those boys who frequently broke the norms of the Mosque-school (who also did

Table 16A - **The Pilrig Boys: Frequency of Breaking the Norms of the Mosque-School**

Degree of Deviation		Frequency of Breaking Norms of the Mosque-School		
		Punishable Misbehaviour in Class	Punishable Misbehaviour during Prayer	Opposing *Hafiz Sahib*'s Authority
Low	1	Once or twice	Never	Never
	2	Two or three times	Never	Never
	3	Two or three times	Never or once	Never or once
High	4	More than three times	Two or three times	Two or three times

not have a good reputation in the community) and the rest of the boys. That is to say that *Hafiz Sahib*'s rating categorised the 60 boys into two categories of conformists and non-conformists. But the analysis of the 60 boys' records (as part of my field-data) about the frequency of breaking the seven norms resulted in a continuum that split *Hafiz Sahib*'s two categories into further two categories of *less* and *more* conformists and non-conformists. This continuum that categorises all the 60 boys – from the least deviant to the most deviant – is tabulated in Table 16A.

The total number of boys in the first category was 16 individuals (26.7%) whereas more than half, 32 individuals (53.3%), fell into the second category. There were 7 individuals (11.7%) in the third category, whereas only 5 individuals (8.3%) fell into the last, the fourth category.

The above categorisation of the Pilrig boys in terms of *less* and *more* deviant was further analysed in the light of ethnographic data (descriptive notes) about each individual. From this combination of the qualitative and quantitative data distinct patterns of behaviour about each of the four categories of the continuum (from the least to the most deviant) emerged. Each of the four categories was named by the dominant theme of its respective

Table 16B - The Pilrig Boys: Frequency of Breaking Community Norms

Degree of Deviation		Frequency of Breaking the General Norms of the Community			
		Attendance at Disco/*Bhangra*	Drinking Alcohol*/Smoking Cigarettes	Going Out with Girls	Involvement in inter-group violence
Low	1	Never	Never	Never	Never
	2	Once or twice	Never or once	Never	Once or twice
	3	Almost every week	Often but not openly	Often but not openly	Once or twice
High	4	Almost every week	Often and openly	Often and openly	Once or twice

* Smoking cigarettes was almost as much prohibited for boys about under 15 as alcohol for all ages; but smoking cigarettes for older boys was, to some extent, tolerated.

pattern of behaviour. This exercise resulted in the development of the four-fold typology of the Pilrig boys: Conformists, Accommodationists, Part-time Conformists and Rebels. Furthermore, the four categories of the Pilrig boys – from the least deviant to the most – was further examined in the light of self-reported delinquency data about the boys. These data show that the degree of deviance among the Pilrig boys is generally correlated to the frequency of committing delinquent acts.

A Typology of the Pilrig Boys[1]

Before going into the details of a behavioural typology of the Pilrig boys that emerged from the field-data, it is important to look back for a moment. In the first part of the book it was mentioned that the Edinburgh's Pakistani community is in the process of becoming a small-scale society within the wider Scottish/British society; it has developed its own social institutions and moral and social order. Furthermore it was pointed out that much effort is made by the community to socialise the young British born Pakistanis to its moral and social values (see Chapter II and III).

However, I have also mentioned in the present chapter that the young British-born Pakistanis also interact with the wider Scottish/British society whose moral and social values are, in some important ways, different from those the boys are socialised to. At school, in the playground, in public places, and through television and the mass-media the British-born Pakistani boys are exposed to the values and morality of the wider society.

This exposure of the British-born Pakistani youngsters to the moral and social values of two cultures has led most British sociologists/anthropologists to draw the conclusion that these youngsters are 'caught between two cultures'. For example Watson (1977 : 3) in his well-known book *Between Two Cultures* (a contribution of twelve social anthropologists) reaches the conclusion that the British-born Pakistanis '. . . are caught between the cultural expectations of their parents (the first-generation migrants) and the social demands of the wider society'. Similarly, Anwar (1985 : 59), a prominent sociologist of race relations in Britain says that 'the children of Pakistani parents born or brought up in Britain are a generation caught between two cultures' (see also Anwar 1978, 1986). And more recently Professor Ahmed (1992 : 10) wrote that the British-born Pakistani youngsters are '. . . not quite British and no longer Asian'. Professor Ahmed further says that these youngsters are referred to by non-resident Pakistanis in Britain as 'BBCDs – British Born Confused *Desi* [native in Urdu]'.

Such works, explicitly or implicitly state that the British-born Pakistani youngsters are a confused and rootless generation who do not know who they are, and what moral and social world they belong to. Not surprisingly this view about the British-born Pakistanis is followed by the mass-media, by the average British citizen, including the Pakistanis in the UK them-selves (see Section III, Chapter I).

The present study supports the view that the British-born Pakistani boys, indeed, are exposed to the values of two cultures and to the pressures each produces for conformity. However this study finds the 'caught between two cultures' thesis, which suggests that the second-generation Pakistani young-sters are confused individuals is an over-simplification and, in some ways, a misleading generalisation. This study reveals that individual boys in the Pilrig sample responded to the pressures of the two cultures in different ways, rather than all simply being confused by and caught between them. Every one of the 60 boys in the Pilrig sample has worked out solutions to the pressures and contradictions of the two cultures. Some of these boys chose a full conformity to their Islamic/Pakistani culture, where others rebelled against it and tried to follow a very different social and cultural life-style. There were others who found out a synthesis between the two extremes. The differential responses of the Pilrig boys to the pressures and contradictions of their community's culture and to that of the wider society are described in the following four-fold behavioural typology.

1. Conformists

As the concept of conformity connotes, the conformist boys in Pilrig are full-time followers of the moral and social norms (particularly those rele-vant to the behaviour of youngsters) of Edinburgh's Pakistani community. In fact the moral and social world of these boys lies within the narrower boundaries of the community - within the boundaries of the family, the *Biraderi* and the Mosque. Their vision of life and understanding of 'right' and 'wrong' strongly reflect the values of their families and the Mosque. A group of the conformist boys described their vision of life in this way:

...you must believe that there is one God, *Allah*. *Allah* is the lord of kind-ness to mankind and Mohammad (P.B.U.H.) is the messenger of *Allah*. You should pray five times a day and you should go to *Jom'a* [Friday congregational prayer]. When you pray you should face the *Ka'aba* [*Makka*] and follow *Hafiz Sahib* silently. Never disobey your father and mother. Never disobey *Hafiz Sahib* and other elders. You should never ever eat *Haram* meat [pork, ham and meat that is the result of un-Islamic way of slaughtering of animals] or drink beer and wine. You should never go out with girls. You should not dance or watch dirty films; don't tell lies, or steal or get into a fight. You should not make friends with *Kafirs* [infi-dels]. Don't make birthday parties; don't touch dogs.

This vision of life and the definition of 'right' and 'wrong' is not only a description of the 'ideal culture' of the community. For the conformist boys there is no separation between the 'ideal' and the 'real' culture. As was demonstrated in Tables 16A and 16B the conformist boys in the Pilrig sample most often obeyed almost all norms of the Mosque-school and of the community.

The overwhelming majority of the conformists are among the youngest boys who count for about a fourth (26.66%) of the Pilrig sample. Due to their comparatively younger ages, the conformist boys are, to a greater extent, insulated from the effects of the surrounding culture. Therefore, these boys seemed to recognise only one moral order - the one they refer to as 'ours'; the moral and social order of the surrounding society, according to the conformist boys was 'theirs', and these boys 'had nothing to do with it'. The Pilrig conformists had a clear sense of their belonging to the moral and social order of their own community - a small-scale moral and cultural entity.

However, it seems that the older the Pilrig boys grew, the more they recognised the existence of the surrounding moral and social order - the one with which they have to deal and accommodate some of its elements. There are very few conformists who grew older but did not follow the 'accommo-dationist' trend. Some of the few conformists who grew older but did not respond to some of the demands of the wider social environment felt alien-ated even among their own friends. They tend to favour religious and polit-ical extremism.

I will return to the relationship between age and the four behavioural types later. First, it is important to describe the next type of the Pilrig boys-the accommodationists.

2. Accommodationists

Similar to their conformist friends the second type of the Pilrig boys have a clear sense of their belonging to the moral and social order of their com-munity that they see as different from that of the surrounding society. These boys positively identify themselves with their distinct culture. Nevertheless, for the accommodationists the boundaries between the moral/social order of their own community and that of the wider society are not as rigidly and sharply drawn as they are for the conformists. First of all, according to these boys, there are certain common grounds and shared values between the two moral/social orders that should be understood and further explored. The accommodationists particularly refer, in this regard, to the common grounds between Islamic and Christian teachings. But whenever conflict appears between the two, accommodation is often a possibility, the boys believe.

For the accommodationist boys, adopting certain British values/social manners and making certain situational compromises with the culture of the wider society are not only an acceptable price to pay for successful interaction with the wider society, but these are necessary requirements for living in a modern multi-cultural society as a 19 year old boy in Pilrig said:

> ... This is not Pakistan. We live in Britain. Actually we are British Pakistanis; we live with British people. We ought to change some of our manners and behaviour so that we don't look odd or stupid. We ought to wear ties on some occasions and bow-ties on other occasions. I don't drink alcohol but I do join my Scottish friends – girls and boys – in parties. I sometimes dance with them. I don't think these things are wrong; our religion is not as strict as some people think.

The boy added 'please don't take me wrong. I don't mean that we should compromise on everything; no compromise on principles!' The above passage clearly indicates that the accommodationist boy points to the desirability and even the necessity of a degree of deviation from the 'ideal culture' of Edinburgh's Pakistani community. He knew that attendance at discos, dancing and mixing with unrelated women are taboos according to the 'ideal culture' of the community. In fact the accommodationist boys deviated in practice from some of the norms of the Mosque-school and the community, on some occasions. This is clearly demonstrated in Tables 16A and 16B where the accommodationists occasionally broke some of the norms of the Mosque-school and the community. But, perhaps surprisingly, this extent of deviation is tolerated in the community. The accommodationists boys are seen as 'good boys' in the community/Mosque. The majority (53.33%) of the Pilrig boys fall into this category.

It should be mentioned that while most of the accommodationist boys in Pilrig are not ready to 'compromise on principles', some of them go a little beyond this: these comparatively older boys favour broader interpretations of some Islamic principles and seek modification of some of the established cultural values. For example, they do not follow the restriction that meat must always be prepared by the Islamic way of slaughtering (*Halal*); and they believe that they will try to know their future wife and to have more say in the arrangement of their marriages.

In sum, the accommodationists, generally, adopt certain British values, and modify their behaviour and attitudes to fit the social demands of the wider society. But these boys do remain loyal to the fundamental religious and cultural values of their community.

3. Part-Time Conformists

While the accommodationists, generally, justify their deviation from some of the less fundamental moral and social norms of their community, the part-time conformists violate many of its fundamental moral and social norms. As Tables 16A and 16B show, this category of the Pilrig boys frequently violated most norms of the Mosque-school and of the community. These boys knew that violation of some of the community's norms such as drinking alcohol and relationships with women outside marriage are taken very seriously by the agencies of social control of the community. But, most of the part-time conformists justified their violations, as a group of them put it: '...most boys in the community do these things; they have girlfriends and drink [alcoholic drinks] secretly.' But, in fact only a minority of the Pilrig boys violated these fundamental norms of the community. For some other of the part-time conformists most of the moral and social values of Edinburgh's Pakistani community were irrelevant in Britain as one of these boys told me '...Do in Rome what Romans do.'

Despite their wide-scale deviation from the community's moral/social norms, the part-time conformists tried to cover up their deviations from the community. These boys maintained their links with the community through attending *Jom'a* and *Eid* prayers and other cultural/religious gatherings to show that they were respectable members of the community. These deviant boys' part-timeness in conformity resembles the part-timeness in crime of Ditton's (1977) 'part-time criminals'. The latter were persons who indulged in regular 'fiddling' (embezzlement, fare-dodging etc.) while pretending to be honest individuals. However, Ditton's 'fiddlers' had partial roles in crime whereas the Pilrig part-time conformists had a partial role in conformity.

In fact through their part-timeness in conformity many of the Pilrig boys managed to deceive and therefore prevent, to a considerable extent, the community's agencies of social control defining them as deviants. But, because of the suspicious attitudes of the community's conventional members towards these boys, they saw themselves as potential targets of the label 'bad boys'. These boys admitted that they behaved in this deceitful-way to avoid damaging their family's *Izzet* and bringing a bad name to it. And this, in turn, will have serious consequences for the boys themselves - the part-time conformists, in Pilrig, tried to 'have their cake and eat it'!

Despite their deviation from the fundamental moral/social values of their community, many of the Pilrig's part-time conformists still have a relatively strong sense of their ethnicity and cultural identity. Many of them identified themselves with their Pakistani/Islamic cultural roots. But they placed stronger emphasis on the secular aspects of their distinct ethnicity rather than on its religious aspects. It may be appropriate to call these boys 'Cultural Muslims'. The part-time conformists constituted only a little more than a tenth (11.66%) of all the boys in the Pilrig sample.

It must also be mentioned that a few boys among the Pilrig's part-time conformists did not have a clear sense of their cultural identity and belonging. Confused and disillusioned, this latter group may be described as boys who are genuinely 'caught between two cultures'.

4. Rebels

The last category in the continuum - from the least to the most deviant - of the Pilrig boys are rebels. The young Pilrig rebels not only openly violate many moral/social norms of Edinburgh's Pakistani community, but they also challenge them. Tables 16A and 16B clearly indicated that rebels among the Pilrig boys more frequently violated norms of the Mosque-school: they more frequently 'misbehaved' in the class, during prayer(s) and opposed *Hafiz Sahib*'s authority, as compared to the rest of Pilrig boys. Similarly, the rebels violated the moral/social norms of the community (outside the Mosque-school) more frequently as compared to the conformists and accommodationists among the Pilrig boys. Although the rebels violated the community's moral/social norms (attending discos/night-clubs, drinking alcohol, and going out with girls/having a girlfriend) almost as frequently as part-time conformists, the former violated these norms openly while the latter did so in relative secrecy.

For the rebels in Pilrig the existing moral/social arrangements in the community are '...an old story' - a story of the first-generation Pakistani migrants and a story of Pakistan. Many of the community's moral/social norms, particularly restrictions on foods, drinks, and on matters related to an individual's private life, are not acceptable to these boys. They seriously challenge the relevance of these norms. Some boys among this category of the Pilrig sample resemble Merton's (1964) rebels - 'rebels with a cause'. They seek to substitute much of what they call the 'old fashioned' and 'backward' moral/social arrangements in the community by new alternatives. But the majority of the Pilrig rebels rebel against these moral/social arrangements just because they '....want to have fun; to enjoy life...', as three of the rebels put it. The boys further added that ' All the stupid restrictions just don't make sense to us; we are just not bothered about them; we don't give a damn about what people say'. Unlike the first group ('rebel with cause') - the second group of the Pilrig rebels have a confused sense of their cultural identity; they do not know where they actually belong.

The Pilrig rebels' deviations from the community's norms have been strongly reacted to by its agencies of social control. The Pilrig rebels have earned a reputation of 'bad boys' in the community. Many parents advise their sons to avoid the company of 'bad boys'. Due to social pressures within the family and the kinship group, some of the rebels had left their parents' houses and live alone. They are, in many ways cut off from the community - they are a kind of 'social outcasts'. However the majority of the Pilrig rebels live with their families. Their parents tolerate their rebellious sons' behaviour and the community's criticism of them. Parents of these boys say that they have no alternative but to '....hope that they will return to the right way after they grow older and get married' as the parents of two of the Pilrig rebels said. These young Pakistani rebels formed only a minority (8.33%) of the total sample of the 60 Pilrig boys.

It is important to mention that rebels among the Pilrig boys had an important role in stimulating social/cultural change in the community. This may be very briefly described in the following subsequent cases of the marriage of two Pilrig rebels. The importance of these two cases is that the two young rebels rebelled against and broke the convention of 'arranged marriage' in the community. Despite enormous pressures from their parents, kin and the community one of the boys flatly rejected his arranged marriage and later got married to a girl of his choice. Similarly, the second rebel extr-ordinarily insisted on marrying a girl that he knew. Despite strong opposition from his parents the boy finally succeeded in marrying the girl whom he had known for a long time.

These two cases have shaken the community and are still a major topic of gossip and discussions in the community. After these and some other similar events many parents of marriageable sons and daughters told me that they will have to reconsider the institution of 'arranged marriage'. If many other girls and boys within the community persistently deviate from some of its norms it my be predicted that the community is undergoing a gradual cultural/social change - the rebels are definitely the pioneers!

Having put forward this description of the four-fold typology of the Pilrig boys - from the least to the most deviant - it is now important to look at the relationship between age and deviance.

Age and Deviance

Age is one of the most important sociological variables in the explanation of crime and delinquency. Criminological research has consistently shown that crime and delinquency reach their peak at certain points in teenage years (see McClintock and Avison 1968; Greenburg 1979; Hirschi and Gottfredson 1983; Wilson and Hernstein 1985; Farrington 1986; Anderson et al 1990; Gottfredson and Hirschi 1990, Sapson and Laub 1993). The relationships between age and deviance in the sample of 60 Pakistani boys in the Pilrig Mosque/community centre can be seen in Table 17.

Table 17 reveals that the youngest of the Pilrig boys was 10 and the oldest was 21 years at the time the questionnaire of the present study was completed. The table further reveals that over two fifths (41.66%) of the boys in the sample were 10 to 12 years old; almost a fifth (18.33%) of the boys were 13 to 15 years old; only a small minority (8.33%) of these boys were 16 to

18 years old, whereas almost a third (31.66%) of them were 19 to 21 years old.

Table 17 further reveals that a large majority (68.75%) of the conformist boys in the sample were aged 10 to 12 years, whereas only one fourth of them were in the 19 to 21 age group; a small minority (6.25%) of the conformists were aged between 13 to 15 years. Similarly, more than two fifths (40.62%) of the accommodationist boys were aged 10 to 12 years and more than a fifth (21.87%) of them were between 13 to 15 years old. A small minority (3.12%) of the boys in this category were aged 16 to 18 years whereas about a third (34.37%) of them fell into the 19 to 21 age-group.

These data show that the majority of each of the conformist and accommodationist boys (non-deviant categories) are comparatively younger persons: three-fourths of the conformists and about two-thirds (62.49%) of the accommodationists are in age groups 10 to 12 and 13 to 15 years. But this pattern is almost the other way round in the age-distribution among the part-time conformists and the rebels (deviant categories): only 14.28 percent of the part-time conformists are aged 10 to 12 years old, and 28.57 percent of them are in the 13 to 15 years age group. But the majority (57.14%) of these boys fall into the 16 to 18 age-group. Similarly, only one fifth of the rebels were 13 to 15 years old, whereas four fifths of them fell into the 19 to 21 age-group. These data indicate that the older the boys in Pilrig sample the more deviant they are. This is confirmed by Kendall's Tau b showing moderately strong positive correlation (0.21) between age and the degree of deviance among the Pilrig boys.

The age distribution of the Pilrig boys clearly indicate that the majority of these boys deviated from and openly rebelled against their community's norms after their 16th birthday. These results are very similar to the findings of important British, Scandinavian, and American studies. For example Farrington (1992) found that the median age of conviction for most offences (shoplifting, robbery, burglary and theft from vehicles) showed that the prevalence of offending in this study reached to a peak at 15-17 years of age. The ANYS's findings are identical to those of the Stockholm Metropolitan Project which found that peak age of offending in the Stockholm study was 15-17 (Wikström 1990).

It is worth mentioning that the fact that the oldest boys in the Pilrig sample were 21-year-old 'deviants' does not imply that deviation from the community's norms stops at this age. In fact some of the ethnographic data of the present study indicates that rebellious youngsters in Edinburgh's Pakistani community continue to remain involved in 'deviant' activities until their mid to late twenties. Stories of the adolescent life of some respectable members of the community - now in their mid thirties - very much resemble those of the part-time conformists and rebels in the Pilrig sample. These ex-deviants/rebels told me while laughing that '...we retired

Table 17 - Age and the Four Behavioural Types in the Pilrig Sample

Typology	Age				
	10-12	13-15	16-18	19-21	All
	% (No.)	% (No.)	% (No.)	% (No.)	% (No.)
Conformists	68.75 (11)	6.25 (1)	– (0)	25.00 (4)	26.66 (16)
Accommodationists	40.62 (13)	21.87 (7)	03.12 (1)	34.37 (11)	53.33 (32)
PT Conformists	14.28 (1)	28.57 (2)	57.14 (4)	– (0)	11.66 (7)
Rebels	– (0)	20.00 (1)	– (0)	80.00 (4)	08.33 (5)
Total	41.66 (25)	18.33 (11)	8.33 (5)	31.66 (19)	100.00 (60)

Tau b = 0.21   Sig. 0.03

after getting married and starting our own business'. However these ex-rebels say that they did not rebel against some of the most well established values/norms of the community including arranged marriage. But the Pilrig rebels did!

The data at hand showing moderately strong relationship between age and deviance among the Pilrig boys, in fact, explains the very degrees of social control to which these boys are subject in the course of their adolescent and adult life. The British-born Pakistani boys in the Pilrig sample lived in a relatively insulated and protected social and cultural world of the family and the community until they reach the age of 15 or 16, or the age of *Bolugh* (puberty). Because until this age they depended, to a greater extent, on the social and emotional support of their parents and kin, and therefore were more socially controlled, fewer of them involved in deviant behaviour. But, since these boys became relatively free from the family and the community's social control after the age of around 15 or 16 (the age of *Bolugh*), a larger number of them deviated from the norms of their community. In the same vein the fact that most non-conformist Pakistani boys returned to conventional life style after they got married and started in business explains the extent of social control to which they are subject in their mid/late twenties. Marriage and business socially bond these youngsters to the community's social institutions and to its moral and social order; hence they become more socially controlled.

What has been so far discussed in this chapter aimed at providing a general introductory background to the empirical examination of deviance among the Pilrig boys. In the following pages the discussion will focus on the explanation of deviance among the Pilrig boys within the theoretical framework of Travis Hirschi's version of social control theory.

Note

[1] It is worth saying that the proposed typology of the Pilrig boys is not necessarily generalisable to all second-generation young Pakistanis in Britain. But such a possibility may exist. This is because almost all second-generation young Pakistanis are exposed to pressures and contradictions between the two cultural/social worlds in which they live. The second-generation youngsters are very likely to seek various possibilities to find solutions to these pressures and contradictions. The proposed typology has explored such possibilities.

Moreover, due to the relatively small size of the Pilrig sample (60 boys) it is not claimed that the proposed typology is complete. In fact there were some clues in the present data that pointed to the possibility of splitting the four types to a further two categories each. For example among the conformists there were those younger boys who were mainly exposed to the values of their families/community and therefore devoutly conformed to them. But, there were also a few 'older conformists' who failed to accommodate and adopt certain values of the wider society. This latter category of older conformist tended to favour extreme interpretation of Islamic teachings.

Similarly, among the accommodationists there were those who compromised on minor religious and social norms/values, and not on fundamental principles. But, some accommodationists interpreted even fundamental religious/social values in a broad way. Finally the rebels could be divided into 'rebels with cause' (organised groups with alternative social agendas) and to 'rebels without cause' (who just rebel against the existing norms just for the sake of rebellion). Further expansion and development of the proposed typology is a task to be left for other researchers.

5 Attachment

Introduction

In this chapter, the first and the most important element of Travis Hirschi's (1969) social control theory - attachment - is empirically examined. After a brief theoretical exploration of the concept, attachment is defined as an individual's (mainly a child/adolescent's) affectionate involvement in others ('Significant others') and, hence, becoming sensitive to their views, wishes, and expectations. Attachment to parents - the most important form of attachment from the social control theorists' point of view - is examined first in this chapter. To operationalise attachment to parents, in the context of the present study, 'Intimacy of communication with parents', 'giving importance to parents' *Nasihat* [advice], and 'affection to parents' were considered as indicators of the concept. Results of this empirical investigation are mainly quantitatively analysed.

Attachment to parents often leads to the psychological presence of parents in the child's mind, even when they are absent. This aspect of attachment that is referred to as 'Indirect control' (Nye 1958) is discussed under the sub-heading of 'Parental supervision'. That is, parental supervision, in this sense, is the extent of the child's perception of parents' knowledge about his/her whereabouts; it is not actual supervision and surveillance. Within this theoretical context the relationship between the Pilrig boys' perception of their 'parents' knowledge about their whereabouts' and about their 'company' (when they were away from home) and deviance were empirically examined. Parental supervision was categorised into three forms: 'neglectful', 'moderate' and 'too strict'. Moreover, this discussion was further supplemented by examining the relationship between 'parental discipline and deviance/delinquency. Parental discipline in this context is defined as the use of certain measures of direct control by parents after the child did something that was 'wrong' in their view. Within this context the relationships between 'neglectful', 'moderate' and 'too strict' forms of parental discipline were empirically investigated.

After attachment to parents, attachment to the school and the teacher(s) is strongly emphasised in control theory. In order to examine the relationship between attachment to the school and deviance in the Pilrig sample, 'liking the school', 'caring about teacher(s)' opinions, and the extent of 'attendance at school' were considered as indicators of the independent variable. The analysis and interpretation of the findings are mainly based on quantitative data.

Subsequently, the relationship between attachment to friends and deviance is examined. To operationalise attachment to friends, in the context of the Pilrig sample, 'importance of friends', 'respect for best friends opinions', and 'identification with best friends' were considered as indicators of this form of attachment. Because friendship among Edinburgh's Pakistanis often took place within the context of kinship, the quantitative results of the findings were analysed in the light of qualitative data. Finally, the question of whether attachment to delinquent friends has any relationship with deviance is examined. The relationship between the numbers of 'friends picked up by the police' and 'suspended from the school' and deviance in the Pilrig sample are empirically investigated. The quantitative findings are analysed in the light of ethnographic data.

Attachment

From childhood we normally develop our initial affective relations with persons who are available in our immediate social environment. Normally, we are born to parents whose emotional, material and social support is vital to us during our childhood and adolescence. After our parents we usually interact more intimately and frequently with our other family members, i.e. brothers and sisters and with our close kin as well. At school, in our neighbourhood locality and in the playground we often make close friends. We meet many other people too. But we do not feel emotionally close to everybody. We develop affectionate relationships and feel emotionally close only to some individuals. They are individuals whose existence has meaning in our lives; we relate to and identify with them; we share our thoughts and feelings with them; and therefore they become 'significant others' to us. In the context of Hirschi's social control theory (1969) attachment refers to this kind of affectionate involvement of human individuals in 'significant others', and therefore becoming sensitive to their feelings, wishes and expectations and to their ideas and opinions.

The relevance of attachment to delinquency and crime is that in fantasy deviance is a possibility to us all. But what often makes us choose not to follow that path is our affective human relationships that have more worth to us (emotional, physical or material) than the joy, thrill and/or benefit that we may get from deviance. So, whenever we think about deviation or going against the opinions and expectations of others, we think twice - we think twice not because the 'significant others' may physically force us to conform or punish us for our deviance; but because we feel so close to them (or closely identified with them) that even in their absence, they are profoundly present in our consciousness - we find it very difficult to betray those feelings; we do not want them to be hurt or embarrassed when they see us going against their expectations and opinions should they come to know about our acts. Described in this way, attachment is a flexible variable; the degree of its intensity varies across individuals with the fluctuating human affectionate involvement in one another. Theoretically the least attached (and the totally detached) individuals are more likely to deviate - they are individuals who are unaffected by the constraint of attachment; and therefore they are relatively free to deviate.

In exploring the relationship between attachment and crime/delinquency, modern theorists and researchers mainly focus on three sources of attachment: parents, school and friends. The most important of all these sources are parents.

I: Attachment to Parents

...the emotional bond between the parent and the child presumably provides the bridge across which pass parental ideals and expectations. If the child is alienated from the parent, he will not learn or will have no feeling for moral rules... (Hirschi 1969:86)

Parents are normally conventional figures who have the responsibility of socialising their children to society's conventional morality and values. In most cultures parents teach their children the 'wrongs' and 'rights' of the society and pro-conformity behaviour. Even parents who themselves are involved in deviant/criminal behaviour are very unlikely to intend or desire that their children become criminal and anti-social individuals (see Box 1981:126). Because parents are normally conventional figures, they naturally expect their children to conform to society's moral norms and rules. Although the degree of the internalisation of society's moral rules may vary from individual to individual, most children, know how parents and society's other conventional figures expect them to behave.

Parents may persuade, manipulate, or even physically force their children to live up to theirs and to societal expectations. But, this is not what the control theorist means by 'attachment to parents'. As mentioned earlier, the control theorist's emphasis, in this regard, is on the emotional bond between the child and his/her parent and to the extent to which he/she cares and is sensitive to their expectations and conventional opinions. Thus, the control theorist hypothesises that those young people who are strongly attached to their parents are more likely to care about to their opinions, and therefore, they are less likely to violate society's conventional rules and norms. Conversely, those young people who are weakly attached to their parents, or whose attachment has been destroyed or has not been made at all are free to violate society's rules and norms.

In the subsequent research literature and in those prior to Hirschi's social control theory, the concept of attachment has not been operationalised in a standard way. That is to say, that the 'items' that have been used for 'measuring' attachment, to some extent, vary from one study to another (either in content, form or both) reflecting different dimensions of attachment, and its different contexts. Various indicators, including 'affection and love', 'interest and concern', 'support and help', 'trust', 'encouragement', 'lack of rejection', 'desire for physical closeness', 'amount of interaction or positive communication and identification', have been identified as bases for measuring the concept. By and large all these various measures have been negatively correlated to delinquency. The empirical evidence showing negative correlation between attachment to parents and delinquency is massive and well documented (see Glueck and Glueck 1950; Nye 1958; McCord et al 1962; Hirschi 1969; Farrington 1973; Hirschi and Hindelang 1977; Hagan 1979; Box 1981; Wiatrowski et al 1981; West 1982; Eliott et al 1985; Patterson and Dishion 1985; Cernkovich and Giordano 1987; Sampson and Laub 1993).

In the present research, however, much attention was paid to the operationalisation of attachment to parents within the cultural and social context of the Pakistani family in Edinburgh. As was mentioned in Chapter II, the Pakistani family in Edinburgh is, in general, a very close-knit social unit where children are usually emotionally and socially dependent on their parents. Parents are normally the first people with whom these children share their intimate thoughts and feelings. Thus, 'intimacy of communication' was selected as the first indicator of attachment to parents.

In the same vein, for the Pakistani children in Edinburgh, their parents were the first people to whom they turn for *Nasihat* (advice). It was generally accepted among the 60 boys in Pilrig, Edinburgh, that their parents 'know best'. Thus, parents' *Nasihat* as an important feature of parent-children interaction and a central element in the socialisation of Pakistani children in Edinburgh was considered as the second indicator of attachment to parents.

Finally, since most young Pakistanis in Pilrig felt 'excluded' from the wider society (see Chapter IV) they tended to strongly relate to and positively identify with men in their own 'closed' community - a community that is in the process of becoming a small-scale society within the wider society (see Chapter I). Fathers were the most immediate 'role-models' for the Pilrig Boys to identify with. Thus 'positive identification' with father and the 'feeling of closeness' to mother (the latter are 'role-models' only for daughters in the Pakistani male-dominated culture) were selected as last indicators of attachment to parents.

Intimacy of Communication with Parents

To measure intimacy of communication between the Pilrig boys and their mothers/fathers, they were asked: 'How often do you share your thoughts and feelings with your mother?' (using the same item for each parent separately). Answer categories 'always' and 'often' (scored 3 and 2) accounted for much intimacy of communication, whereas 'sometimes' and 'hardly ever' (scored 1 and 0) measured little intimacy of communication.

Table 18 - Intimacy of Communication with Mother and the Level of Deviance

| Typology | Intimacy of Communication with Mother | | |
	Little	Much	Total
	% (No.)	% (No.)	% (No.)
Conformists	31.25 (5)	68.75 (11)	100.00 (16)
Accommodationists	50.00 (16)	50.00 (16)	100.00 (32)
PT Conformists	100.00 (7)	00.00 (0)	100.00 (7)
Rebels	100.00 (5)	00.00 (0)	100.00 (5)
Total	55.00 (33)	45.00 (27)	100.00 (60)

Tau b = -0.41, Sig. 0.000

Table 18 shows that the majority (68.75%) of the conformist boys have much intimate communication with their mothers, whereas a significant minority (31.25%) of them have little intimate communication with their mothers. Among the accommodationists, exactly one half of them have much intimate communication with their mothers and the other half have little communication with their mothers. For these two non-deviant categories of the boys the figures by themselves may not seem very striking. That is to say that higher percentages of the non-deviant categories of the Pilrig boys were expected to have had more intimate communication with their mothers than the table shows. However the figures become much more striking when compared with the two deviant categories of the boys: none of the part-time conformists and rebels have much intimate communication with their mothers. It is this discriminatory power of the attachment variable (or intimacy of communication, as an indicator of attachment) between deviants and non-deviants which the control theorist emphasises. Furthermore, the statistical test of correlation coefficient shows very strong inverse correlation (-0.41) between the amount of intimacy of communication with mother and the level of deviance. That is to say that the less the intimacy of communication between the Pilrig boys and their mothers the higher their degree of deviation from the normative standards of their community.

As far as the intimacy of communication with father is concerned, Table 19 indicates that fewer conformist boys (56.25%) have much intimate communication with their fathers as compared with the figure for the mother

Table 19 - Intimacy of Communication with Father and the Level of Deviance

Typology	Intimacy of Communication with Father		Total
	Little	Much	
	% (No.)	% (No.)	% (No.)
Conformists	43.75 (7)	56.25 (11)	100.00 (16)
Accommodationists	50.00 (16)	50.00 (16)	100.00 (32)
PT Conformists	71.43 (5)	28.57 (2)	100.00 (7)
Rebels	100.00 (5)	00.00 (0)	100.00 (5)
Total	55.00 (33)	45.00 (27)	100.00 (60)

Tau b = -0.24, Sig. 0.0219

(68.75%). Among the accommodationists the figures for the father are, interestingly, the same as those for mother. However, a significant minority of the part-time conformists (28.57%) have much communication with their fathers, whereas not one of them has much communication with their mothers. As expected none of the rebels has much intimate communication with either of their parents.

The comparison between percentages in the first and third categories of the boys regarding the degree of intimacy of communication with each parent indicates some clear variations. These variations suggest that intimacy of communication with mother discriminates more markedly between deviants and non-deviants than intimacy of communication with father. The comparatively larger figure for the inverse correlation between intimacy of communication with the mother and the level of deviance (-0.41) than that in the case of the father (-0.24) confirms this: it indicates very strong correlation between the independent and dependent variables in the mother's case, whereas this correlation is moderately strong in the case of the father. Nevertheless, the general conclusion regarding intimacy of communication with the father and the mother is consistent with the assumption of control theory: the more the Pilrig boys intimately communicated with their parents, the less they deviated from the norms of the Pakistani community in Edinburgh.

While the above interpretation of Table 18 meets the theoretical expectations, its row-wise picture apparently challenges the common view and research (Henley 1986; Shaw 1988) that '[Asian (Pakistani)] parents and children have close and warm relationships'. According to the tables less than half of all the boys (45%) have much communication with their mothers, and it is exactly the same case with fathers. This issue will be dealt with while examining the direction of communication between parents and children, in the next section. First, it is important to look at the relationship between parents' advice and deviance.

Parents' Nasihat (Advice)

Having analysed the relationships between intimacy of communication and the level of deviance, the question arises as to whether the Pilrig boys' mere sharing of thoughts and feeling with their parents may have been superficial: a ritualistic practice without the actual acceptance of parents' thoughts and ideas. If the communication between the boys and their parents had actually been intimate they are expected to give importance to and listen to their parents' advice. In Islam giving importance to parents advice, *Nasihat*, is a religious duty of children; and among Edinburgh's Pakistanis it is considered a sign of close and 'healthy' relationships between children and their parents. Thus taking into account this particular socio-cultural context the

Pilrig boys were next asked 'How important is your mother/father's *Nasihat* (advice) to you?'   (Separate answer boxes were used for each parent). Answer categories: 'Very important' and 'Fairly important' accounted for Much importance and 'Not very important' and 'Not important at all' for 'Little importance.

Table 20 - Mother's Advice and the Level of Deviance

Typology	Mother's Advice		Total
	Of Little Importance	Of Much Importance	
	% (No.)	% (No.)	% (No.)
Conformists	6.25 (1)	93.75 (15)	100.00 (16)
Accommodationists	3.12 (1)	96.87 (31)	100.00 (32)
PT Conformists	42.86 (3)	57.14 (4)	100.00 (7)
Rebels	100.00 (5)	00.00 (0)	100.00 (5)
Total	16.67 (10)	83.33 (50)	100.00 (60)

Tau b = -0.48,   Sig. 0.000

The data in Table 20 clearly show that for the overwhelming majority of both the conformist and the accommodationist categories (non-deviant boys) their mother's advice is of much importance; only for insignificant minorities in each category is their mother's advice of little importance. This is very much in line with what is theoretically expected. What is of some surprise and unexpected is that for more than half (57.14%) of the part-time conformists (deviant category) their mother's advice is also of much importance to them. But on the other hand none of the rebels (the most deviant category) regard their mother's advice of much importance. I will return to the interpretation of this finding shortly. But first, it is impor-

Table 21 - Father's Advice and the Level of Deviance

| | Father's Advice | | Total |
Typology	Of Little Importance	Of Much Importance	
	% (No.)	% (No.)	% (No.)
Conformists	00.00 (0)	100.00 (16)	100.00 (16)
Accommodationists	00.00 (0)	100.00 (32)	100.00 (32)
PT Conformists	14.29 (1)	87.81 (6)	100.00 (7)
Rebels	60.00 (3)	40.00 (2)	100.00 (5)
Total	6.67 (4)	93.33 (56)	100.00 (60)

Tau b = -0.41,   Sig. 0.000

tant to look at the relationship between the father's advice and deviance, in the Pilrig sample.

As can be seen in Table 21, for all of the two non-deviant categories of the boys their fathers' advice is of much importance to them. What is interesting is that for an overwhelming majority of the part-time conformists (87.81%) their fathers' advice is also of much importance; and it is a similar situation in the case of their mothers' advice. It can be inferred from this observation that despite deviating from much of the conventional morality of their community, the part-time conformists dare not to challenge parental authority, particularly their fathers' authority. Even if these boys do not feel close to their fathers (see Table 23), the father is still an 'economic father' and a 'social' one. That is to say that the father is the powerful head of the family, of its property and business. By challenging their fathers' authority, the part-time conformists would be endangering their economic future; they will be taking the risk of depriving themselves from the comfort that they enjoy in their 'fathers' house' (though often considered as the 'family's house'). However, for the majority (60%) of the rebels in the sample their fathers' advice is of little importance to them, where none of them say that their mothers' advice is of much importance. The fact that no one among the rebels give much importance to the mother's advice is probably because the mother is not the economic head of the family (though she may be the social head) and therefore her power to impose economic sanctions on her 'rebellious' sons is limited. Nevertheless, both the mother's and the father's advice is very strongly correlated with deviance, with a slightly larger correlation figure for the mother's advice (-0.48) than that for the father's advice (-0.41). Table 21 further reveals that the overwhelming majority of all the Pilrig boys give much importance to their parents' advice: 83.33% to mothers' advice and 93.33% to fathers' advice.

At this point, it seems appropriate to recall what we noticed in Table 18 and 19 that only a minority of all the Pilrig boys (45%) have much intimate communication (sharing thoughts and feelings) with each parent. Considering parents-children sharing thoughts and feelings as a major criterion of their 'close relationships' the above result apparently conflicts with the common view that: 'Asian parents and children have very close and warm relationships'. But if the nature and direction of parent-children communication in the present study is more carefully examined the apparent conflict disappears: while sharing of thoughts and feelings with parents, and parents' advice are both basically a communication between parents and children, the direction of each is different: in the 'intimacy of communication' case ('How often do you share your thoughts and feelings with your mother/father?') the flow of communication is from the child to the parent; the child is the initiator. But in the case of parents' advice' ('How important is your mother/fathers' advice to you?') the flow of communication is from the parent(s) to the child, with an element of authority/respect loaded in the term 'advice'. Taking into account this distinction, the comparison between Tables 18 and 19 reveals that an overwhelming majority of Pakistani boys still have much communication with their parents (93.33% give much importance to their fathers' advice and 83.33% to their mothers'). However the dominant pattern of parent-children communication is that the boys tend to be more recipients in communicating with their parents rather than active initiators.

Affection to Parents

Up to this point, the general pattern has been that boys who have much intimacy of communication with their parents also give much importance to their advice. Now, the question is, to what extent do the Pilrig boys affectionately relate and feel close to their parents? Thus, all the 60 boys were asked 'How close do you feel to your mother?' , which was used as a third and last measure of attachment to the mother. Answer categories 'Very close' and 'Fairly close' accounted for much feeling of closeness, whereas 'Not very close' and 'I do not feel close to my mother, at all' for little feeling of closeness to the mother.

Table 22 - Feeling of Closeness to Mother and the Level of Deviance

| Typology | Feeling of Closeness to Mother | | Total |
	Little	Much	
	% (No.)	% (No.)	% (No.)
Conformists	6.25 (1)	93.75 (15)	100.00 (16)
Accommodationists	3.12 (1)	96.87 (31)	100.00 (32)
PT Conformists	42.86 (3)	57.14 (4)	100.00 (7)
Rebels	80.00 (4)	20.00 (1)	100.00 (5)
Total	15.00 (9)	85.00 (51)	100.00

Tau b = -0.43,   Sig. 0.000

The findings in Table 22 show that exactly the same numbers of each of conformist (93.75%), the accommodationists (96.87%) and the part-time conformist (57.14%) categories of the boys for whom their mothers' advice was of much importance, also have much feeling of closeness to their mothers. Among the rebels, for none of whom their mothers' advice was of much importance, only a minority (20%) have much feeling of closeness to their mothers. These findings show that the relationship between affection for mother and the level of deviance, generally, follows the same pattern as that of the relationships between 'intimacy of communication', with and 'importance of the mother's advice' and the level of deviance. That is, the less the Pilrig boys have feelings of closeness to their mothers the greater is their deviation from the conventional morality of their community. Furthermore, feeling of closeness to mother is very strongly correlated to the level of deviance (-0.43). Table 22 also reveals that a large majority (85%) of all the Pilrig boys have much feelings of closeness to their mothers. This is a confirmation of the ethnographic findings of this study according to which most of the Pilrig boys were emotionally and socially dependent on their parents, particularly on their mothers.

It should be mentioned that because of the male-dominated culture of the community under study, boys are encouraged to follow their fathers as 'role-model' whereas girls are encouraged to follow their mothers as 'role-models'. Thus 'positive identification with father' rather than 'feeling of closeness' was selected as the third indicator of the Pilrig boys' attachment to their fathers. All the boys in the Pilrig sample were asked a separate question: 'How much would you like to be the kind of person your father is? Answer categories 'In every way' and 'In most ways' accounted for much positive identification with the father, whereas 'In some ways' and 'Not at all' little positive identification with the father.

Table 23 - Positive Identification with Father and the Level of Deviance

Typology	Positive Identification with Father		Total
	Little	Much	
	% (No.)	% (No.)	% (No.)
Conformists	50.00 (8)	50.00 (8)	100.00 (16)
Accommodationists	21.87 (7)	78.12 (25)	100.00 (32)
PT Conformists	57.14 (4)	42.86 (3)	100.00 (7)
Rebels	100.00 (5)	00.00 (0)	100.00 (5)
Total	40.00 (24)	60.00 (36)	100.00 (60)

Tau b = -0.12, Sig. -0.153

Unlike the empirical data that have been analysed so far with regard to the attachment variable, the findings of Table 23 are, to some extent, unexpected and problematic: only half of the conformist boys express feelings of much positive identification with their fathers. It becomes more puzzling to note that more than two fifths (42.86%) of the part-time conformists (a deviant category) also express much feeelings of identification with their fathers. Despite the facts that more than three fourths (78.12%) among the accommodationists (non-deviants) express much feelings of positive identification with their fathers; and despite the fact that none among the rebels do so, the question remains as to why only half of the conformists among the Pilrig boys express a strong sense of positive identification with their fathers?

One possible interpretation of these data may be that the conformist boys are generally among the youngest (10-12 year olds) of the Pilrig boys (see Table 17). Unlike their older class fellows who help their fathers in their work-place, the young conformists spend most of their time at home with their mothers. Because these younger boys have little chance to interact with their fathers, they may not see them as 'role-models' at all (see Chapter II where some mothers complained that their husbands have little time for their children). Thus, fewer conformist boys in the Pilrig sample positively identify themselves with their fathers.

At any rate, the findings of Table 23 fail to support the control theory strongly; the small correlation coefficient figure (-0.12) indicates that 'Positive identification with father' is weakly correlated with the level of deviance. At this point, it should be recalled that 'feeling of closeness' was strongly correlated with Deviance. This situation raises the question: is affection to one parent sufficient in controlling Deviance/Delinquency? Control theory does not have a straightforward answer to this question. Hirschi gives a 'maybe' support to the idea that attachment to one parent is sufficient in controlling delinquency: 'It may be, for example, that the boy strongly attached to his mother is unlikely to be delinquent regardless of his feelings toward his father; it may be that strong attachment to both parents adds little in the way of control' (Hirschi 1969:103; see also Hirschi 1983:62; and Gottfredson and Hirschi 1990:103). If this argument can be accepted, then a one-parent family may be as efficient in controlling delinquency/deviance as a two-parent family.

On the same token, then the strong inverse correlation between 'feeling of closeness to mother' and the dependent variable in the present study 'may be' sufficient to support control theory, without having strong correlation between 'Positive identification with father' and the dependent variable.

Finally, it is worth mentioning that the majority (60%) of all the boys express much 'Positive identification' with their father.

To sum up, consistent with social control theory and with much of the existing body of research, the present data show that the less the Pilrig boys share their thoughts and feelings with their parents, the less they give importance to their parents' advice, and the less affectionate feelings they have toward their mother, the more they deviate from the normative order of their community (positive identification with father did not have a strong relationship with deviance).

After analysing the relationships between attachment to parents and deviance, now it is important to look at the relationship between certain direct and indirect supervision/disciplinary measures by parents and the level of deviance among the Pilrig boys.

Parental Supervision and Discipline

The importance of parental supervision in controlling delinquency has long been recognised by theorists and researchers of delinquency. But the emphasis of researchers on different aspects of parental supervision have led to contradictory findings and to unresolved controversy over the topic that are discussed as follows:

For social control theorists parental supervision, in terms of restrictive monitoring, punishment and the use of other disciplinary techniques (direct control) has little impact on controlling delinquency. For example Nye (1958:7) argued that these techniques can be effective so far the child is 'within the physical limits of the house'. Following this line of reasoning Hirschi stated that:

> So called 'direct control' is not, except, a limiting case of much substantive or theoretical importance. The important consideration is whether the parent is psychologically present when temptation to commit a crime arises. (Hirschi 1969:88)

Receiving empirical support in his study for the argument Hirschi reached the conclusion:

> ...that the child is less likely to commit delinquent acts not because his parents actually restrict his activities, but because he shares his activities with them; not because his parents actually know where he is, but because he perceives them as aware of his location. (Hirschi 1969:89-90)

What is crucial in this view is the child's perception that his parents have a full knowledge of his whereabouts and his company. Thus, because of 'sharing' his social and psychological life with parents, the child is most likely to avoid going to places, accompanying persons and doing things that he knows his parents disapprove of. This psychological presence of the parents in the child's mind seems to be an outcome of parent-child attachment (not necessarily attachment itself, as it may be thought) that operates as an 'indirect control' over the child's behaviour. This position is further strengthened by the fact that Hirschi did not find support for the effectiveness of disciplinary techniques (or direct controls) in reducing delinquency. On the contrary, in Hirschi's study (1969:102, note 35), the use of disciplinary techniques by parents was positively (though weakly) related to delinquency. This finding has further support in a body of relatively earlier research. For example in a study by Sears et. al. (1957) the parents' use of punishment had a positive correlation with the children's misconduct. Similarly Berkowitz (1973) suggested that punishment may have an adverse effect on children's behaviour.

However, recent delinquency researchers have found that parental discipline and direct control have inverse relationships with delinquency. Patterson (1980:89-90) in his study of 'children who steal' reveals that '...parents of stealers do not track; they do not punish, and they do not care'. But Patterson's findings (1980) do add that it is not the severity and frequency of punishment by parents that reduces children's misbehaviours. Instead, it is the contingency and consistency of punishment.

More recent studies have found that direct controls by parents are as effective, in controlling children's delinquent behaviour, as indirect controls (Cernkowich et al 1987; Wells and Rankin 1988). Some of the studies in this category furthermore focused closely on the interaction between parental attachment and direct control by parents. For example another well quoted study by Patterson (1982) generally concludes that punishment by parents was more effective in reducing misbehaviour among children when they were strongly attached to their parents. While this conclusion is in line with relatively earlier research by Becker (1964) and with the finding of Eron et al. (1971), a more recent study by Rankin and Wells (1990) contradicts it. In their study of the effects of parental attachment and the different dimensions of direct control by parents (contingency, consistency and strictness of punishment), Rankin and Wells did not find a clear-cut interaction among these variables:

> Punishment that is too strict, frequent or severe can lead to greater probability of delinquency regardless of parental attachments....The adverse effects of both weak attachments and frequent/severe punishment on delinquency appear to be independent (additive) rather than multiplicative or interactive. (Rankin and Wells 1990:163)

In sum, the research findings that I have mentioned in this section indicate that the effects of the different aspects of parental supervision and discipline on children's delinquency and misconduct are not very clear - the controversy continues.

With regard to the present study it should be mentioned again that the use of the questionnaire was preceded by more than one year of participant observation. During this period it was possible to find out about the nature and forms of supervision and discipline that parents actually used. I reached the conclusion that parental supervision in Edinburgh's Pakistani community included, all of indirect, direct and disciplinary measures. On the one hand, parents monitored and imposed some direct restrictions (on different occasions and on different levels) over their children's (sons') behaviour. At the same time the use of different disciplinary measures such as slapping/hitting, threats of throwing out of the house, and shouting and calling bad names were observable. I shall call all these direct measures by parents in controlling their children's behaviour 'parental discipline'. On the other hand the more common aspects of indirect parental supervision, the subconscious presence of the parents in the child's mind (as a result of successful attachment to parents) were clearly at work. I shall call these indirect supervisory measures by parents 'parental supervision'.

a: Parental Supervision

As mentioned above, parental supervision in the social-psychological context of the present study means the Pilrig boy's perception that his parents are aware of his whereabouts and of his company when he is away from home. Thus, all the Pilrig boys were asked: 'Do your parents know where you are when you are away from home for recreation? ' (separate response boxes were provided for each parent). Response categories 'He/she always knows' and 'he/she often knows' (scored 2 each) accounted for 'Moderate' supervision; 'He/she sometimes knows' and 'he/she does not care about my whereabouts when I am away from home' (scored 1 each) accounted for 'Neglectful' supervision; and 'he/she does not allow me to go for recreation unless I am accompanied by him/her or close relatives' and 'he/she does not allow me to go for recreation at all' (scored 3 each) accounted for 'Too strict' supervision.

As can be seen in Table 24 that a large majority (87.50%) of the conformist and exactly three quarters of accommodationist boys think that they are under a moderate supervision of their fathers. Among the part-time conformists only a small minority (14.29%) think in this way. Instead, a vast majority of them (85.71%) think that their fathers are neglectful about their supervision. Not surprisingly all the rebels think that their fathers are neglectful regarding their supervision.

It is evident from these results that larger proportions of the deviant boys (part-time conformists and rebels) perceive their fathers as neglectful about their whereabouts and about their companions. The results of the data at

**Table 24 - Father's Supervision (Knowledge of Child's Whereabouts)
and the Level of Deviance**

| Typology | Father's Supervision (Knowledge of Child's Whereabouts) | | | |
	Neglectful	Moderate	Too Strict	Total
	% (No.)	% (No.)	% (No.)	% (No.)
Conformists	12.50 (2)	87.50 (14)	00.00 (0)	100.00 (16)
Accommodationists	15.62 (5)	75.00 (24)	9.37 (3)	100.00 (32)
PT Conformists	85.71 (6)	14.29 (1)	00.00 (0)	100.00 (7)
Rebels	100.00 (5)	00.00 (0)	00.00 (0)	100.00 (5)
Total	30.00 (18)	65.00 (39)	5.00 (3)	100.00 (60)

Tau b = -0.43   Sig. -0.000

hand further indicate that more than two thirds (65%) of all the boys perceive their fathers as moderate about their supervision; less than a third
(30%) as neglectful; and only a very small minority (5%) perceive their
fathers as too strict about their supervision.

With regards to mothers' supervision, Table 25 indicates that more conformists and accommodationists (100% and 87% respectively) than those in
the case of fathers' supervision (87.50% and 75% conformists and accommodationists respectively) perceive their mothers as moderately supervising
them. But also, more part-time Conformists (42.86%) as compared to those
in the fathers' case (14.29%) perceive their mothers' supervision in this way.
However, none of the rebels think of either of their parents as moderately
supervising them. Instead, all of them perceive their mothers (as well as
their fathers) as neglectful about their supervision, when they are away from
home. In addition to this, and quite importantly, almost four fifths (78.33%)
of all the boys think that they are under a moderate supervision of their
mothers, whereas only about three fifths (65%) of all the boys think so
about their father. Only one fifth of all the boys think of their mothers as

Table 25 - Mother's Supervision (Knowledge of Child's Whereabouts) and the Level of Deviance

Typology	Mother's Supervision (Knowledge of Child's Whereabouts)			
	Neglectful	Moderate	Too Strict	Total
	% (No.)	% (No.)	% (No.)	% (No.)
Conformists	00.00 (0)	100.00 (16)	00.00 (0)	100.00 (16)
Accommodationists	9.37 (3)	87.50 (28)	3.12 (1)	100.00 (32)
PT Conformists	57.14 (4)	42.86 (3)	00.00 (0)	100.00 (7)
Rebels	100.00 (5)	00.00 (0)	00.00 (0)	100.00 (5)
Total	20.00 (12)	78.33 (47)	1.67 (1)	100.00 (60)

Tau b = -0.53   Sig. 0.000

neglectful regarding their supervision, while a third of them think in this way about their fathers. Interestingly enough only insignificant minorities of all the boys (1.67% and 5% for mother and father respectively) say that their parents are too strict.

Moreover, the present data show a larger figure of inverse correlation coefficient between mother's supervision and the level of deviance (-0.53) as compared to that between father's supervision and the dependent variable (-0.43). However, in both cases the independent and the dependent variables are very strongly correlated.

Alongside the emphasis of Edinburgh's Pakistani parents over their children's whereabouts, they place almost an equal emphasis over the companions of their children. They instruct their children to be highly selective, not only about their peers, but also about their companions, in general. Most parents encourage their sons and daughters to spend their leisure time with persons belonging to 'good' families and who have good a reputation in the community. They are warned to avoid the company and friendship of persons who drink alcohol, use drugs, gamble and persons with unconventional lifestyles and appearances, e.g. skinheads and boys who wear earrings. Most parents do not discourage their sons (especially) to make friends with boys from the indigenous British population 'as long as they are decent boys', a group of parents told me in an *Eid-milan* party (a communal dinner a few days after the end of the fasting month of *Ramadan*). However, some parents showed reservations '...but the problem is that it is normal for the Scottish teenagers to have girlfriends and even to drink alcohol. But these things are wrong in our community. If our children mix with them, they get confused'.

Keeping these considerations in mind, the boys were asked next: 'Do your parents know who you are with when you are away from home for recreation?' Since the format and the response categories of this question are identical to the previous question (except the phrase 'who I am with' instead of 'my whereabouts') a repetition of the response categories is avoided here. Also an identical scoring order and measuring scale: 'Neglectful', 'Moderate' and 'Too strict' are used for both of the questions.

Tables 26 and 27 indicate that three quarters of the conformists and two

Table 26 - Father's Supervision (Knowledge of Child's Company) and the Level of Deviance

| Typology | Father's Supervision (Knowledge of Child's Company) | | | |
	Neglectful	Moderate	Too Strict	Total
	% (No.)	% (No.)	% (No.)	% (No.)
Conformists	18.75 (3)	75.00 (12)	6.25 (1)	100.00 (16)
Accommodationists	31.25 (10)	62.50 (20)	6.25 (2)	100.00 (32)
PT Conformists	57.14 (4)	42.86 (3)	00.00 (0)	100.00 (7)
Rebels	100.00 (5)	00.00 (0)	00.00 (0)	100.00 (5)
Total	36.67 (22)	58.33 (35)	5.00 (3)	100.00 (60)

Tau b = -0.35   Sig. 0.001

thirds of the accommodationists among the Pilrig boys have the perception that they are under a moderate supervision of their fathers when they are away from home with friends. Among the part-time conformists about two fifths perceive their fathers as moderately supervising them when they are away from home with friends, whereas none of the rebels perceive their fathers in this way. Instead 57.11 percent of the part-time conformists and all the rebels think of their fathers as neglectful in their supervision. These results show that it is majorities of the deviant categories of the boys (part-time conformists and rebels) who think of their fathers supervision as neglectful.

The overall picture of this set of data shows that about three fifths (58.33%) of the boys in this sample perceive themselves under a moderate supervision of their fathers; a little more than one third (36.67%) under a neglectful supervision; and only a small minority (5%) of them perceive their fathers as too strict.

With respect to mothers, it seems, that their role is again crucial in the supervision of their children (sons). Table 27 reveals that three quarters of

Table 27 - Mother's Supervision (Knowledge of Child's Company) and the Level of Deviance

| Typology | Mother's Supervision (Knowledge of Child's Company) | | | |
| | Neglectful | Moderate | Too Strict | Total |
	% (No.)	% (No.)	% (No.)	% (No.)
Conformists	18.75 (3)	75.00 (12)	6.25 (1)	100.00 (16)
Accommodationists	18.75 (6)	78.12 (25)	3.12 (1)	100.00 (32)
PT Conformists	42.86 (3)	57.14 (4)	00.00 (0)	100.00 (7)
Rebels	100.00 (5)	00.00 (0)	00.00 (0)	100.00 (5)
Total	28.33 (17)	68.33 (41)	3.330 (2)	100.00 (60)

Tau b = -0.33   Sig. 0.003

the conformist boys think that they are under a moderate supervision of their mothers when they are away from home with friends. Exactly the same proportion of them thought so about their fathers. But among the accommodationists, more than three quarters (78.12%) think that they are under a moderate supervision of their mothers, whereas just two thirds of them think so about their fathers. Somewhat unexpectedly, almost three fifths (57.15%) of the part-time conformists also think that they are under a moderate supervision of their mothers, whereas just over two fifths (42.86%) of them think in this way about their fathers. However, none among the rebels think that they are under a moderate supervision of either their mother and father. The rebels, instead, perceive their parents as neglectful regarding their supervision when they are away from home with friends.

Overall, more boys (68.33%) in the total sample think of their mothers' supervision as moderate compared to 58.33% in the case of fathers. Fewer boys (28.17%) think of their mothers as neglectful, compared to 36.67 percent in the case of father's supervision. Only negligible minorities (5% in the case of fathers and 3.33% in the case of mothers) perceive their parents as too strict. Moreover, in both cases there are moderately strong correlation between the different forms of parental supervision and the degree of deviance among the Pilrig boys.

Up to this point the relationships between the form of parental supervision that is mainly indirect (perception of the child that his parents know about his whereabouts and his company) and the level of deviance have been examined. A kind of uniformity of the results, in all the four sets (or tables) of the data has emerged: boys who perceive their parents as moderately supervising them tend to be among the non-deviants. On the other hand, those who perceive their parents as neglectful are, by and large, among the deviant boys. Surprisingly, very few boys have the perception that their parents are too strict in their supervision. Finally, more boys perceive their mothers' supervision as moderate compared to the supervision of their fathers.

After discussing the relationship between perceived 'parental supervision' and deviance, now it is important to look at the reaction of Pakistani parents in Edinburgh, when their children (sons) do something that is wrong in the parents' view.

b: Parental Discipline

As mentioned earlier, the phrase 'parental discipline' in the context of the present study refers to those direct measures that parents take after their children commit acts that are considered as 'wrong'. The disciplinary measures include among other things, corporal punishments, throwing out of house (or the threat of it), shouting and calling 'bad names', and cautioning and persuading not to repeat doing 'wrong' things. Thus, in order to explore the relationship between the various disciplinary measures by parents and the level of deviance, all the Pilrig boys were asked 'When you do something that is wrong in your parents view, do they...'?: (Respondents had the choice of selecting more than one answer category and separate response boxes were provided for each parent.) Answer categories: 'slap/hit you'; 'threaten to throw you from home'; and 'call you bad names' (scored 3 each) accounted for 'Too strict' discipline. 'Advise and encourage you not to repeat it' (scored 2) accounted for 'Moderate' discipline. And finally, answer categories 'ignore it' and 'does not bother about it ' (scored 1 each) accounted for 'Neglectful' discipline.

Table 28 - Father's Discipline and the Level of Deviance

Typology	Father's Discipline			
	Neglectful	Moderate	Too Strict	Total
	% (No.)	% (No.)	% (No.)	% (No.)
Conformists	00.00 (0)	56.25 (9)	43.75 (7)	100.00 (16)
Accommodationists	9.37 (3)	56.25 (18)	34.37 (11)	100.00 (32)
PT Conformists	28.75 (2)	28.75 (2)	42.86 (3)	100.00 (7)
Rebels	20.00 (1)	80.00 (4)	00.00 (0)	100.00 (5)
Total	10.00 (6)	55.00 (33)	35.00 (21)	100.00 (60)

Tau b = -0.20   Sig. 0.040

The data in Table 28 show that just a little more than half (56.25%) of each of the conformist and the accommodationist boys report that their fathers used moderate discipline when they did something wrong. Unlike

Table 29 - Mother's Discipline and the Level of Deviance

Typology	Mother's Discipline			
	Neglectful	Moderate	Too Strict	Total
	% (No.)	% (No.)	% (No.)	% (No.)
Conformists	00.00 (0)	62.50 (10)	37.50 (6)	100.00 (16)
Accommodationists	6.25 (2)	56.25 (18)	37.50 (12)	100.00 (32)
PT Conformists	14.29 (1)	14.29 (1)	71.43 (5)	100.00 (7)
Rebels	20.00 (1)	80.00 (4)	00.00 (0)	100.00 (5)
Total	6.67 (4)	55.00 (33)	38.33 (23)	100.00 (60)

Tau b = -0.06   Sig. 0.304

the pattern of the data related to parental supervision, 43.75 percent of the conformists and 34.37 percent of the accommodationists say that their parents use too strict discipline when they do something wrong. Among the part-time conformists only a little more than a quarter (28.57%) say that their fathers use moderate discipline; about two fifths of them (42.86%) report too strict discipline by their fathers.

Interestingly enough, four fifths of the rebels say that the discipline their fathers use is moderate, and another fifth say that it is neglectful (I will return to the interpretation of this apparently, unexpected finding soon). As a whole a little more than a half (55%) of all the boys say that their fathers use moderate disciplinary measures when they do something wrong. A little more than a third (35%) report that their fathers are too strict, and only 1 in 10 say that their fathers are neglectful.

As far as mothers' discipline is concerned results of the findings in Table 29 do not seem significantly different from those related to fathers' discipline. Among the conformists and the accommodationist boys 62.50 percent and 56.25 percent of them respectively, say that their mothers use moderate discipline, whereas in the case of fathers 56.25 of each of the conformists and the accommodationists report experiencing this type of discipline. 37.50 percent of each these two categories of the boys said that their mothers were too strict as compared to 43.75 percent and 34.37 percent who said their fathers were too strict. However, among the part-time conformists only 14.29% of the boys say that their mothers use moderate discipline. Instead: about twice as large a number (71.43%) of them as that in the case of fathers' discipline say that their mothers are too strict in disciplining them. Four fifths of the rebels report that each of their parents use moderate disciplinary techniques when they do something wrong; the rest (one fifth) report a neglectful discipline by both their fathers and mothers.

Again, exactly as in the case of fathers' discipline, more than half (55%) of all the boys in the sample experienced moderate discipline by each parent; 38.33 percent of all the boys report experiencing too strict discipline by their mothers, whereas 35 percent of them report this experience with their fathers. While only 6.67% of all the boys report a neglectful supervision by their mothers, one in ten (or 10%) of them report a neglectful discipline by their fathers.

Now, if we look back and compare the data that relate to parental supervision (Tables 24 to 27) to that that relate to parental discipline (Tables 28 and 29) significant contrasts between the results of these two sets of data appear. In the first set of data the bulk of all the boys (in each of the four tables) perceive the way they are supervised by their parents as either moderate or neglectful (though large proportions perceive it as moderate). But, in the second set of the data the bulk of all the boys say that their parents use either moderate or too strict discipline (again larger proportions report moderate discipline). The fact that the large number of non-deviant boys report moderate supervision and moderate discipline by their parents supports the control theorists who say that it is the psychological presence of parents in the child's mind rather than the use of direct control that is crucial in controlling deviance/delinquency. But the problem with the last set of data (parental discipline) is that 'facts' are dealt with as if they were 'speaking for themselves'. That is to say that we (many researchers and I) label 'hitting/slapping'; 'throwing out of home etc.' as 'too strict' discipline, and then examine relationships between the various types of discipline and deviance. The important point is whether the boys, deviants and non-deviants see these disciplinary techniques in the way we label them or differently. To explore this point further the boys were asked: 'What do you think about the kind of discipline your parents use?' Response categories were 'Too strict'; 'Just fair' and 'Too lax' (loose) (separate answer categories were used for each parent).

According to Tables 30 and 31 a large majority of all the boys (interest-

Table 30 - Perception of Father's Discipline and the Level of Deviance

| Typology | Perception of Father's Discipline | | | |
	Neglectful	Moderate	Too Strict	Total
	% (No.)	% (No.)	% (No.)	% (No.)
Conformists	00.00 (0)	93.75 (15)	6.25 (1)	100.00 (16)
Accommodationists	3.12 (1)	84.37 (27)	12.50 (4)	100.00 (32)
PT Conformists	00.00 (0)	71.43 (5)	28.57 (2)	100.00 (7)
Rebels	00.00 (0)	100.00 (5)	00.00 (0)	100.00 (5)
Total	1.67 (1)	86.67 (52)	11.67 (7)	100.00 (60)

Tau b = 0.07, Sig. 0.263

ingly, 86.67% in the case of each parent) say that the discipline their parents use is 'fair'; small minorities of 11.67 percent and 10 percent say that their father and mother (respectively) are too strict. Negligible minorities of 1.67 percent and 3.33 percent say that their fathers' and mothers' discipline (respectively) is 'too lax'.

These results would seem to mean that many Pakistani boys do not consider 'hitting/slapping'; 'threats or throwing out of home' etc. as 'Too strict' disciplinary measures. Rather they see these measures as fair - a legitimate exercise of parental authority. However, the data in Tables 30 and 31 show that some Pakistani boys (mainly the deviant categories) also see 'ignoring' and 'not bothering' with their 'wrong-doings' as 'Just fair', rather than 'Too lax' discipline. But there is an obvious difference between the two situations. In the first, because of their internalisation of the cultural values of their community, the boys (mainly non-deviants) do not see the obviously painful disciplinary acts by their parents as harsh or too strict. In this situation what should be considered are the ways the boys see these disciplinary acts; not the nature of these acts. However in the second situation it does not

Table 31 - Perception of Mother's Discipline and the Level of Deviance

| Typology | Perception of Mother's Discipline | | | |
	Neglectful	Moderate	Too Strict	Total
	% (No.)	% (No.)	% (No.)	% (No.)
Conformists	00.00 (0)	100.00 (16)	00.00 (0)	100.00 (16)
Accommodationists	3.12 (1)	84.37 (27)	12.50 (4)	100.00 (32)
PT Conformists	00.00 (0)	71.43 (5)	28.57 (2)	100.00 (7)
Rebels	20.00 (1)	80.00 (4)	00.00 (0)	100.00 (5)
Total	3.33 (2)	86.67 (52)	10.00 (6)	100.00 (60)

Tau b = 0.06   Sig. 0.287

seem reasonable to consider 'ignoring' and 'not bothering' about children's 'wrong-doings' by their parents as fair (as described by, mainly, the deviant boys). This kind of parental supervision (if it can be called supervision at all) is obviously 'Neglectful' and 'Too lax'. So in this second situation what should be counted are the actual supervisory measures rather than the description of the boys.

If this argument is acceptable, then we will have somewhat different pictures of Tables 30 and 31 from the way they look at present: there will be more boys whose supervision by their parents is 'Too lax' - but probably too few to change the present picture of these tables dramatically.

In conclusion, the position arguing that indirect parental supervision (the psychological presence of parents in the child's mind) is more important than direct disciplinary controls in controlling delinquency receives cautious support from the data at hand.

Nonetheless, the present data yielded some relatively concrete results: boys who perceive their parents as moderately supervising them tend to be among the non-deviants, whereas those who perceive their parents as neglectful tend to be among the deviant boys. These results are almost identical with the findings of the well known English study:

> A particularly noticeable characteristic of parents of delinquents in the study was carelessness or laxness in matters of supervision. They were less concerned than other parents to watch over or to know about their children's doings, whereabouts and companions . . . (West 1982 : 57).

Similarly, findings of another study in England by Wilson and Heriott (1980) are in line with this conclusion. After examining the relationships between attachments to parents, parental supervision and discipline, and deviance in the Pilrig sample, now it is appropriate to look at attachment within the context of the school.

II: Attachment to the School

From the social control perspective school is seen as an important social institution (after the family) responsible for the transmission of societal values and conventional morality to the younger members of society. In fact the school is seen as a unique social institution that bridges the family to the larger conventional society. According to Hirschi (1969 : 110) 'Between the conventional family and the conventional world of work and marriage lies the school, an eminently conventional institution.' This implies that the school is next to the family in the development of the child's social bond to society. The school socialises youngsters to society's values and morality ('beliefs') and trains them for successful 'involvement' in conventional activities, and 'commitment' to conventional lines of action. Not only the school performs this future-orientated function of bonding to society through its social consequences; but attachment to the school itself (positive sentiments and respect to teachers, to school authority, and to school's values and norms) partly constitutes the child's bond to society.

In probing relationships between attachment to the school and delinquency, Hirschi (1969:132) suggests a 'causal chain' that 'runs from academic incompetence to poor school performance to disliking of school to rejection of school authority to the commission of delinquent acts.' However, it must be mentioned that in this 'causal chain' academic competence is assumed to be only indirectly related to delinquency so far as attachment to the school is concerned. In the logic of social control theory 'academic competence' (satisfactory scholastic performance) is considered only instrumental to the child's attachment to school; it is not attachment itself.

In other words, academic competence positively influences the child's attitude towards the school. (Relationships between academic competence and deviance in the Pilrig sample are analysed in Chapter VI where it is shown that the two variables are strongly correlated). It is then the liking or disliking of the school that is assumed to have direct relationships with conformity or deviance.

Thus from the view point of the social control theorist the child who does not like school and does not care about his teachers' opinions is weakly attached to the school. Therefore he/she is more likely to commit delinquent acts. There is much empirical evidence showing inverse relationships between liking school and delinquency (Glueck 1950; Jensen and Eve 1976; Thomas and Hyman 1978; Johnson 1979; Wiatrowski et al 1981; Kaplan and Robbins 1983; Agnew 1985, Gottfredson and Hirschi 1990; Sampson and Laub 1993).

Liking the School and Caring about Teachers' Opinions

To examine relationships between attachment to the school and deviance the Pilrig boys were first asked a direct question: 'In general, do you like school?' 'Like it in every way' and 'Like it in most ways' (score 3 and 2 respectively) accounted for 'Much liking' of the school, whereas 'Like it in some ways' and 'Dislike it' (scored 1 and 0 respectively) accounted for 'Little liking' of the school (separate response categories were provided for each of the local and the Mosque-schools).

Table 32   shows sharp and consistent differences between deviant and non-deviant boys as regard to their degree of liking the local school. Likewise, similar differences (though less consistent) can be seen between deviant and non-deviant boys in the case of the Mosque-school as Table 33 indicates. While 87.50 percent and 75 percent of the conformist and accommodationist boys (respectively) like the local school much, 68.75 percent and 71.87 percent of the two categories (respectively) express much liking for the Mosque-school. Exactly the same proportions (57.19%) of the part-time conformists say that they like both the local and the Mosque-schools a lot. But only two fifths of the rebels (40%) say that they like the local school much, whereas none of them like the Mosque-school much. Moreover, fewer boys (63.33%) in the total sample express much liking for the Mosque-school as compared to those in the local school (73.33%). As expected, both liking the local school and liking the Mosque-school are inversely correlated with the level of deviance. The correlation coefficients in both cases (local school: -0.26 and Mosque-school: -0.22) are moderately strong.

Boys who like school and find it rewarding and relevant to their future are more likely to respect its prevailing norms and values and the legitimacy of the school authority. A central figure in this regard is the teacher. This is particularly true in Islamic culture. The teacher in Islamic culture is not

Table 32 - Liking the Local School and the Level of Deviance

Typology	Liking the Local School		Total
	Little	Much	
	% (No.)	% (No.)	% (No.)
Conformists	12.50 (2)	87.50 (14)	100.00 (16)
Accommodationists	25.00 (8)	75.00 (24)	100.00 (32)
PT Conformists	42.86 (3)	57.14 (4)	100.00 (7)
Rebels	60.00 (3)	40.00 (2)	100.00 (5)
Total	26.67 (16)	73.33 (44)	100.00 (60)

Tau b = -0.26   Sig. 0.01

only respected because of his official status, but as a person of knowledge and a model of high moral standards. The teacher is commonly referred to as 'the spiritual father'. With such a central place of the teacher in the school, the Pilrig boys were next asked: 'Do you care what your teachers think of you? 'Very much' and 'a lot' accounted for 'much' caring about teachers' opinions, whereas 'not very much' and 'not at all' for 'little' care.

Both Tables 34 and 35 show a clear consistency between the decreasing number of boys who care much about their teachers' opinions (in both schools) and the increasing degree of their deviation from the Pakistani community's norms: three quarters of the conformists say that they care much about their teachers' opinions both in the local and in the Mosque schools, whereas fewer (59.37%) accommodationists say this about their teachers in the Mosque-school as compared to their teachers in the local school (65.62%). Among the deviant categories of the boys about two fifths (42.86%) of the part-time conformists and one fifth of the rebels say that they care much about their teachers opinions. These last two categories are further less sensitive to their teachers opinions in the Mosque-school: only

Table 33 - Liking the Mosque-School and the Level of Deviance

Typology	Liking the Mosque-School		Total
	Little	Much	
	% (No.)	% (No.)	% (No.)
Conformists	31.25 (5)	68.75 (11)	100.00 (16)
Accommodationists	28.12 (9)	71.87 (23)	100.00 (32)
PT Conformists	42.86 (3)	57.14 (4)	100.00 (7)
Rebels	100.00 (5)	00.00 (0)	100.00 (5)
Total	36.67 (22)	63.33 (38)	100.00 (60)

Tau b = -0.22   Sig. 0.03

28.57 percent of the part-time conformists and none of the rebels care much about their teachers opinions in the Mosque-school. Instead the large majority (71.43%) of the part-time conformists and all the rebels care little what their teachers in the Mosque-school think of them.

The above findings, indicating moderately strong inverse relationships between caring about teachers' opinions, and the level of deviance are further supported by the correlation coefficients between the two variables. However the independent variable is more strongly correlated to the level of deviance in the case of the Mosque-school (-0.36) than in the case of the local school (-0.26).

From comparing the attitude of the deviant categories of the boys to their teachers in each of the local school and in the Mosque-schools an important question arises: why do much larger proportions of the deviant boys care little (or not at all) about the opinions of *Hafiz Sahib*(s) than about the opinions of their teachers in the local school?

There may be more than one answer to the question in point. Nonetheless, placing the question in its social context may help in provid-

Table 34 - Caring about Teachers' Opinions and the Level of Deviance (Local School)

| Typology | Caring about Teachers' Opinions (Local School) | | |
	Little	Much	Total
	% (No.)	% (No.)	% (No.)
Conformists	5.00 (4)	75.00 (12)	100.00 (16)
Accommodationists	34.37 (11)	65.62 (21)	100.00 (32)
PT Conformists	57.14 (4)	42.86 (3)	100.00 (7)
Rebels	80.00 (4)	20.00 (1)	100.00 (5)
Total	38.83 (23)	61.67 (37)	100.00 (60)

Tau b = -0.26   Sig. 0.01

ing a more plausible explanation. As described in Chapter III the social organisation of the Mosque-school fails to provide a social situation that is conducive to the development of the Pilrig boys' attachment to the *Hafiz Sahibs* (teachers of the Mosque). Development of emotional attachment to persons and to institutions is normally a voluntary process in a relaxed and congenial communicative situation. But for many reasons, mainly the lack of sufficient classroom facilities, lack of effective communication between the *Hafiz Sahibs* and the students and the method of teaching, *Sabaq* becomes an uninteresting monotonous activity for many boys. The lack of interest of some of these boys which is often accompanied by *Shararat* (troublesome behaviour) is automatically reacted to by various kinds of punishments, including physical. Frustrated and angry, some of the boys question the very relevance of *Sabaq* to their future: 'there is no point in reading the *Quran* in Arabic without understanding its meaning', a few boys told me. This kind of situation creates a degree of estrangement between these boys, *Hafiz Sahibs* and the Mosque-school, rather than attachment to them. Thus, boys who have no emotional attachment to persons in authori-

Table 35 - Caring about Teachers' Opinions and the Level of Deviance (Mosque-School)

Typology	Caring about Teachers' Opinions (Mosque-School)		
	Little	Much	Total
	% (No.)	% (No.)	% (No.)
Conformists	25.00 (4)	75.00 (12)	100.00 (16)
Accommodationists	40.62 (13)	59.37 (19)	100.00 (32)
PT Conformists	71.43 (5)	28.75 (2)	100.00 (7)
Rebels	100.00 (5)	00.00 (0)	100.00 (5)
Total	45.00 (27)	55.00 (33)	100.00 . (60)

Tau b = -0.36   Sig. 0.01

ty (and controlling institutions) in effect deny the legitimacy of their authority; and therefore they feel no obligation to care what persons in positions of authority think of them.

Nevertheless in the total sample a little more than half (55%) of the boys say that they care much what their teachers think of them in the Mosque-school. But a larger number (61.67%) say so about their teachers in the local school.

Attendance at the School

Up to this point, analysis of the present data shows that liking the school and caring about teachers opinions are inversely correlated with the level of deviance. The more the Pilrig boys liked their schools and the more they cared about their teachers' opinions, the less deviant they were. Now, boys who have favourable sentiments to their school and teachers are expected to be interested in attending the school regularly. They are expected to give priority to attending school over other things to do at home, shop or elsewhere. In order to examine the relationship (if any) between the degree of regularity of school attendance and the level of deviance, the Pilrig boys were asked: 'During the past school year, for how many days were you absent from school, because you had important work to do at your home/shop?" 'More than three weeks' and 'about two weeks' (scored 0 and 1 respectively) accounted for 'little' regularity in school attendance. 'less than a week' and 'never' (scored 2 and 3 respectively) accounted for 'much' regularity .

Table 36 - Regularity of Attendance at the Local School and the Level of Deviance

| Typology | Regularity of School Attendance (Local School) | | |
	Little	Much	Total
	% (No.)	% (No.)	% (No.)
Conformists	18.75 (3)	81.25 (13)	100.00 (16)
Accommodationists	28.12 (9)	71.87 (23)	100.00 (32)
PT Conformists	14.29 (1)	85.71 (6)	100.00 (7)
Rebels	80.00 (4)	20.00 (1)	100.00 (5)
Total	28.33 (17)	71.67 (43)	100.00 (60)

Tau b = -0.18   Sig. 0.06

As can be seen in Table 36 the large majority of the conformists (81.25%), accommodationists (71.87%) and (unexpectedly) a larger majority of the part-time conformists (85.71%) report much regularity in attending the local school. However, the rebels differ significantly from the rest: only one fifth (20%) of them report much regularity of attending the local school.

As far as the Mosque-school is concerned about two thirds of the conformists (62.50%), a half of the accommodationists (50%) and again unex-

Table 37 - Regularity of Attendance at the Mosque-School and the Level of Deviance

| Typology | Regularity of School Attendance (Mosque-School) | | |
	Little	Much	Total
	% (No.)	% (No.)	% (No.)
Conformists	37.50 (6)	62.20 (10)	100.00 (16)
Accommodationists	50.00 (16)	50.00 (16)	100.00 (32)
PT Conformists	42.86 (3)	57.14 (4)	100.00 (7)
Rebels	100.00 (5)	00.00 (0)	100.00 (5)
Total	50.00 (30)	50.00 (30)	100.00 (60)

Tau b = -0.20   Sig. 0.04

pectedly 57.14 percent of the part-time conformists report much regularity of attending the Mosque-school. None of the rebels report much regularity in attending the Mosque-school. In fact all of the rebels attended their *Sabaq* less regularly, in the past year.

The above presentation of the data shows that 'regularity of school attendance' as an indicator of attachment to school discriminates less sharply as compared to 'liking the school' and 'caring about teachers' opinions' between the deviant and the non-deviant categories of the boys, in both the local and in the Mosque-schools. This is further reflected in the relatively strong (but not very strong) inverse correlation between regularity of attendance in the Mosque-school and the level of deviance (-0.2). The correlation is weak between the two variables (-0.18) in the case of the local school. It should be mentioned that the fact that larger majorities of the part-time conformists report much regularity in school attendance not only makes the distinction between the deviant and non-deviant boys less clearer. It also raises the question that why does a larger proportion of the part-time conformists as compared to the non-deviant boys report much regularity in attending the local school. Similarly, in the case of the Mosque-school more part-time conformists attend the *Sabaq* than the accommodationists.

One possible interpretation is that the part-time conformists (as the label connotes) are individuals who frequently deviate from their community's norms, and yet do not want to break their relationships with the community. Therefore to demonstrate their allegiance with the community and also to cover up their deviations, regular attendance of the Mosque-school may be one way of playing the game. Evidence for this was clearly observable during *Ramadan*: some boys after taking part in the special late night long prayers during *Ramadan* (*Taravih*) quietly slipped away to night clubs. The prayer normally took about three hours. The boys used to arrive early and queue near the entrance so that they could be seen by everybody. After being seen by the estimated three hundred worshippers in the front queues standing attentively facing Macca, the boys quietly left the Mosque, facing downwards towards Edinburgh's night clubs!

Finally, the data shows that a much larger proportion (71.67%) of all the boys attended the local school more regularly as compared to their attendance of the Mosque-school (50%).

To sum up, those boys who did not like much the local and the Mosque-schools, did not care much what their teachers thought of them, and did not regularly attend the two schools were markedly among the deviant categories. All the three variables were inversely correlated with the level of deviance. However, regularity of school attendance was not as strongly correlated with the level of deviance as were academic competence, liking the school and caring about teachers' opinions. The correlation coefficient between regularity of school attendance and the dependant variable was stronger in the case of the Mosque-school as compared to the local school. But, the correlation coefficient, between all the independent and their dependent variables were stronger in the case of the local school as compared to the Mosque-school. Larger proportions of all the boys expressed more liking, cared more about their teachers' opinions and attended more regularly the local school than the Mosque-school.

III: Attachment to Friends

In criminological theory, the connection between peer group, delinquency, and non-delinquency has been approached in various ways. The presently more dominant approaches in this regard are those of the 'cultural deviance' and of the 'social control' theorists (see Wilson and Herrnstein 1985:291-9).

First, there is the view of the theorists of 'cultural deviance' who contend that association with delinquents leads to the delinquency of those who are not delinquents. Among the first academic proponents of this view is Edwin Sutherland (1924) who is well known for his 'Differential Association' theory. According to Sutherland's theory that was further developed with the co-authorship of his student and colleague Donald Cressey (1978:81) 'A person becomes delinquent because of the excess of definitions favourable to violation of law over definitions unfavourable to violation of law.' That is, individuals learn deviant and delinquent 'values', attitudes and behaviour from association with their criminal delinquent friends. Other theorists within the 'cultural deviance' approach maintain that membership in a particular socio-economic class, sub-group, or delinquent sub-culture leads to delinquency and crime (Millar 1958; Cohen 1955; Cloward and Ohlin 1960). Although these theories differ from each other in how and why delinquent peers and particular subcultures and groups 'cause' delinquency and crime, the common ground between them is that young persons are strongly influenced by the 'values' and expectations of their delinquent/criminal friends and associates.

Since the emergence of the earlier versions of the 'cultural deviance' perspective, there have been numerous studies which show that many juvenile offences have been committed by persons belonging to a criminal group (Shaw and Mackay 1930; Cohen 1955; Klein 1969; Hindelang 1971,1976; Erickson 1971; Erickson and Jensen 1977; Greenwood, Petersilia, and Zimring 1980 and Sampson and Laub 1993). These data are generally thought as empirical support for the thesis of 'cultural deviance' theory.

The second major view about the connection between peer group and delinquency, and more importantly, non-delinquency, is that of control theorists. These theorists, while looking at the same data that are used as support for the 'cultural deviance' theory, reach a different conclusion. The social control theorists maintain that delinquents are involved in delinquency before they join a gang or other delinquents. Because they are delinquents, they have common interests in delinquency, and therefore they form/join a delinquent gang. The Gluecks' (1960) well known and influential study of five hundred delinquent boys strongly supported this position. The Gluecks found that their delinquents had been involved in delinquency before they joined the juvenile gangs. The control theorists used these data to argue that, since gang membership comes after delinquency, it is logically impossible for it to be a cause of delinquency.

Thus, from the social control perspective, it appears that, membership of a delinquent gang is a choice that the delinquent makes, rather than the result of 'bad influence' by delinquent peers. But the question is why do delinquents make such a 'bad' choice? Hirschi's (1969:40) answer is that delinquents do not have much of a 'good' choice - they have lost their stake in conformity:

The lack of attachment to others and the absence of commitment to individualistic success values lead to association with delinquents [that is, with others similarly lacking in attachment and commitment]. Since delinquents are less strongly attached to conventional adults than non-delinquents, they are less likely to be attached to each other. (Hirschi 1969:140)

There appear to be two important points in the above quoted passage: first, Hirschi says that because of their low stakes in conformity (broken/weak social bond to conventional persons and institutions, and poor scholastic achievements), delinquents associate with other boys who are in a similar situation. The second point in Hirschi's quotation is that despite their apparent 'hanging around' with each other, delinquents are less attached to their delinquent peers. In other words, delinquents are persons with no attachments or weak attachments, even to their own peers.

To return to the first point, the present data has clearly supported the control theorists' position, so far as the relationships between a low stake in conformity and delinquency is concerned. Throughout this chapter it has been confirmed that weak attachments to parents, to school and poor scholastic achievements were, in general, correlated with deviance.

As far as the second point is concerned - delinquents are less attached to their peers - the data at hand, generally, *fail* to support Hirschi's assumption. For 'testing' Hirschi's assumption about attachment to peers, the 'population' of this study were asked three questions. The first was: 'How important are your friends in your life?' 'Very important' and 'fairly important' accounted for 'much' importance. 'Not very important' and 'not important at all' accounted for 'little' importance. As can be seen in Table 38, results of the present data do not show significant differences between deviant and non-deviant boys, as regard to the degree of importance of friends to them. In fact large majorities (though with slight differences) of all the four categories of the boys say that friends are of much importance to them in their lives. The statistical calculation of the data further confirms that there is no correlation (0.01) between the importance of friends and the level of deviation.

However the mere importance of friends in one's life does not, necessarily, indicate closeness to them. Friends may be important for 'instrumental reasons' e.g., playing football with them, but not much more. Closeness among peers would require, among other things, intimacy, mutual trust and therefore respect for one another's opinion in making certain decisions in life. Thus, the boys were asked next: 'How often do you respect your best friends' opinion about the important things in your life? would you say:' 'Always' and 'often' accounted for 'much' respect, whereas, 'sometimes' and 'hardly ever' for 'little' respect for best friends' opinions.

According to Table 39, about two thirds of each of the conformists (62.50%) and of the accommodationists (65.62%) say that they have much

Table 38 - Importance of Friends and the Level of Deviance

| Typology | Importance of Friends | | Total |
| | Little | Much | |
	% (No.)	% (No.)	% (No.)
Conformists	25.00 (4)	75.00 (12)	100.00 (16)
Accommodationists	18.75 (6)	81.26 (26)	100.00 (32)
PT Conformists	28.75 (2)	71.43 (5)	100.00 (7)
Rebels	20.00 (1)	80.00 (4)	100.00 (5)
Total	21.67 (13)	78.33 (47)	100.00 (60)

Tau b = 0.01   Sig. 0.45

respect for their best friends' opinions in the important matters in their lives. Among the deviant categories of the boys, a little more than two fifths of the part-time conformists (42.86%) and exactly two fifths of the rebels say that they have much respect for their best friends' opinions about the important things in their lives, that is to say that majorities of the last two categories have little respect for their best friends' opinion. These results do not meet the theoretical expectations in the present study; the differences between the deviant and the non-deviant categories as regard to the degree of their respect to best friends' opinions are not very striking. This fact is confirmed by the weak (Tau b = - 0.11) inverse correlation between the degree of respect to best friends' opinions and the level of the Pilrig boys' deviation from the normative standards of Edinburgh's Pakistani community.

Besides respect for friends' opinions another indicator of attachment to peers which is often used by control theorists and researchers is 'positive identification' with peers. So, all the boys in the Pilrig sample were asked a third and final question regarding their attachment to their peers: 'How much would you like to be the kind of person your best friends are?' 'In

**Table 39 - Respect for Best Friends' Opinions and the Level of
Deviance**

| Typology | Respect for Best Friends' Opinions | | |
	Little	Much	Total
	% (No.)	% (No.)	% (No.)
Conformists	37.50 (6)	62.50 (10)	100.00 (16)
Accommodationists	34.37 (11)	65.62 (21)	100.00 (32)
PT Conformists	57.14 (4)	42.86 (3)	100.00 (7)
Rebels	60.00 (3)	40.00 (2)	100.00 (5)
Total	40.00 (24)	60.00 (36)	100.00 (60)

Tau b = -0.11,   Sig. 0.16

every way' and 'in most ways' accounted for 'much' identification with best
friends: and 'in some ways' and 'not at all' accounted for 'little' identification.

Table 40 does not show significant differences between the deviant and
the non-deviant categories of the boys as regard to the degree of their identification with their best friends. The statistical test further confirms that the
degree of identification with best friends and the degree of deviance among
the Pilrig boys are not correlated (Tau b = 0.08)

The data so far analysed, in this section, show that the results of Tables
38, 39 and 40 do not support the control theorists' assumption that delinquents are less attached to their peers than non-delinquents. This raises the
question why the control theorists' assumptions about the connection
between attachment to parents and school and deviance have been generally confirmed, in the present study, but not their assumption about the connection between attachment to peers and deviance.

One answer could, simply, be that the facts do not fit Hirschi's assumptions. That is that attachment to peers ('best friends') has less important

Table 40 - Identification with Best Friends and the Level of Deviance

	Identification with Best Friends		
Typology	Little	Much	Total
	% (No.)	% (No.)	% (No.)
Conformists	81.25 (13)	18.75 (3)	100.00 (16)
Accommodationists	56.25 (18)	43.75 (14)	100.00 (32)
PT Conformists	85.71 (6)	14.29 (1)	100.00 (7)
Rebels	60.00 (3)	40.00 (2)	100.00 (5)
Total	66.67 (40)	33.33 (20)	100.00 (60)

Tau b = -0.08, Sig. 0.25

effects in controlling deviance among the Pilrig boys as compared to the effects of attachments to parents and to the school. But it seems that a more accurate answer to the question is hidden in the cultural complexities of the patterns of friendship with kin and friends among Edinburgh's Pakistanis. As described in Chapter II, individuals in this particular community are not only closely related to each other through their immediate families. They are also closely tied to one another through extended families and through networks of kinship/friendship (the *Biraderi*) relationships. The younger Pakistani boys' experiences of racial discrimination, exclusion and rejection in the wider society have particularly led to their withdrawal from the wider society; and this, in turn, resulted in their need for 'sticking together, walking together, and going out together' as the ethnographic data of this study reveals (see Chapter IV).

Thus, alongside their close and warm relationships with members of their immediate families, Pakistani children frequently and closely interact with children within their kin-group. Since this interaction is positively encouraged by parents and adult kin, the Pakistani children normally develop close ties of friendship and identify with children within the kin-group. As will be further examined later in this chapter, the intra-kin relationships of friendship among these youngsters are often so close that they often refer to each other as '*Bhaie jan*' (brother/elder brother) or '*Cazan*' (cousin). They often have strong attachments and identify with each other. This is not to say that Edinburgh's Pakistani boys do not have friends among boys outside their kin-group and among non-Pakistani boys; they often do and call these boys 'best friends'. But this pattern of friendship, generally, seems to be business-like, 'instrumental' and 'diplomatic', rather than based on intimacy, mutual trust and identification. Hence, it would appear, that it is attachment to '*Bhaie Jan*' and '*Cazan*' that plays a crucial role in controlling deviance among the Pilrig boys; non-kin and non-Pakistani boys are just called 'best friend' without a real sense of attachment to them.

If this interpretation of the present data that relates attachment to 'best friends' is correct, then it is very unlikely for the Pakistani boys to be influenced by the 'values' and expectations of their delinquent 'best friends'.

Delinquent Friends

It was mentioned in the previous section that according to the more influential versions of cultural deviance theory - 'Differential Association' - association with delinquent peers leads to the delinquency of those who are not delinquents. Delinquency researchers have generally 'tested' this assertion by the number of one's friends who were picked up by the police or were suspended from school. Borrowing from these schools, both the cultural deviance and control theory traditions, the following measures were used to examine relationships (if any) between attachment to delinquent friends and deviance among the Pilrig boys. Hence, all of the 60 boys were asked: 'Among your friends, has any one had trouble with the police or been to the 'Children's Hearing'[The Scottish juvenile justice and welfare system]?' Answer categories were: 'none', 'one', 'two or three' and 'more than three'.'

As can be seen in Table 41, there were no significant differences between the deviant and the non-deviant boys in having 'best friends' who had trouble with the police or been to the 'children's hearing' panel. Nor did the number of such friends significantly discriminate between the two categories of the boys. The statistical test of correlation co-efficient, furthermore, showed that there is no relationship between the degree of deviation and the number of delinquent friends (Tau b=.07).

Since having trouble with the police or being to the 'children's hearing' panels are not the only criteria for the officially defined delinquency, the Pilrig boys were asked next: 'Among your best friends, has anyone been suspended from school?' (the same answer categories as those for the pre-

Table 41 - Number of Friends who had Trouble with the Police and the Level of Deviance

Typology	Number of Friends Who Had Trouble with Police				
	None	One	2-3	4+	Total
	% (No.)	% (No.)	% (No.)	% (No.)	% (No.)
Conformists	62.50 (10)	12.50 (2)	25.00 (4)	00.00 (0)	100.00 (16)
Accommodationists	59.37 (19)	28.12 (9)	06.25 (2)	06.25 (2)	100.00 (32)
PT Conformists	71.43 (5)	14.29 (1)	00.00 (0)	14.29 (1)	100.00 (7)
Rebels	20.00 (1)	40.00 (2)	40.00 (2)	00.00 (0)	100.00 (5)
Total	58.33 (35)	23.33 (14)	13.33 (8)	05.00 (3)	100.00 (60)

Tau b = 0.07   Sig. 0.25

vious question were used).

The findings in Table 42 show that there are only small differences between the deviant and the non-deviant boys as regard to having a 'best friend' (or a number of best friends) who have been suspended from school. A positive correlation (0.16) exists between the number of best friends who were suspended from school and the level of deviance. These findings show that having one or more 'best' delinquent friend(s) did not affect the values and behaviour of Pilrig boys significantly. This conclusion, it seems, contrasts with many studies on the subject to which I referred earlier. But this should not be surprising. 'Simple facts' without placing them in their 'social' contexts can be less meaningful and, occasionally, misleading. As suggested earlier, because of the duality of patterns of friendship in this particular community, the Pilrig boys tend to have strong ties of friendship within their kinship group. Friendship outside kinship is often instrumental and business-like. Thus, delinquent friends who fall into the latter category are less likely to be a source of influence over the non-deviant boys, in the Pilrig sample. Friends who play a crucial role in this respect are '*Bhaie jan*'

Table 42 - Number of Friends Suspended from School and the Level of Deviance

Typology	Number of Friends suspended from School				
	None	One	2-3	4+	Total
	% (No.)	% (No.)	% (No.)	% (No.)	% (No.)
Conformists	68.75 (11)	18.75 (3)	12.50 (2)	00.00 (0)	100.00 (16)
Accommodationists	50.00 (16)	34.37 (11)	12.50 (4)	03.12 (1)	100.00 (32)
PT Conformists	57.14 (4)	28.57 (2)	00.00 (0)	14.29 (1)	100.00 (7)
Rebels	20.00 (1)	60.00 (3)	20.00 (1)	00.00 (0)	100.00 (5)
Total	53.33 (32)	31.67 (17)	13.33 (9)	03.33 (2)	100.00 (60)

Tau b = 0.16   Sig. 0.07

and '*Cazan*'. Although '*Bhaie jan*' and '*Cazan*' are to be expected, and normally are a source of pro-conformity influence, this is not always the case. Close associates of a deviant/delinquent '*Bhaie jan*' or '*Cazan*' are often their deviant young kin. The clearest evidence for this point, during my participant observation in the Mosque-school, was that most of the Pilrig boys were in groups of three, four or five. Boys belonging to a group often sat together in the class; studied together; and some also made trouble together.

An interesting observation, in this respect, was that the boys Who were later identified as 'deviants' had their own groups; and there was a similarly strong tendency among the 'non-deviant' boys. But even more interestingly, it later became clear that members in each group were brothers and/or close kin. If a group comprised 'deviant' boys – part-time conformists and rebels – its members often included real brothers and/or close kin (though the older deviant boys tended not to be in the same group of deviant boys in which their real brother was). Similarly, groups of non-deviant boys included either real brothers and/or close kin. Both deviance and non-deviance among Pilrig boys tended to occur within tight circles of brothers and/or kin; and, thus it may be said that despite the apparent lack of (quantitative) empirical support, delinquent friends are, probably, a source of 'bad' influence over the non-deviant boys in the Pilrig sample. But, it is very likely that it is the influence of delinquent/deviant '*Bhaie Jan*' and '*Cazan*' that matters in this regard. The so-called 'best friends' in the wider sense appear to be of less importance.

Now the question is whether it is a deviant/delinquent '*Bhaie Jan*' and/or '*Cazan*' who influenced the other members of a deviant group; or whether members of a deviant group had a low stake in conformity to begin with and then they were attracted by a deviant real brother, '*Bhaie Jan*' and/or '*Cazan*' who had much in common with them, and 'recruited' them into their 'gang'.

The data presented throughout this chapter suggest that the rebels and the part-time conformists (deviant boys) had, significantly, weak attachments to their parents, to their school, and had poor scholastic achievements, as compared to the conformists and the accommodationists. Because of their common background in having a low stake in conforming behaviour, the deviant (real) brothers and/or cousins had common interests in deviance, and therefore, they formed their own groups.

It may be said that the deviant boys had weak attachments to their parents and poor scholastic achievements, because they were (first) 'spoiled' by their '*Bhaie Jan*' and/or '*Cazan*'. But, the difficulty with this argument is that it raises the question why were the conformists and the accommodationist boys in their own groups of non-deviants? Obviously, it cannot logically be argued that the non-deviant boys were first positively influenced by their conformist '*Bhaie Jan*' and '*Cazan*' and then they developed strong attachments to parents and school. Attachments to parents (almost) always take place before attachments to kin and friends in Edinburgh's Pakistani community; this is probably the case in all social groups.

Looking back at the different theoretical assumptions, it may be summarised : the assumption that delinquents/deviants are persons with a low stake in conformity (weak attachments to parents to school and low scholastic achievement) already had sufficient support by the data that were presented in the earlier sections of this chapter. But the assumption that delinquents/deviants are less attached to their peers than non-delinquents/non-deviants was not supported by the present quantitative data: there was no significant relationship between 'importance of friends', 'respect of best friends opinion', 'identification with best friends' and deviance and conformity. However, interpreting these results in the light of ethnographic data, it was suggested that attachment to friends in Edinburgh's Pakistani community normally occurs within the kin group, rather than with 'best friends' outside it. It is attachment to '*Bhaie Jan*' and/or '*Cazan*' that is more likely to be important in controlling deviance among the Pilrig boys. The so called 'Best Friends' of the Pilrig boys seem to be just for 'hanging around with' for instrumental reasons.

Likewise, the theoretical assumption that association with delinquents/deviants leads to delinquency did not have clear-cut support from the data collected by quantitative measures in the present study. There was no correlation between 'having a best friend' (or a number of them) who had been in trouble with the police or had been to the 'children's hearing panel' and the level of deviance. There was only weak positive relationship between having 'a best friend (or a number of them) who was suspended from school' and the dependent variable.

However, the ethnographic evidence suggests that deviants among the Pilrig boys were often in groups of their deviant kin. Members of these groups might have been influenced by the 'values' and behaviour of their deviant members. It was argued further that it is most likely that the potential deviants joined groups of the deviants because they all had a low stake in conformity (weak attachments to parents, teachers and poor scholastic performance), and hence they had more in common with the deviant boys than with the non-deviant in the Pilrig sample.

Following this empirical examination of attachment as the most important element of Hirschi's social control theory, its other three elements - commitment, involvement and belief - are examined in the next chapter.

6 Commitment, Involvement and Belief

Introduction

After the empirical examination of attachment, the other three elements of Hirschi's Social Control Theory – commitment, involvement and belief – are examined in this chapter. Each one of the three elements of Hirschi's theory is individually operationalised in the social, cultural and religious context of Edinburgh's Pakistani community; the analysis of each of the three elements constitutes a section of the chapter.

First the concept of commitment is theoretically examined, and is defined as an individual's social investments in conventional behaviour. In operationalising commitment, 'educational success', 'aspirations for higher/professional education', and 'family *Izzet* (honour)', are considered as indicators of the concept. Results of the empirical findings are discussed and interpreted under the sub-headings: 'commitment and education' and 'commitment and family *Izzet.*'

Involvement, which is the behavioural counterpart of commitment is discussed in the second section of the chapter. After a theoretical and conceptual examination of the concept, involvement is operationally defined as an individual's participation in conventional activities with the effect that he/she has little time for thinking about crime and delinquency, let alone committing it. However, the concept is further sharpened, and it is argued that involvement in all conventional activities does not contribute to controlling crime/delinquency; instead, it is inhibitive involvement - participation in those conventional activities that strengthen an individual's social bond to society/ community's conventional order - that is effective in controlling crime/delinquency. To operationalise involvement, 'time spent on homework' and 'participation in the activities of Mosque/community' are considered as the main indicators of the concept; the 'feeling of nothing to do' is further added to the two indicators of involvement. Results of the empirical findings are discussed and interpreted under the general sub-headings: 'involvement in school-related activities' and 'involvement in Mosque/community-related activities'.

Finally, belief, as the fourth and the last element of Hirschi's social control theory is theoretically and empirically examined in the third section of the chapter. Belief, which is defined as the moral 'validity' or 'legitimacy' of society/community's rules and norms, is operationalised both in the context of Edinburgh's Pakistani (Muslim) community and in that of the wider Scottish society. Thus, 'the extent to which one follows Islamic teachings (in this country)', the extent of agreement with 'one must be honest with all people', and the 'feelings of guilt after doing something dishonest to people', were considered as indicators of belief. The results of the empirical findings are analysed under the sub-headings: 'belief and Islamic teachings' and 'belief and the moral values of society'.

I: Commitment

In the process of our social living, most of us make certain social and material investments in conventional behaviour; most of us engage in certain conventional activities. We work fairly hard to have a place for living, to acquire certain goods for our daily use, and to have a bank account for our present and future sense of security. We also spend our time, our energy and often our money on acquiring educational qualifications, getting married, creating a family and developing a good reputation. We engage in these activities because society rewards us for them. Society's rewards include, among other things, social approval, respectable social status and occupational positions. The more we get engaged in these activities and institutional arrangements, the more we become committed to the conventional lines of action - lines of action that society approves. But, it is at this stage that we realise that we are trapped in a 'golden cage' of our own making. We find out that the investments that we have made in conventional behaviour are too great to be jeopardised by engaging in activities that are considered deviant. Society uses these investments as its 'insurance' that we will conform to its norms!

It is clear from what has been said that commitment is the rationalist element of Hirschi's social control theory. That is to say that most individuals are 'reasoning': they calculate the benefits and costs of behaving in alternative ways, deviant and non-deviant; and then choose those they think more beneficial. It is at this point where much common ground can be found between social control and 'Rational Choice' theories, as Hirschi (1986:113) acknowledges: 'Rational choice theory and social control theory share the same image of man, an image rather different from the image of sociological positivism. Rational choice theory and social control theory are therefore the same theory reared in different disciplinary contexts' (see Hirschi 1986:105-28 for details).

Understood as social and material investments in conventional behaviour the relevance of commitment in controlling crime/deviance comes into prominence when one feels temptation to deviate. It is on this occasion that one must first think about the pros and the cons of a deviant behaviour *vis-à-vis* his/her past investments; as Hirschi (1969:20) put it: 'When, or whenever he considers deviant behaviour, he must consider the costs of this deviant behaviour, the risk of losing the investments he has made in conventional behaviour.'

Commitment, however, is not only investment from the past that has consequences for the present. Commitment is equally future-orientated. It has important consequences for one's future: an ambitious student in school has to work hard to get high marks so that he/she is eligible to enter certain fields of higher and professional education; he/she would try to improve his/her CV for future career prospects. In this way, society's promises for future rewards may keep many young ambitious persons committed to the conventional line of action. Even a higher degree of commitment to conventional lines of action may be required for certain individuals, in order to be eligible for important roles in society. For example, less than the socially 'required' degree of commitment to societal values and morality may endanger the future prospects of ambitious politicians: Gary Hart, presidential candidate in America's 1988 general election was forced to resign because he had an 'affair' outside marriage; John Tower, a proposed defence minister for George Bush's first cabinet was disqualified because of his past reputation as a 'womaniser'; Cecil Parkinson had to resign as chairman of the British Conservative Party in 1983 because of his extra marital relations; and Tim Yeo, a Junior Minister in Prime Minister John Major's cabinet had to resign for very similar reasons in 1994.

But involvement in the kind of behaviour that was mentioned in the above examples may not have any (or important) consequences for the future prospects of an ordinary citizen. This fact points to the relativistic nature of the meaning of commitment to members of different social groups. These groups may be divided by age, gender/sex, class, religion, ethnicity and even occupation in a society. This complexity of the meaning of commitment is nicely described by Howard Becker:

> It is important to recognise that many sets of valuable things have value only within subcultural groups in a society and that many side bets producing commitment are made within systems of value of limited provenience. Regional, ethnic and social class subcultures all provide raw materials for side bets peculiar to those sharing in the culture, as do the variants of those related to differing age and sex status. (Becker 1970:39)

However, Becker does not deny that there are certain social values that have general societal currency, as he adds that 'some systems of values permeate an entire society.'

It seems safe to say that the meaning of commitment can be more adequately understood in the narrower social contexts in which it operates. That is, the degree of emphasis on certain sets of values and standards of morality varies in different social groups. But at the same time, there are some sets of values that enjoy almost the same degree of importance and emphasis across social groupings in a society.

Having examined the meaning of commitment from a theoretical point of view, now the question is: how and in what context is juvenile crime/deviance, operationally, explained in terms of commitment, as an element of Hirschi's social control theory?

For the social control theorist the school is an appropriate social context for explaining juvenile crime/deviance, in terms of social investments that adolescents make in conventional behaviour. The extent of adolescents' educational successes and the degree of their higher educational and occupational aspirations are, generally, considered as key variables in explaining juvenile crime/deviance. In the words of Box:

> To the extent that adolescents become involved in school, have plans or desires for future academic success, experience positive present success from teachers' evaluations, then they have *stake in conformity*. Accordingly, school failures or rejects might perceive that they have little to lose by committing delinquent acts because their future looks bleak without academic qualifications, the key to better paid jobs. (emphasis added) (Box 1981:130)

The above description of school as a proper social context for the study of adolescents' social investments in conventional behaviour, generally, applies to the situation of Pakistani adolescents in Pilrig. As mentioned in Chapter II, formal educational qualifications are highly valued in Edinburgh's Pakistani community. Despite a degree of hidden pessimism of their parents (due to racial discrimination in employment as discussed in Chapter I) the Pilrig boys were highly optimistic about the prospects of their British educational qualifications. Many of the boys strongly aspired to become pilots, lawyers and accountants. Some said that they plan to become managers of their own established businesses, after they graduate from university.

More importantly, educational qualification among Edinburgh's Pakistanis is considered a major criterion for a boy's civility and 'culturedness'; and thus a measure of his social status in the community. As discussed in Chapter II, a Pakistani boy's social status is closely linked with the *Izzet* (honour) of his family and kin. His educational qualification adds to and becomes part of the collectively and dearly achieved *Izzet*, of his family and kin-group. Likewise, the extent of a Pakistani boy's family *Izzet* has a strong bearing upon the degree of his social status in the community and on his 'self-perception'.

Taking into account these interlinks between educational qualification and family *Izzet*, the latter was considered as another indicator to 'measure' commitment. Thus in operationalising commitment, 'educational success', 'higher educational aspirations' and 'family *Izzet*' were considered as indicators of the concept.

Commitment and Education

From the control theorist's perspective commitment to education means to have invested something in it: to be regularly present in a certain place for a certain period of time, to follow certain restricting rules and regulations, to learn the lessons as required, to take the trouble of doing homework after school, and finally to get good marks and succeed from grade to grade is an investment - an investment of time, energy and money in education. Thus, the control theorist contends that the greater the adolescent's educational success the less likely he/she is to get involved in delinquent and deviant behaviour. This statement has been supported by numerous empirical studies. These studies found an inverse relationship between educational success in school and lower levels of involvement in delinquency (see Polk and Pink 1971; European Committee on Crime Problems 1972; Hindelang 1973; Kelly and Pink 1973; West and Farrington 1977; Johnson 1979; Rutter and Giller 1983, Sampson and Laub 1993).

Delinquency researchers, by and large, have used young students' marks in school as the main criterion for ascertaining the level of their educational success. This criterion was also used, in the present study, for measuring the level of educational success of the Pilrig boys in their local schools. Thus the boys were asked:'How were your marks in your class (in the local school) last year?' 'Mostly A's', and 'mostly A's and B's', (scored 3 each category)'mostly B's', and 'mostly B's and C's' (scored 2 each category) accounted for 'high' marks. Response categories 'mostly C's', 'mostly C's and D's' (scored 1 each category) and 'mostly D's' (scored 0) accounted for 'low' marks in class.

Table 43 shows a consistent picture of the relationship between the level of marks (in the local school) and the degree of deviation across the continuum from conformists to rebels: among the non-deviant boys, all of the conformists and 90.62 per cent of the accommodationists said that they got high marks. Among the deviant boys, 85.71 per cent of the part-time conformists and only 40 per cent of the rebels said that they got high marks in the local school.

As the table shows, the number of deviant boys who got high marks is not as small as might be expected. But, compared with the number of non-deviant boys who got high marks, the difference is significant. This is revealed by a moderately strong inverse correlation (-.0.34) between the level of marks in school and the level of deviation.

Moreover, the table shows that an overwhelming majority (88.33%) of all the boys - deviant and non-deviant - got high marks in their local schools.

Table 43 - Marks in School and the Level of Deviance

Typology	Marks in the Local School		
	Low	High	Total
	% (No.)	% (No.)	% (No.)
Conformists	0.00 (0)	100.00 (16)	100.00 (16)
Accommodationists	9.37 (3)	90.62 (29)	100.00 (32)
PT Conformists	14.29 (1)	85.71 (6)	100.00 (7)
Rebels	60.00 (3)	40.00 (2)	100.00 (5)
Total	11.67 (7)	88.33 (53)	100.00 (60)

Tau b = -0.34,   Sig. 0.002

This confirms the common view and official reports stating that 'Asian students do well in school'.

Apart from educational success as an indicator of commitment, aspirations for higher/professional education has a central place in its formation. As higher/professional education is often a necessary means to high-status occupational careers, perceiving of and planning for such a career strengthen one's commitment to conventional goals. Indeed, the plans, ambitions and educational success of a striving and goal-orientated youngster are his/her psychological and social investments in the future. Thus, it is the youngster with (anticipated) prospects of a future career who is going to be a loser by committing delinquent acts; not the youngster who sees his future as bleak and therefore has nothing, or little, to lose by getting involved in delinquency. One control theorist contrasted a 'law-abiding adolescent' with a 'hoodlum' this way:

He [the law-abiding adolescent] gets good marks; he moves easily from grade to grade. He has a basis for anticipating that this will continue until he completes college and takes up a business or professional career. If he applied his energies to burglary instead of homework, he would risk not only the ego-flattering rewards currently available but his future prospects as well. (Toby 1957:16)

Based on this line of reasoning, the hypothesis derived from Hirschi's version of social control theory is that: the higher the student's aspirations for higher/professional education, the less likely he is to get involved in delinquency and deviance. To test this hypothesis the Pilrig boys were asked:'What do you think about going to university (or other institutions of higher and professional education) after your secondary school?'..'Response categories 'want and plan to go' and 'want to go, but I do not know if I will' (scored 3 and 2 respectively) accounted for 'high' aspirations; 'want to go but will probably not go' and 'do not want to go and you are sure that you will not go' (scored 1 and 0 respectively) accounted for 'low' aspirations for higher/professional education.

Results of the data in Table 44 show that 93.75 per cent of the conformist and 78.12 per cent of the accommodationist boys expressed high aspirations for higher/professional education. Comparatively much smaller proportions of the part-time conformists (57.14%) and rebels (60%) had high aspirations for higher/professional education. The statistical test of correlation coefficient indicates a moderately strong inverse correlation (-0.26) between aspirations for higher/professional education and deviance.

Furthermore the data show that about four fifths (78.33%) of all the Pakistani boys in the sample expressed high aspirations for higher and professional education. This indicates that despite the generic feelings of pessimism about job prospects for members of ethnic communities in Scotland, young Pakistanis place strong emphasis on gaining higher educational qualifications. A Pakistani father of two Pilrig boys told me that

...in my experience it is very difficult for us to get good government jobs in this country, even if we have good qualifications. Don't you see many doctors and engineers working in shops? But, I don't mean, you know, that my sons should not go to university. Education is always good, always..

This view was widely shared by members of Edinburgh's Pakistani community, including the British-born youngsters (see Chapter I).

In any case, to turn again to the analysis of our hypothesis, it should be mentioned that it is supported by some other studies as well. These empirical studies found that greater delinquency was associated with lower educational/occupational aspirations (see Elliott 1962; Clark and Wenninger 1962; Gold 1963; Short 1964; Hindelang 1973, Johnson 1979).

Table 44 -Aspiration for Higher/Professional Education and the Level of Deviance

| Typology | Aspiration for Higher/Professional Education | | |
	Low	High	Total
	% (No.)	% (No.)	% (No.)
Conformists	6.25 (1)	93.75 (15)	100.00 (16)
Accommodationists	21.87 (7)	78.12 (25)	100.00 (32)
PT Conformists	42.87 (3)	57.14 (4)	100.00 (7)
Rebels	40.00 (2)	60.00 (3)	100.00 (5)
Total	21.67 (13)	78.33 (47)	100.00 (60)

Tau b = -0.26   Sig. 0.01

To sum up briefly, it can be said that the lower their marks in school and the lower their aspirations for higher/professional education, the more deviant the Pilrig boys were. Put differently, educational success (high marks in school) and aspirations for higher education, significantly contributed towards controlling deviance among the Pilrig boys.

For all that, educational success and aspirations for higher/professional education are only two indicators of the concept of commitment. Family *Izzet* (honour), was picked up as the third and most important indicator of commitment in the socio-cultural context of Edinburgh's Pakistani community.

Commitment and Family Izzet(Honour)

As mentioned in the introductory pages of this chapter, educational success and qualifications among Edinburgh's Pakistanis, are not only considered as means for occupational careers, they also add to a Pakistani boy's social status in the community. But, the individual's social status in this community is closely linked with and is part and parcel of one's collectively achieved family *Izzet* or honour. The social status of the individual and the social status of the group (family, kinship unit etc.) of which the individual is a member interact in complex ways: on the one hand, the individual's place in the community is defined by the level of his family *Izzet*. On the other hand individual achievements are as much a personal gain as they are a contribution to the collectively built family *Izzet* (see Chapter II).

Because of the close interaction between individual and collective social investments, the role of family *Izzet* is very significant in the formation of Pakistani youngsters' commitment to conventional lines of action. Thus, by being involved in delinquent/deviant behaviour, a Pakistani boy may not only endanger his own social status, but more importantly he might be inflicting irreparable damage on his family *Izzet*. The fear of harm to family *Izzet* in controlling 'unconventional' behaviour is shown in the following example: A.S. and R.M. are in their very early twenties. They come from Edinburgh's rich and respectable Pakistani families. Once, the two young boys planned to go for a trip to the Scottish highlands with two local girls that they met in an Edinburgh club. The boys had the choice of driving any one of their families' three cars or van. But the problem was how to drive to the highlands with the girls without being seen by anyone from their families and/or from the community. R.M. suggested that they could drive the van and draw its curtains so that no one could see who are inside. A.S. thought about this for a while. Then he said 'but we never draw the curtains of the wagon. If anyone from my family or some friends see that, they will think that something is going on there.' Then he disappointedly suggests to his friend 'I think it is not worth it. If someone from the community sees us with the girls, they will talk to everybody about us; people will say, look K's and A's (mentioning their father's last names) sons took girls to the highlands; *Izzet ki bat hi*, this is a matter of (family) honour.' R.M. quietly agreed and the planned trip was cancelled. The above description, clearly indicates that *Izzet* operates as a powerful agent of social control in Edinburgh's Pakistani community.

As far as the quantification and measurement of family *Izzet* is concerned, there seems to be some methodological problems: firstly, family *Izzet* is a complex variable that is comprised of its various constituent elements i.e. caste, wealth, occupation, generosity and hospitality(see Chapter II). These elements are then interconnected among themselves in intricate ways. This complexity in the nature of family *Izzet* makes it very difficult to be measured in a more or less objective way. Secondly, whatever the quantifiable nature of the elements of family *Izzet*, its meaning for the individual is highly subjective, that is to say, family *Izzet*, on an individual level, is very much one's perception of his/her social standing as it is seen and evaluated by the community (see Chapter II, Section II). Understanding the notion of *Izzet* and its socially constructed meaning in this way, the Pilrig boys were asked: 'How important is the idea of family *Izzet* (honour) to you personally?' Extremely important and fairly important' (scored 3 and 2 respectively) accounted for 'high' importance of family *Izzet*. Response categories 'not very important' and 'unimportant' (scored 1 and 0 respectively) accounted for 'low' importance given to family *Izzet*.

As expected, Table 45 indicates that all of the conformist and 93.75 per cent of the accommodationist boys say that the idea of family *Izzet* is of much importance to them. Interestingly, all of the part-time conformists (a deviant

Table 45 - Importance of Family *Izzet* and the Level of Deviance

| Typology | Importance of Family *Izzet* | | |
	Low	High	Total
	% (No.)	% (No.)	% (No.)
Conformists	00.00 (0)	100.00 (16)	100.00 (16)
Accommodationists	6.25 (2)	93.75 (30)	100.00 (32)
PT Conformists	00.00 (0)	100.00 (7)	100.00 (7)
Rebels	40.00 (2)	60.00 (3)	100.00 (5)
Total	21.67 (4)	78.33 (56)	100.00 (60)

Tau b = -0.23,   Sig. 0.02

category) also say that the idea of family *Izzet* is of much importance to them. This result may seem unexpected. But in fact, it partly explains why the part-time conformist boys hush up their deviation from their community's normative standards and try to present themselves as conforming individuals. Unlike the rebels, the fear of damaging their family *Izzet* is, probably in part, what has held back the part-time conformists from openly declaring their deviance. Deviating from conventional norms and yet unable to break with their family and the community, the part-time conformists seem to be in the difficult situation of 'wanting the best of both worlds'.

As far as the rebels (who openly declare their deviance) are concerned, a comparatively much smaller proportion (60%) of them say that the idea of family *Izzet* is of much importance to them. This result was very much expected. The statistical examination of the data in Table 45 shows a moderately strong inverse relationship (-0.23) between the importance of family *Izzet* and the level of deviance. Moreover, the data confirms that family *Izzet* is a strongly established idea among Pakistanis in Edinburgh: 93.33 per cent of all the boys in the sample say that the idea of family *Izzet* is of much importance to them.

To conclude, it may be said that after operationalising commitment in the socio-cultural context of Edinburgh's Pakistani community, it was found that all of its three indicators were related to conformity and deviance. The statistical tests of correlation coefficient indicated that there were moderately strong relationships between each of educational success, aspiration for higher/professional education, family *Izzet*, and the level of deviance. However, the relationship between educational success and the level of deviance were slightly stronger as compared to those between each of aspiration for higher/professional education, and family *Izzet* and the dependent variable. Thus the findings of the present study confirm the assumption of social control theorists that deviants/delinquents are people with little (or nothing) to lose; because of their low commitment to conventional line of action (educational success etc.) they are, already losers!

II: Involvement

In Hirschi's (1969) formulation of social control theory, involvement is the behavioural counterpart of commitment. Initially, involvement refers to practical engagement in legitimate activities - the extent to which the individual is bound to formal working hours, deadlines, appointments and to informal obligations and responsibilities in the family, community and in the wider society,such that he/she is too busy to deviate, as Hirschi put it:

> a person may be simply too busy doing conventional things to find time to engage in deviant behaviour. The person involved in conventional activities is tied to appointments, deadlines, working hours, plans and the like, so the opportunity to commit deviant acts rarely arises. To the extent that he is engrossed in conventional activities, he cannot even think about deviant acts, let alone act out his inclinations. (Hirschi 1969:22)

It can be clearly noticed that the central point in the above quoted passage is that the engrossment of individual in doing legitimate things is very likely to inhibit his/her deviation. For example, an adolescent who spends much of his/her working day at the school; then does his/her homework at home or in the library; in the afternoon he/she takes part in sports and other (legitimate) recreational activities; after evening meal with the family he/she might have a chat with parents, watch television or read a novel/comic book; and then it is the time for rest/sleep. If the weekend is also occupied by visiting a family-friend/relative, playing a match or watching a film, then this adolescent, apparently, has no (or little) time for deviation/delinquency; he/she is ' kept busy' .

The idea that 'keeping youths busy' (through recreation, work and other conventional activities) inhibits delinquency has been influential in criminological thinking for a long time. For example one prominent criminologist wrote:

> In the general area of juvenile delinquency it is probable that the most significant difference between juveniles who engage in delinquency and those who do not is that the latter are provided abundant opportunities of a conventional type for satisfying their recreational interests while the former lack those opportunities or facilities. (Sutherland 1956:37)

Likewise more practically orientated approaches to the problem of delinquency follow a very similar line of thinking:

> ...if I were forced to select a single approach that struck me in my travels as coming closer to a whole solution [to the problem of delinquency] than any other, it could be summed up in the four letter word (work). (Tunley 1962:258)

In fact, these ideas have been translated into policies in the general area of delinquency-prevention programmes, to varying degrees. Getting youngsters involved in education, employment, recreation and the like has been a central theme behind many projects for the prevention of delinquency, in the UK and in the USA. An example of such projects is the New York-based Mobilisation for Youth Project (MFY). The proposal for this project said: ...in summary, it is our belief that most delinquent behaviour is engendered because opportunities for conformity are limited (MFY proposal, quoted in Downes and Rock 1982:233). Thus, the MFY project was designed to provide jobs, educational opportunities for youngsters and to get them involved in the community organisation (see Hagan 1987:312). Similarly many crime prevention programmes in the UK strongly emphasise providing training and work opportunities for young people.

It appears from what has been said up to this point that involvement in anything conventional or legitimate inhibits delinquency. But does it?

Surprisingly, no, according to Hirschi's data. Hirschi's findings (1969:190, footnote 7) showed that measures of time spent on watching television, reading comic books and playing games were even positively related to the commission of delinquent acts (though the relationships were very weak). These results forced Hirschi to admit the flaws of what he previously hypothesised:

> What tricked us into rather naïve acceptance of a straightforward involvement hypothesis.... is the idea that 'delinquency' is a more or less full-time job, a common enough idea in delinquency theory but highly inappropriate when applied to an explanation of delinquent acts. Most 'conventional' activities are neutral with respect to delinquency; they neither inhibit nor promote it (Hirschi 1969:190)

So, if most conventional activities are neutral with regard to delinquency, then involvement in what kind of conventional activities inhibit it? Hirschi's findings (1969:194-96) showed that time spent on homework and on other school-related activities such as projects, assignments and the like were negatively related to the commission of delinquent acts (these relationships were generally strong). The amount of time spent on homework was, particularly, crucial with respect to inhibiting delinquency. Not only because homework as a relatively 'recurring obligation' restricted boys from engagement in activities that are conducive to delinquency such as 'killing time' with friends, going to pubs and riding around in a car. But, more importantly, spending time on homework and on other school-related activities, Hirschi (1969:192) says '....affects student's performance in school, and may thus operate on delinquency through its effects on attachment and commitment to the school.' That is to say that involvement in those conventional activities is most likely to be inhibitive of delinquency that contribute towards strengthening one's social bond to the conventional order of society - not all conventional activities, that are, merely, time-consuming. I shall refer to involvement, in this new sense, as inhibitive involvement.

For the Pilrig boys there is a wide range of conventional activities that appear to be directly contributing towards the strengthening of their social bond to the normative order of their community. Apart from homework and other school-related activities, the Pilrig Mosque/community centre provides numerous educational, religio-cultural, social and (sometimes) recreational opportunities and events both for its young and older members. These events and opportunities range from gathering for daily (five times), weekly (*Jom'a*), and the annual prayers of the two *Eids* (Islamic festivals) to the collective celebration of many other social and religious occasions. Moreover, sometimes specific recreational events are organised by the Mosque/community centre in city halls in Edinburgh (see Chapter III Section II for details). The degree of social and/or religious obligation of taking part in these events may vary from one to another, but almost none of these events are 'neutral' with respect to deviation from the community's normative order. The spiritual and cultural socialisation of the younger members of the community to its moral and normative order is particularly targeted in these events.

Thus, in the context of the present study the operationalisation of involvement in inhibitive conventional activities was not confined only to time spent on homework, as with Hirschi and many other delinquency researchers. Participation in activities in the Mosque/community centre was considered as the second indicator of involvement in conventional activities that are inhibitive of deviance/delinquency. Moreover, the feeling of 'nothing to do' was added to the two indicators of involvement. Strictly speaking, this variable was not considered as an indicator of involvement in inhibitive conventional activities. Rather the purpose was to know how the abundance of unutilised leisure time for youngsters is related (if at all) to conformity and deviance. So, the data produced by asking this question has no implications for testing the involvement hypothesis and therefore for social control theory. But first, it is important to examine the relationship between the amount of the time spent on school-related activities (homework) and the level of deviance, among the Pilrig boys.

Involvement in School-Related Activities

As mentioned previously, the Pilrig boys attend two schools - the Mosque-school and the local Scottish schools. The Mosque-school, which mainly aims at the religio-cultural socialisation of the younger members of Edinburgh's Pakistani (Muslim) community, has an informal social organisation(see Chapter III). Despite its strict educational/disciplinary regime in the 'classroom' the school does not assign its students any homework. But the local Scottish schools, in general, require homework regularly. Most of the Pilrig boys said that their teacher in the local schools frequently assigned them projects, drawings, solution of problems etc. The boys called all these home-based school assignments homework. Thus, against this background of their school-related activities the Pilrig boys were asked:

'On average, how long each day do you spend on your homework, outside school?' 'More than four hours' and 'about two hours' (scored 3 and 2 respectively) accounted for 'much' time spent on homework, 'less than an hour' and 'you are hardly given any homework' (scored 1 and 0 respectively) accounted for 'little' time spent on homework.

Table 46 indicates that more than two fifths (43.75%) of the conformist and about a third (34.37%) of the accommodationist boys say that they spend much time on their homework, daily. But among the deviant categories of the boys only about one sixth (14.29%) of the part-time conformists and one fifth of the rebels say that they, daily, spend much time on their homework.

Table 46 - Time Spent on Homework and the Level of Deviance

Typology	Little	Much	Total
	Time Spent on Homework		
	% (No.)	% (No.)	% (No.)
Conformists	56.25 (9)	43.75 (7)	100.00 (16)
Accommodationists	65.62 (21)	34.37 (11)	100.00 (32)
PT Conformists	85.71 (6)	14.29 (1)	100.00 (7)
Rebels	80.00 (4)	20.00 (1)	100.00 (5)
Total	66.67 (40)	33.33 (20)	100.00 (60)

Tau b = -0.17, Sig. 0.07 (Recalculated Tau b = -0.22, Sig. 0.03

Despite the fact that the majority of the Pilrig boys in all four categories spend little time on their homework, the number of non-deviant boys who spend much time on their homework is larger as compared with the deviant boys. However, the statistical calculation of these data does not show a strong inverse (-0.17) relationship between the amount of time spent on homework and the level of deviance.

These results not only fail to support the (inhibitive) involvement hypothesis, they also raise an important question: the fact that only one third of all the Pilrig boys (deviants and non-deviants) spend much time on their homework daily casts doubt on the essence of the inhibitive involvement thesis according to which it operates on delinquency through attachment and commitment to school. In other words, according to the hypothesis of inhibitive involvement the boys, who are highly attached and committed to school are also expected to spend much time on their homework. But, the findings of the present study revealed (see Chapter V and the first part of this Chapter) that much larger proportions of the Pilrig boys were highly attached and committed to school compared to those who spent much time on their homework, (one third). The link between time spent on homework and attachment and commitment apparently does not exist.

A most likely answer to resolve this apparent contradiction seems to be hidden in the present data themselves: after a careful look into the data, Table 46 reveals that 13 out of 60 respondents say that they 'were hardly given any homework'. Most of these 13 boys who were in their early years of primary schools did revise their lessons at home under their parents' supervision. But they did not call this 'homework' because it was not assigned by their teachers. Importantly all these boys fall in the non-deviant categories.

This second look into the data indicates that much more than half of the (55%) Pilrig boys spent much time, daily, on their homework. The statistical recalculation of the data shows a strong correlation (-0.22) between the amount of time spent and the level of deviance. This new picture of the data is consistent with the previous findings about the attachment and commitment of the Pilrig boys to school. Thus 'inhibitive' involvement probably does operate through its effects on attachment and commitment to school, as Hirschi suggested.

In any case, so far as it relates to the social world of the Pilrig boys, homework is only one side of the involvement that inhibits delinquency/deviance; its other side is participation in the Mosque/community-related activities.

Involvement in Mosque/Community-Related Activities

It was mentioned in the first part of this chapter (and described in detail in Chapter III, Section II) that the Pilrig Mosque/community centre provides a wide range of educational, social, religio-cultural and recreational activities for its members. It was also mentioned that a special emphasis is placed on the participation of youngsters in these social activities so that they are more 'adequately' socialised to the conventional order of their community - the small-scale society in the wider Scottish/British society. However, since involvement in Islamic educational activities or *Sabaq* (attendance at the Mosque-school) has already been discussed in Chapter V, the data in this section relate to participation in the social, religio-cultural and recreational activities in the Mosque/community centre. Thus, the Pilrig boys were asked: 'Other than for your *Sabaq*, how often do you go to the Mosque (for praying and/or other gatherings)?' 'More than once a week' and 'only for *Jom'a* prayer' (scored 3 and 2 respectively) accounted for 'more frequent' participation in the Mosque/community-related activities. 'only for some major occasions' (such as *Eids*, *Milad-un-Nabi* etc.) and 'I hardly every go' (scored 1 and 0 respectively) accounted for 'less frequent' participation.

According to table 47 about four fifths (81.25%) of the conformist and about two thirds (59.37%) of the accommodationist boys say that they participated in the Mosque/community-related activities, more frequently. Among the deviant categories of the boys only about two fifths (42.86%) of the part-time conformists and no one of the rebels participated, more frequently, in the Mosque/community - related activities.

These results show marked differences between the deviant and the non-deviant categories of the Pilrig boys with respect to the degree of their participation in the activities of the Mosque/community centre. Moreover there is a very strong inverse relationship (-0.37) between the frequency of participation in the activities of the Mosque/community centre and the degree of deviance. Put differently, the more frequently the Pilrig boys participated in their community's social, cultural and religious life, the less they deviated from its norms. These findings strongly support the control theorist's position that involvement in those legitimate activities that strengthen one's social bond to the conventional order of community/society contributes towards controlling deviance/delinquency. Furthermore, the overall picture of Table 47 shows that about two thirds (58.33%) of all the Pilrig boys say that they participate more frequently in the Mosque/community-related activities.

Up to this point, it has been noticed that 55 percent of all the Pilrig boys spend much time on their homework, and almost two thirds (58.33%) of them participated, more frequently, in the social, religious and cultural life of their community. Now, the issue is that those of the Pilrig boys who do not spend much time on their homework and do not participate more frequently in the social, cultural and religious life of their community may not have other 'meaningful' ways to occupy their leisure-time. They may, therefore, look for 'something to do'; 'something exciting' that may include involvement in deviance/delinquency. Hirschi's findings (1969:193) showed that the feeling of 'nothing to do' (or feeling of boredom) were positively related to the commission of delinquent acts. That is to say that the more often the boy in Hirschi's study felt that 'there is nothing to do' the more likely he was to commit delinquent acts. Is this true in the case of the Pilrig boys? To try to answer this question, the Pilrig boys were asked: 'How often do you feel that there is nothing to do?' 'Often' and 'sometimes' (scored 0 and 1 respectively) accounted for a 'more frequent' feeling of 'nothing to do', whereas 'rarely' and 'never' (scored 2 and 3 respective-

Table 47 - Participation in the Mosque/Community-Related Activities and the Level of Deviance

| Typology | Participation in Mosque/Community-related Activities | | |
	Less Frequent	More Frequent	Total
	% (No.)	% (No.)	% (No.)
Conformists	18.75 (3)	81.25 (13)	100.00 (16)
Accommodationists	40.62 (13)	59.37 (19)	100.00
PT Conformists	57.14 (4)	42.86(32) (3)	100.00 (7)
Rebels	100.00 (5)	00.00 (0)	100.00 (5)
Total	41.67 (25)	58.33 (35)	100.00 (60)

Tau b = -0.37   Sig. 0.001

ly) accounted for a 'less frequent' feeling of 'nothing to do'.

Surprisingly, the present data indicate that more boys among the non-deviant categories said that they feel more frequently, that 'there is nothing to do' as compared to the deviant boys. As can be seen in Table 48, more than two thirds (62.25%) of the conformist and a majority (56.25%) of the accommodationist boys say that they more frequently feel that 'there is nothing to do'. Although a majority (57.14%) of the part-time conformists also say that they more frequently feel that there is nothing to do, but only one fifth of the rebels say so. These results do not, apparently, confirm Hirschi's finding (1969:193) according to which the feelings of 'nothing to do' were inversely related to the commission of delinquent acts. Instead, the results of the present data tend to show a positive but weak (0.14) relationship between the frequency of a feeling of 'nothing to do' and the level of deviance.

The findings of the present study tend to suggest that those of the Pilrig boys who do not spend much time on their homework and do not often participate in the community's social, cultural and religious life have alterna-

Table 48 - The Feeling of 'Nothing to do' and the Level of Deviance

Typology	Feeling of 'Nothing to do'		Total
	Less Frequent	More Frequent	
	% (No.)	% (No.)	% (No.)
Conformists	37.50 (6)	62.50 (10)	100.00 (16)
Accommodationists	43.75 (14)	56.25 (18)	100.00 (32)
PT Conformists	42.86 (3)	57.14 (4)	100.00 (7)
Rebels	80.00 (4)	20.00 (1)	100.00 (5)
Total	45.00 (27)	55.00 (33)	100.00 (60)

Tau b = 0.14,   Sig. 0.12

tive ways of occupying their leisure-time. But these alternative ways may include involvement in 'non-legitimate' activities. In fact, some of the deviant boys, particularly the rebels, spent their leisure time in night clubs and *Bhangras,* as part-time workers. These boys obviously have 'something to do' and they might be 'having a good time'. But, working in a night club and *Bhangra* for a member of Edinburgh's Pakistani community is considered as an undesirable and even 'deviant' activity.

To conclude, the findings of the present study generally support the control theorist's assumption that involvement in legitimate activities (those that strengthens one's social bond to the conventional order) contribute towards controlling deviance/delinquency. Operationalised in the context of Edinburgh's Pakistani community, both of the two indicators of (inhibitive) involvement - time spent on homework and participation in the activities of the Mosque/community centre were inversely related to the level of deviance. However, the relationship between the latter variable to the level of deviance is stronger than that of the former.

Furthermore, the present findings show that 55 percent of all the Pilrig boys spent much time daily on their homework, whereas 58.33 percent of them participated more frequently in the activities of the Mosque/community centre.

Surprisingly, the present findings did not support Hirschi's findings of a negative relationship between the feeling of 'nothing to do' (feeling of boredom) and the commission of delinquent acts. Interpreting this discrepancy between the present and Hirschi's findings, it was suggested that some of the deviant Pilrig boys who did not occupy their leisure time with culturally defined 'meaningful' ways (homework and participation in the activities of the Mosque/community centre) had alternative ways of 'something to do'. These alternative ways tended to be defined as 'deviant' on the community's standards.

III: Belief

The fourth and the last element of social bond in Hirschi's (1969) social control theory is belief. It refers to an individual's sense of the 'moral validity' or 'legitimacy' of the conventional norms and rules of society - the extent to which individuals feel moral obligation to obey the rules of society.

Individuals may obey society's norms and rules out of their religious convictions - because these rules/norms originate from divine teachings and orders. Or alternatively, they may obey the rules and norms of society because doing so is 'right', 'fair' and 'legitimate'. Whatever the source of individuals' belief - religious, secular or both, the main point is about the extent to which they accept the idea that the rules of society should be obeyed.

The phrase 'the rules of society' implies that the control theorist assumes the existence of a common value system in society. Indeed, this is one of the main assumptions on which control theory is based. The control theorist assumes that almost all members of a society share at least some of the fundamental societal values that are central to the maintenance of social order and for the mere survival of the society. It is the acceptance of this shared morality by members of a society that is termed 'belief' in Hirschi's version of social control theory. However, the control theorist's assumption about the existence of a common value system, or a shared normative order in society raises an important question when he proceeds to explain deviation from societal norms/rules: if almost all members of society - the law-abiding and the offender - believe that violating society's rules is wrong, then how come that one violates them and the other does not?

More than a decade before the emergence of the presently dominant version of social control theory, Sykes and Matza, who also assume the existence of a degree of shared morality in a society (see for the details of this point, Chan 1981:120 and Vold and Bernard 1986:242) attempted to answer this question. The delinquent while believing in the conventional rules of society, Sykes and Matza (1957:464-70) say, neutralises 'the internal and external demands for conformity'. Through the 'techniques of neutralisa-tion' (denial of responsibility, denial of injury, denial of victim, the con-demnation of accusers, and appeal to higher loyalties) he/she creates a 'moral vacuum' - a situational and temporary freedom from moral obstacles to the violation of rules.

However, Hirschi and the proponents of his version of social control the-ory are not very impressed by this answer. Their complaint is that the answer contains a motivational element which comes particularly to the sur-face when this issue is later dealt with by Matza. In his *Delinquency and Drift*, Matza (1964) says that the mood of 'desperation' and the 'will to delinquency' that motivate the potential delinquent to 'make things happen' occur *after* the 'moral vacuum' has been created. In other words Matza con-tends that a special motivational force pushes the potential delinquent into delinquency. But in the logic of control theory, no special motivation is needed for the potential delinquent in order to break the rules. A better answer, and one consistent with the implicit logic of control theory, to the question in point, therefore, is that:

> ...there is variation in the extent to which people believe they should obey the rules of society and, furthermore, that the less a person believes he should obey the rules, the more likely he is to violate them. (Hirschi 1969:26)

Thus, Hirschi argues that neutralisation is unnecessary, because weak belief (or the absence of belief) means that neutralisation has already occurred. In fact, despite these apparently different arguments there is not an essential difference in Hirschi's and Sykes and Matza's positions. Weak belief and temporarily neutralised belief can both result in 'moral holidays' - situa-tional violation of rules without completely abandoning the belief. However, the strength of Hirschi's position is that it is more consistent with the basic assumptions of control theory with which Sykes and Matza and Matza's later works (1964) are also identified.

To leave theoretical issues aside, researchers have found it very difficult to directly measure individuals' inner religious and moral beliefs. Nevertheless, they have attempted to measure individuals' attitudes towards certain religious and moral issues which are considered as indicators of their beliefs. There have been many empirical studies that have explored the rela-tionship between religious and/or moral beliefs (or attitudes) and delin-quency. For example some studies found that rejection of religious values was positively related to delinquency (Clayton 1969; Burket and White 1974; Cochran and Akers 1989). Other studies reported that acceptance of moral values and respect for law and the police were inversely related to delinquency (Hirschi and Stark 1969; Waldo and Hall 1970; and Burket and White 1974). Some other studies focused on exploring the relationship between belief and obeying rules. For example a more recent empirical study has reached the following conclusion:

> People obey the law because they believe that it is proper to do so...their responsiveness leads people to evaluate laws and the decisions of legal authorities in normative terms, *obeying the law if it is legitimate and moral* and accepting decisions if they are fairly arrived at. (emphasis added) (Tyler 1990:178)

More common-sense examples of the connectedness between the moral validity and legitimacy of rules/norms and obeying them can be found on a broader societal level. One such example can be the implementation of the Poll Tax (community charge) in Scotland (during the years 1989-92). About 50 percent of the people in Scotland did not obey the rules about paying the Poll Tax - why? Of course, it is naïve to try to find only one straightforward answer to such a complex question with many social and political dimensions. Nevertheless there is much reason to say that a major factor in the disobedience over the Poll Tax regulation was due to its perceived lack of moral validity and legitimacy. This was for, at least, two major reasons

First, how can a 'welfare state' require those citizens (and residents) of the country who live on the poverty line to pay a tax that they cannot afford to pay? The state requires both the rich and the poor to pay the Poll Tax (though a reduced amount of tax for the poor). People who cannot afford to pay the Poll Tax are very likely to find these rules unfair and therefore will not feel a moral obligation to obey them.

Secondly, the legislation about the Poll Tax did not reflect the social and political consensus that is supposed to constitute the basis of the legitimacy of rules in a democratic society. Apart from the fact that the Conservative government in the UK did not represent the majority of the people in Scotland, it is an open secret that the government itself did not reach a consensus on the existing form of the legislation about the Poll Tax. (The dramatic downfall of Mrs Thatcher is widely attributed to her insistence on making this unpopular decision, and hence, a political mistake.) Therefore, the rules about the Poll Tax did not enjoy a full legitimacy, not only for the Scots, but also for many citizens of the UK. The massive and violent anti-Poll Tax rallies in London and Glasgow were strong social indicators of this. More interestingly, Mr T. Sheridan the leader of the anti-Poll Tax movement in Scotland was elected as a councillor while still in prison for not paying the poll tax!

As this is not the place to go into further details of the relationships between belief and its broader socio-legal and political dimensions, it is important to focus now on the analysis of the normative context of belief in Edinburgh's Pakistani community.

The Normative Context of Belief

Before looking at the relationship between belief and the level of deviance in the Pilrig sample of the 60 Muslim Pakistani boys, it is important, first, to answer the question: belief in what? - in the norms/rules of the Muslim Pakistani community or in those of the wider Scottish/British society?

There does not seem to be an either/or answer to this question as may be thought. It is true as has been argued in Chapter I that Edinburgh's Pakistani community is, in many respects, a small-scale society within the larger Scottish/British society. With the passage of time the community has developed its own unique social, cultural, religious, quasi-political, economic and recreational institutions that meet the various needs of members of the community in a more or less sustained maaner. As a Muslim community in a non-Muslim society the religious institution, the Mosque, has a dominant role in the general life of the community. Islamic teachings generally guide the social institutional life of the community and are supposed to be followed by individual members of the community. This has brought about a broad normative consensus and shared morality in the community. That is to say that Islamic teachings, generally, constitute the basis of 'rights' and 'wrongs' in the community (see Chapter III).

Nevertheless, what has been said neither means that this community is a holy community of God's men and women, nor does it mean that most of its 'wrongs' and 'rights' essentially differ from the norms and values of the wider Scottish/British society. This is particularly true with regard to those norms and values that are relevant to the Scottish/British criminal law. The present discussion is not the place to go into the details of this issue. It may be sufficient to say that, on the one hand theft, murder, child-abuse and many other crimes are considered serious 'wrongs', in the community, as they are so considered in the wider society. On the other hand honesty, good-neighbourliness, helping the poor, the elderly and the disabled - positively sanctioned in the Scottish/British society - are among the 'rights' of Edinburgh's Pakistani community. There are other issues on which the community takes a compromising stand: Neither is it easy to find a man with more than one wife in the community; nor is a Pakistani user of alcohol punished by lashes, nor are adulterers stoned to death (though these behaviours are strongly disapproved of as mentioned in Chapter III and IV).

In sum the Edinburgh Pakistani community, on the one hand, has cultural and religious values that are specific to it. On the other hand the community shares most of the values of the larger Scottish/British society, particularly those relevant to the criminal law. Thus a fruitful enquiry into the relationship between belief and conformity and deviance in Edinburgh's Pakistani community must take into account this complex nature of normative order of the community.

Operationalising belief in this multi-dimensional social and normative context will have to, first of all, take into consideration the Islamic dimension. Thus, the extent to which 'following Islamic teaching' was considered as the first indicator of belief in the moral validity of rules/norms. 'Honesty with all people' was selected as the second indicator of belief in the moral validity of rules/norms. 'Honesty with all people' is not only one of the core Islamic values, it is also central to the Christian values and to secular morality. Finally 'feelings of guilt' - the social-psychological manifestation of the presence of belief - after breaking rules was considered as the third indicator of belief in the moral validity of rules/norms. Let us first examine the relationship between the extent of belief in Islamic teachings and the level of deviance.

Belief and Islamic Teachings

As mentioned earlier, Islamic teachings constitute the basis of normative order in Edinburgh's Pakistani community. Islamic teachings cover a wide range of issues related to 'rights' and 'wrongs' that come under the general categories of *Awamir* and *Nawahi* (obligations and prohibitions) on both private/individual and on public/social levels. On the private/individual level these teachings include matters ranging from basic Islamic virtues such as generosity, modesty, chastity, perseverance, courage, manners in clothing, greetings, talking, walking, to drinking and eating. On the social and broader public level Islamic teachings have specific sets of rules for social institutional life in the spheres of family, government, economy and even on issues related to interfaith and international relations.

However, there exists a more or less clear-cut dichotomy of Islamic teachings according to the degree of their obligation (compulsoriness) to the Muslim believer. *Fardz* and *Wajib* include duties of the highest degree of obligation. *Sunnah* are in the second and *Mustahab* are in the third and the lowest degree of obligation. There are other local/cultural customs and rituals which are also mixed (and sometimes confused) with Islamic teachings and possess a degree of obligation. All these four levels of Islamic teachings involve duties or obligations. There are others that involve prohibitions. But since omission of many of the obligations naturally become and fall into one or another level of prohibition, it seems sufficient to mention the obligatory Islamic teachings for the present purpose.

Now, the crucial question for Edinburgh's Muslims and probably for

Muslims throughout Britain is this: how much of the Islamic teachings can Muslims afford to follow in this country? Answers of different Muslim individuals and groups vary according to the extent they find Islamic teachings relevant to their daily lives and therefore, according to their interpretation of them. This is, probably, a major reason for the existence of extremist, moderate, liberal/secular tendencies in the following of Islamic teaching in the UK. It was this socio-religious context in which the Pilrig boys were asked: 'How much of the Islamic teachings do you think we should follow in our daily lives in this country?' 'All Islamic teachings from A to Z (*Fardz, Wajib, Sunnah* and *Mustahab*)' and 'the major Islamic teachings (*Fardz* and *Wajib*)' (scored 3 and 2 respectively) accounted for a 'greater extent' of following the Islamic teachings. 'Only those of the Islamic teachings that involve rituals and ceremonies (which are part of our cultural identity such as ceremonies of *Eids*, marriage, funeral, etc.)'. and 'it is no longer necessary for us to follow Islamic teachings' (scored 1 and 0 respectively) accounted for a 'lesser extent' of following the Islamic teachings.

Table 49 indicates that all the conformists and 96.87 percent of the accommodationist boys say that we (Muslims in Edinburgh) should follow Islamic teaching to a greater extent, in our daily lives. However, among the deviant boys, less than three fifths (57.14%) of the part-time conformists and only one fifth of the rebels say that we should follow Islamic teachings to a greater extent, in our daily lives. The statistical test of the data shows that there is a very strong inverse relationship (-0.51) between the extent to follow Islamic teachings and the level of deviance in the Pilrig sample. These results strongly support the control theorist's assumption that the less one believes in the rules/norms of society, the more likely he/she is to violate them.

Moreover, an overwhelming majority (86.67%) of the Pilrig boys say that we (Muslims in Edinburgh) should follow Islamic teachings to a greater extent in our daily lives. Only 13.33 percent of the boys say that we should follow Islamic teachings to a lesser extent. More importantly according to the present data none of the Pilrig boys say that 'it is no longer necessary for us to follow Islamic teachings'. Nevertheless, significant proportions among the deviant boys are in favour of following the cultural/ceremonial aspect of Islamic teachings (not those aspects that relate to prohibitions and obligations); 42.86 percent of the part-time conformists and 80 percent of the rebels say that we should follow 'only those of the Islamic teachings that involve rituals and ceremonies'.

This observation, furthermore, reveals that even the deviant boys, particularly the rebels see at least some aspects of Islamic teachings as relevant to the social and cultural life of their community. The deviant boys seem to recognise that the ceremonial aspects of Islam define and draw the social boundaries of Edinburgh's Pakistani community – a small-scale 'closed'

Table 49 - The Extent of Following Islamic Teaching and the Level of Deviance

Typology	The Extent of Following Islamic Teachings		Total
	Lesser Extent	Greater Extent	
	% (No.)	% (No.)	% (No.)
Conformists	00.00 (0)	100.00 (16)	100.00 (16)
Accommodationists	3.12 (1)	96.87 (31)	100.00 (32)
PT Conformists	42.86 (3)	57.14 (4)	100.00 (7)
Rebels	80.00 (4)	20.00 (1)	100.00 (5)
Total	13.33 (8)	86.67 (52)	100.00 (60)

Tau b = -0.51,   Sig. 0.000

society within the wider society. This would seem to indicate that, despite their deviation from the community's fundamental moral values, they feel the need for a kind of cultural/social belonging to the Pakistani community in Edinburgh. At this point it seems appropriate to expand the present analysis, and have a look at the relationship between belief in the general moral values of society and deviance in the Pilrig sample.

Belief and the Moral Values of the Wider Society

It was mentioned earlier that belief in the context of social control theory does not have to have its source in religious teachings and convictions. Belief in society's rules/norms may as often originate from religious convictions as from secular moral values or from both. Thus, the important point in this respect is the extent of individuals' moral obligation to abide by certain accepted sets of norms and values of society, whatever the source of the obligation may be. For example a devout believer in Christian, Islamic or Jewish teachings may not steal because stealing is prohibited by God.

Similarly a non-religious member of society may refrain from stealing but for a different reason: it is 'wrong' to steal - it is against the accepted social and moral values of society, and against its laws.

One of the general moral and social values that seems to be shared by followers of different religions and by non-religious members of British society is 'honesty with all people'. Taking into account this general social/moral context of British society, the British-born Pakistani boys in Pilrig were asked: 'To what extent do you agree with the statement: 'One must be honest with all people?' 'Agree strongly' and 'agree' (score 3 and 2 respectively) accounted for a 'greater extent' of agreement with the statement. . Response categories 'disagree' and 'strongly disagree' (scored 1 and 0 respectively) accounted for a 'lesser extent' of agreement with the statement.

Interestingly enough, Table 50 indicates that exactly the same proportion of the conformist and accommodationists boys (100% and 96.87% respectively) who said that we should follow Islamic teachings to a greater extent also say that they agree with 'one must always be honest with all people' to a greater extent. Likewise, exactly the same (comparatively smaller) proportions of the part-time conformists and rebels (57.14% and 20% respectively) who said that they should obey Islamic teachings to a greater extent also say that they agree with the statement 'one must be always honest with all people' to a greater extent.

The perfect consistency between the two sets of data (Table 49 and Table 50) may indicate that positive attitudes toward or/and belief in religious teachings positively influence one's attitudes toward general moral values. This seems to be more likely to occur when religious teachings are in agreement with the generally accepted societal values, as in the present case.

The existence of a very strong inverse relationship (-0.51) between the extent of agreement with 'one must be honest with all people' and the level of deviance strongly support the control theorist's assumption the less one believes that he/she should obey the rules/norms of society, the more likely he/she is to violate them.

As mentioned earlier because of the difficulty (even impossibility) of direct measurement of individuals' inner beliefs in religious or/and moral values, researchers in this area have attempted to measure individuals' attitudes towards these issues. The evaluation and measurement of individuals' attitudes have been considered as indications of individuals' inner orientations and beliefs in religious and moral values. Following this research pattern, the data that have been analysed up to this point were based on questions that were designed to measure attitudes towards Islamic teaching and the moral values of British society. However, the next question is designed to attempt to measure the extent of the presence or absence of belief in an

Table 50 - The Extent of Agreement with 'One must be honest with all people' and the Level of Deviance

Typology	Extent of Agreement		Total
	Lesser Extent	Greater Extent	
	% (No.)	% (No.)	% (No.)
Conformists	00.00 (0)	100.00 (16)	100.00 (16)
Accommodationists	3.12 (1)	96.87 (31)	100.00 (32)
PT Conformists	42.86 (3)	57.14 (4)	100.00 (7)
Rebels	80.00 (4)	20.00 (1)	100.00 5)
Total	13.33 (8)	86.67 (52)	100.00 (60)

Tau b = 0.5l   Sig. 0.000

indirect way – the extent to which individuals feel guilty after behaving dishonestly with people. Thus, the Pilrig boys were asked: 'How guilty do you feel when you do something dishonest, even to a stranger?' 'Extremely guilty' and 'quite guilty' (scored 3 and 2) accounted for a greater feeling of guilt, whereas 'not very guilty' and 'not guilty at all' (scored 1 and 0) accounted for little feeling of guilt.

According to Table 51 the overwhelming majority of the conformist and the accommodationist boys (93.75% and 90.62%, respectively) said that they feel guilty after doing something dishonest to people. Among the deviant categories of the boys, comparatively smaller proportions of the part-time conformists and the rebels (44.86% and 60%, respectively) say that they feel guilty after behaving dishonestly. The comparison of the above results to those in Tables 49 and 50 reveals that the more positive the attitudes of the Pilrig boys toward Islamic teachings and toward the general moral values of British society, the more guilty they feel after doing some dishonesty to other people. This indicates that the attitudes of the Pilrig boys toward Islamic teachings and to the moral values of British society repre-

Table 51 - Feelings of Guilt and the Level of Deviance

Typology	Feeling of Guilt		Total
	Little	Much	
	% (No.)	% (No.)	% (No.)
Conformists	6.25 (1)	100.00 (15)	100.00 (16)
Accommodationists	9.37 (3)	90.62 (29)	100.00 (32)
PT Conformists	57.14 (4)	42.86 (3)	100.00 (7)
Rebels	40.00 (2)	60.00 (3)	100.00 (5)
Total	16.67 (10)	83.33 (50)	100.00 (60)

Tau b = -0.33   Sig. 0.003

sent their beliefs in these teachings and values. This may be because feelings of guilt normally result after the 'betrayal' of pre-existing internalised beliefs and moral principles.

To sum up, it may be said that after operationalising belief in the context of the multi-dimensional normative order of Edinburgh's Pakistani community, it was found: the less positive the Pilrig boys' attitudes towards (or the less they believed in) Islamic teachings and the moral principle of 'honesty with all people', the more they deviated from the norms of their community. Likewise, the less these boys felt guilty after doing something dishonest to people, the more deviant they were. All of the three independent variables - 'the extent to which Islamic teachings are followed'; the extent of agreement with 'one must by honest with all people'; and the 'feeling of guilt' after doing some dishonesty to people - were very strongly related to the level of deviance (though the correlation between last indicator of belief and deviance was moderately strong). These results strongly support the assumption of Hirschi's control theory that the less a person believes he should obey the rules/norms of society, the more likely he is to violate them.

Moreover the findings showed that 86.67 percent of all the Pilrig boys said that 'we (Muslims in Edinburgh) follow Islamic teachings to a greater extent', whereas only 13.33 percent said that 'Islamic teachings should be followed to a lesser extent, by us'. But no one said that 'it is no longer necessary for us to follow Islamic teachings'. Likewise, 86.67 percent of all the Pilrig boys agreed with 'one must be honest with all people', whereas, only 13.33 percent agreed with the statement to a lesser extent. Finally, 83.33 percent of these boys said that they felt guilty after doing something dishonest to people. However 16.67 percent of the boys said that they felt less guilty after behaving dishonestly with people.

Summaries and Conclusions

This book began with a general examination of the historical development of the Pakistani community in Scotland and in Edinburgh. Within a broad historical and social/structural context, the examination more specifically focused on the analysis of the social organisation of Edinburgh's Pakistani community, its social and moral order, the ways members related to it, conformed to or deviated from its demands. In sociological terms the analysis centred on two fundamental aspects of the social organisation of the community – social control and social deviance. Although social control and deviance constitute two separate parts of the book, the two are closely interlinked in the present analysis: On the one hand, the various agencies of social control draw the boundaries of the moral and social order of the community; they define what is deviance and how to respond to it. On the other hand, deviance alerts the agencies of social control to the threats it poses to the existing moral and social order, and activates its control mechanisms in response. This dialectic between social control and deviance often leads to the redefinition of the latter, which in turn stimulates social change in the community.

One of the central arguments, particularly in the first part of the thesis, is related to the dialectic of the interaction between the Scottish Pakistani population and the wider Scottish society – to the reaction of the wider society to the presence of the South Asian migrants and the latter's social responses. It has been argued that the large-scale migration of people from the Indian sub-continent and the existing racial prejudice and stereotypes about them are a consequence of the long British colonial rule over what are now Pakistan, Bangladesh and India. Racial stereotypes about the culture and character of these 'coloured' British colonial subjects were established in Scotland through the stories of the returning Scottish soldiers, missionaries, the writing of colonial administrators, and even through school and children's books. The arrival of the early migrants to Scotland from the Indian sub-continent who were destitute and poor colonial subjects, further confirmed the already established racial stereotypes and prejudice about them. Thus, the general reaction to the presence of these colonial migrants in Scotland was one of rejection. This was further translated into exclusionary practices against them. The historical evidence shows that these South-Asian migrants were not only excluded from the social, cultural and political institutional life of the wider society, but they were also subject to a great deal of racial violence and harassment.

Despite successive anti-discriminatory legislation, anti-racist social and political movements, and progressive-liberal writings, racial discrimination and violence against these 'coloured' migrants have not only continued, but have increased. More importantly recent empirical evidence shows that Pakistanis are more subject to racial violence than other minority groups in Britain. These figures, moreover, show that members of Britain's ethnic minority groups, particularly Pakistanis and Bangladeshis, have been excluded from those important spheres of social life that constitute the basic elements of citizenship in a democratic welfare society. These include the spheres of employment, housing, sports and social cultural entertainment, and political institutional life of the wider society. Such exclusionary practices and discrimination against Scotland's Pakistani population have had important social implications for them: a sense of rejection, of non-citizenship and consequent feeling of insecurity. The Pakistani population, in turn responded to their exclusion and its social and psychological consequences by turning into themselves, and to their own traditional cultural, social and human resources. They have been left with no choice but to sustain their own mini-economic, cultural, and political institutions that have gradually separated them from the wider society, and continue to do so.

There is much empirical evidence showing strong relationships between exclusionary practices against Britain/Scotland's Pakistani population in the labour market and their self-employment, which is gradually forcing Pakistanis to form small communities of shopkeepers. The evidence further shows a close connection between discrimination against Pakistanis in housing and their clustering in certain areas of many cities in Britain, although this is less observable in Edinburgh. Nevertheless, there is some recent evidence showing that Pakistanis in Edinburgh increasingly tend to live close to each other in certain areas of the city. Similarly exclusionary practices against young Pakistanis in sports and in places of social/cultural entertainment play a determining role in the emergence of independent Pakistani sports clubs and teams and in the development of *Bhangras* (the Pakistani's equivalent of Western disco clubs). More importantly the exclusion of Britain's Pakistani population from the political and institutional life of the wider society has created a new political consciousness among them; it has created the need for political and social action, demanding their legal, social and political rights as equal citizens of the country. The campaign for Muslim schools to be given grant-aided status (like Catholic and Jewish schools) and for Islam to be covered by the Blasphemy Law are cases in point. The creation of 'The Muslim Parliament of Great Britain' is a response by Pakistani Muslims to their political exclusion.

All this points to a strong reactive element in the making of a 'closed' Pakistani community in Edinburgh and in Scotland - a community which draws increasingly sharper social boundaries between itself and the wider society; a community whose members search for social belonging, cultural identity and inclusion within these social and cultural boundaries. Empirical evidence from Edinburgh's Pakistani community shows that the search for social belonging and identity is particularly strong among the second-generation, British-born Pakistanis who encounter racial discrimination more directly and experience exclusionary practices more frequently than their parents. The data presented in Chapter IV shows that the second-generation Pakistanis identify more strongly with their 'Pakistaniness' than with their 'Britishness'. However, the same data also show that the second generation, who, by and large, take pride in their ethnicity, interpret the religious and cultural values of their community in a modern and relatively secular way. They generally place stronger emphasis on those aspects of the social order of their community that are deemed essential to the preservation of their religious and cultural identity. The second generation Pakistanis who will succeed their fathers as leaders and members of the Pakistani community favour a cohesive and distinctively Pakistani community to which they can belong and identify with as Muslims and Pakistanis; but at the same time, they favour a community that is modern and based on a more flexible version of religious and cultural values.

I will discuss the ways that the British-born young Pakistanis relate to the existing moral and social order of Edinburgh's Pakistani community later. First it is important to look at one of the central themes of the book - the social order of the Edinburgh Pakistani community and its maintenance (social control). The present study reveals that four fundamental social institutions constitute the social and moral order of the community. They at the same time operate as agencies of social control within the community. These four social institutions are the family, the *Biraderi* (social network of kinship/friendship relationship), the Mosque and the Pakistan Association, Edinburgh and the East of Scotland (P.A.E.E.S.).

The Pakistani family in Edinburgh is the most important agency of social control in the community. The present study reveals that the Pakistani family in Edinburgh continues to be an extended/joint social unit. However, it is a 'modified' extended/joint family that has adapted itself to the new circumstances after migration to Scotland. Although members rarely live together under one roof or in adjacent houses/flats, the Pakistani family in Edinburgh is often a branch of an extended family in Scotland, England and/or in Pakistan. It has largely preserved and reinforced its traditional structure and functions.

The most important features of the British Pakistani family are socialisation of the British-born young Pakistanis and 'parental authority' that operate as important mechanisms of social control. Amid pressures from the dominant culture of wider society, the socialisation of the British-born children to Islamic/Pakistani values plays an important role in their social bonding to the Pakistani community's moral and social order. In order to counteract encroachments of the wider society's values, the socialisation process of the British-born Pakistani children is extended to the Mosque-school where they are taught the fundamentals of the Islamic belief system and are trained for active participation in the cultural and religious life of the community. In some cases these children are sent to Pakistan for their cultural and religious socialisation. The basic socialisation process is further backed up by 'parental authority'; it is the 'legitimate' right of parents to exercise (external) control over their children so that they conform to the community's norms. Parents' main sources of authority are cultural and religious values and their control over the family's property/business. Both the socialisation process and parental authority, as mechanisms of social control play an important role in the social bonding of the young Pakistanis to the community, and in regulating their behaviour according to its norms. Thus, it is concluded the Pakistani family in Edinburgh operates as a relatively powerful agency of social control of the community.

The second important agency of social control in Edinburgh's Pakistani community is the *Biraderi* . The 'effective' *Biraderi* in the present study is defined as a social institution where members have close and complex reciprocal relationships in a kinship/friendship framework. The most important aspect of the 'effective' *Biraderi* is *Lina Dina* (Taking and Giving). *Lina Dina,* or a form of institutionalised reciprocity constitutes the machinery of this social institution. The continuous (sometimes even inherited) taking and giving of gifts, favours and services strongly binds the donor(s) and the recipient(s) through lasting moral and social obligations to each other. The act and ceremony of gift-giving that often takes place during a public gathering (mainly weddings) is not only a communication between the donor(s) and the recipient(s), but also between them and onlookers within their *Biraderi* between their own *Biraderi* and a rival *Biraderi* and those in the apparently 'passive' community. By giving away a specific gift (often in the context of pre-existing *Lina Dina*), the donor(s) not only sends a specific message - respect, disrespect, solidarity and continuation of *Lina Dina* or stopping it - to the recipient(s) – but they also send the same messages to members of their own *Biraderi*, to those in rival *Biraderis* and to the general community. Continuous *Lina Dina* of gifts, favours and services create mutual social and moral obligations and interdependence among members of the *Biraderis* and strongly bond them to each other. This in turn, results in a communitarian structure of the *Biraderi* where *Izzet* and *Bizati* (Honour and Dishonour) operate as effective mechanisms of social control.

Izzet is a profoundly established notion in Edinburgh's Pakistani community. An individual or a family's *Izzet* is a complex package of various elements that are intricately interwoven. The most important of these elements among Edinburgh's Pakistanis are: belonging to high caste; a large number of men in the family (or extended family); social/political influence in

Britain and/or in Pakistan; high professional and educational qualifications; generosity; a reputation for honesty; religiosity; and wealth. But the mere objective existence of these elements may not necessarily constitute *Izzet*. The community's evaluation of the claimants of *Izzet* against these closely interlinked elements is a necessary condition. Thus, *Izzet* in the present study is defined as an individual/group's perception of its social standing as it is seen and evaluated by the community.

Izzet is important for Edinburgh's Pakistanis, because it qualifies individuals and families for equal membership of the community – a respectable Muslim and Pakistani. Members who have 'less' *Izzet* are treated as less than equal members of the community. Less than a certain degree of *Izzet* or its loss leads to *Bizati* (Dishonour). *Bizati* brings disgrace to individuals and families. The *Bizat* (Honourless) is looked down on; people avoid association with him/her and do not trust him/her in business and other transactions; he/she loses the chance of marriage with respectable members of the *Biraderi*. These social sanctions against the *Bizat* often extend and apply to his/her close kin and friends too. In extreme cases, the unrepentant and indifferent *Bizat* is labelled as *Bisharm Adami* (shameless person). The *Bisharm Adami* is practically excluded from the community. Because he/she is socially and culturally excluded from the community, it is difficult to find any *Bisharm Adami* in person within the community. But he/she profoundly exists in the collective memory of the community as an extreme example of *Bizati*. Since violation of the community's norms leads to the decrease or loss of *Izzet;* and since its lack disqualifies individuals and families from respectable and equal membership of the community, *Izzet* (and *Bizati)* operates as a powerful mechanism of social control in this particular community.

The bonding processes of members of Edinburgh's Pakistani community into its social and moral order within the family and the *Biraderi* are further extended to and find practical expression in, the collective activities and social arrangements in the Mosque and in the Pakistan Association, Edinburgh and East of Scotland (P.A.E.E.S.). The Mosque not only functions as a place for individual and collective worship and the celebration of religious and cultural occasions, but also caters for the religious education of the British-born Pakistani children. The regular classes of Islamic teachings, or *Sabaq*, are mainly the continuation of the socialisation process of these children to the Islamic belief system, and to Islamic morality. However, in the *Sabaq*-class in the Mosque strong emphasis is placed on the practical aspects of Islamic education - the young Pakistani boys are taught to read (and to some extent to write) Arabic and Urdu scripts; and are required to memorise these sections from the Holy *Quran* that are essential for performing prayers. This socialisation process enables the British-born young Pakistanis to participate practically in complex rituals and collectively performed worship. It integrates them into the social and religious world of the adults, and prepares them for respectable membership of the Pakistani and Muslim community in Edinburgh and in Scotland. Hence, it is not surprising that a very large number of young Pakistanis participate in the most important congregational worship of *Jom'a* (Friday) and *Eid-al-Fiter* (that marks the first non-fasting day at the end of *Ramadan*).

The *Jom'a* congregational worship is one of the most important regular religious and social events. It is a weekly 'compulsory' worship (from the Islamic point of view) which includes sermons, collectively performed, ritualistic prayer and extended preaching about *Awamir* and *Nawahhi* (Islamic obligations and prohibitions). The *Jom'a* prayer may be the fulfilment of a religious obligation and a sacred religious occasion for seeking forgiveness for 'sins' from the individual worshipper's point of view; or it may be an occasion to preach about Islamic morality and remind the faithful of the *Awamir* and *Nawahi*, the life after life, the Heaven and Hell from the *Hafiz Sahib*'s perspective. But from the sociologist's point of view the most important function of the *Jom'a* congregational worship is profoundly social: the highly organised assembly of the faithful in straight rows facing *Ka'aba* (the Holy House in Mecca), the collective and simultaneously performed rituals of *rok'o* (bowing) and *sajda* (putting the fore-heads to the ground), the 'USs' and 'WEs' of the sermons, the wordings of the preaching, and the collective seeking of forgiveness from *Allah* all point to the collective expression of shared beliefs and deeply held sentiments. It is a collective expression of a sense of community and of shared social bonds to a moral and social order. The warm embracings and shaking of hands in the end of the *Jom'a* worship further confirm this. All this, in turn, has important implications for social control - a renewal of membership and loyalty to the common moral community; and a public commitment to abide by the demands of its moral and social order.

This commitment to a common moral and social order finds further practical expression during the fasting month of *Ramadan*. Absolute abstention from food, drink, smoking and conjugal relationships, for the period of a month is a practical translation of belief into practice. The sharing of food every evening for a collective breaking of fasting (*Iftar*), the sharing of happiness on the *Eid*-day (the festival that marks the first non-fasting day), further back up the faithful's shared beliefs and sentiments by their deeds. But the happiness of the *Eid*-day must be shared by members of the moral community, including those who, during the past year, had had grievances against each other. It is on this occasion that 'annoyed brothers' are reconciled. The mediation of the community leaders on this occasion is most effective as a mechanism of social control. The mediatory practices of the community leaders also take place within a structured context of the Pakistan Association, Edinburgh and the East of Scotland (P.A.E.E.S.).

The P.A.E.E.S. provides a semi-formal framework for the various social arrangements, activities and institutional practices within the community. The Association as an organised body which represents Edinburgh's Pakistani community to the wider society, makes policies and executes them through its formal organisational structure. The most central apparatus in the organisational structure is the 'executive committee' that consists of some of the influential leaders of the community who are also called 'office bearers'. Social control in the P.A.E.E.S. is closely linked to the social bases of its leaders' power. The most important bases of the power of these leaders are their control over the economic, managerial and institutional/political resources, and their family *Izzet* and social prestige in the community. However, they exercise authority through a mixture of semi-formal and informal mechanisms that often involve mediation. The main spheres where the P.A.E.E.S's leaders exercise authority are domestic issues (i.e. divorce, separation, domestic violence etc.), business-related problems, and feuds

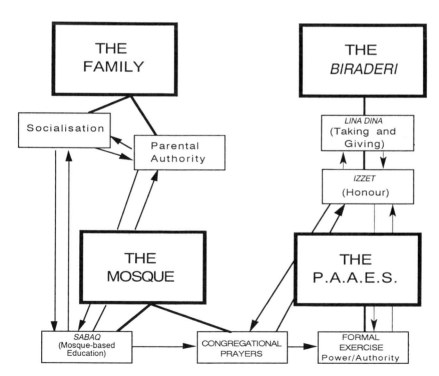

Diagram 2 -   Interrelationships Among Various Mechanisms of Social Control in Edinburgh's Pakistani Community

between individuals and/or families within the community. Only in some cases may the P.A.E.E.S.'s exercise of authority take a purely official form, such as termination of the offender's membership in the Association,withdrawal of official assistance etc. Non-conformists nevertheless become the subject of further informal sanctions through invoking pressures from the kinship groups. Thus, the P.A.E.E.S. operates as a semi-formal and informal agency of social control in Edinburgh's Pakistani community.

It must be mentioned that the various mechanisms of social control that operate within each of the four social institutions of Edinburgh's Pakistani community closely interact with one another and are interrelated in complex ways. The interrelationships between these various mechanisms are illustrated in Diagram 2.

Diagram 2 shows that the seven fundamental mechanisms of social control that operate within the social institutional frameworks of the family, the *Biraderi*, the Mosque, and P.A.E.E.S. interact with one another both in direct and indirect ways. The diagram illustrates the existence of relatively complex interrelationships between 'socialisation', 'parental authority' and *Sabaq*. As the diagram illustrates, each of the three mechanisms directly strengthen and mutually support one another. Among these three mechanisms of social control, the *Sabaq* acts as an important bridge between the British-born young Pakistanis and the adult community – it integrates the former to the community through their participation in congregational worship, collective ceremonies and rituals. This, in turn, has a strong bearing on the individual and family *Izzet* of the regular participants as equal and *Sharif* (decent) members of the 'moral' and cultural community. Likewise, people with a certain degree of *Izzet* are strongly expected to participate in the community's regular collective religious and cultural activities. However, the relationship between *Lina Dina* and the formal exercise of authority are indirect - *Lina Dina* operates mainly through *Izzet* in enabling members of the community to gain positions of leadership in the P.A.E.E.S. and to exercise power/authority. The overall picture of the diagram shows that interaction among the various mechanisms in turn strongly interlink the four social institutions of Edinburgh's Pakistani community, constituting a structure of social relationships and social control in this small-scale society.

What has been said has highlighted the various institutional arrangements, processes and mechanisms that have contributed to the formation of the social order of Edinburgh's Pakistani community and to its maintenance. These conclusions are generally based on the analysis of (mainly) ethnographic data presented in the first part of the book - social control. It is important to recall that social control in the context of Edinburgh's Pakistani community was defined as the extent to which the community's social institutions promote order and regulate behaviour through the social bonding of members to its social and moral order.

The question of how strong second-generation members' social bonds were to the conventional order of the community, was examined in the second part of the book - social deviance. In order to explain deviance in terms of the strength or weakness of individuals' social bonds, Travis Hirschi's (1969) social control theory was used as a theoretical framework for the study of 60 deviant and non-deviant Pakistani boys in Edinburgh - the Pilrig boys. Hirschi's theory and its assumptions were examined against empirical data in the Pilrig sample. Results of the relationships between the degree of strength of each element of the social bond - attachment, commitment, involvement and belief - and the degrees of deviance among the Pilrig boys (conformists, accommodationists, part-time conformists, rebels) are summarised and illustrated below.

Attachment is considered as the most important element of the social bond. It refers to a person's affectionate relationships with other individuals (and institutions) and therefore becoming sensitive to their opinions, feelings and expectations. The most important sources of attachment in the present study were parents, the school and friends. Results of the empirical examination of the relationships between each dimension of attachment and deviance in the Pilrig sample are illustrated in Diagram 3.

Diagram 3 shows that each indicator of attachment to the mother ('intimacy of communication', 'importance of advice'and 'feeling of closeness') is very strongly correlated with deviance among the Pilrig boys. But with regard to the relationship between attachment to the father, only 'importance of father's advice' is very strongly correlated with deviance. The relationships between 'intimacy of communication' with father and deviance are moderately strong. 'Positive identification' with the father, however, has weak relationships with the dependent variable. Thus, it can be concluded that attachment to the mother plays a more important role in controlling deviance among the Pilrig sample than attachment to the father.

As far as the relationships between attachment to the school and deviance are concerned, Diagram 3 shows a slightly different picture from that of attachment between parents and the dependent variable. The relationships between 'liking the school' and 'caring about teachers' opinions', in the case of both the local (Scottish) school and the Mosque-school are (moderately) strong. While the relationship between the third indicator of attachment to the school ('regularity of attendance') and deviance is also (moderately) strong in the case of the Mosque-school, it is relatively weak in the case of the local school. Nevertheless the relationships between attachment to both the local and to the Mosque-school and deviance are in general moderately strong.

There are, however, some surprising results in this study. Diagram 3 illustrates that there are not strong (and therefore significant) relationships between any one of the three indicators of attachment to friends ('importance

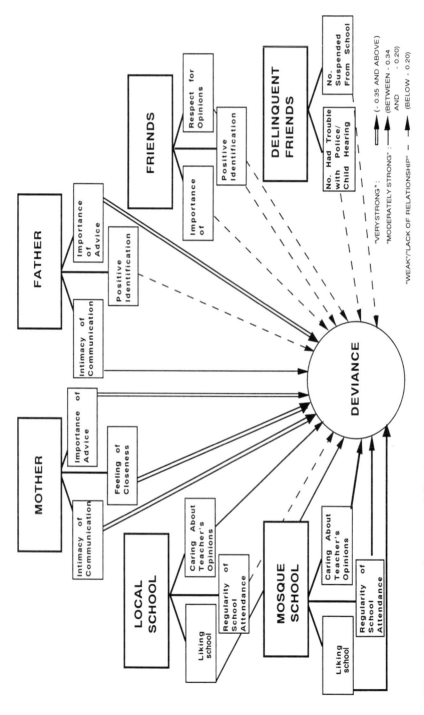

Diagram 3 -   Attachment and Deviance

of friends', 'respect for best friends' opinions', 'positive identification with best friend') and deviance among the Pilrig boys. Similarly, these results reveal that there are no significant relationships between having friends who had trouble with the police (or who have attended the children's hearings) or had been suspended from the school and deviance in the Pilrig sample. These results, showing that attachment to 'best friends' has no role in controlling or promoting deviance in the Pilrig sample, must be treated with caution. As discussed in Chapter V, the cultural context of friendship in Edinburgh's Pakistani community is deeply rooted in kinship relationships. 'Best friends' outside the social networks of kinship tend to have little importance in influencing a young Pakistani's behaviour. Young kin who are called 'brothers' and 'cousins' play a crucial role in this respect.

As far as the other three elements of social bond - commitment, involvement and belief - are concerned, Diagram 4 illustrates the relationships between each of these elements and deviance among the Pilrig boys. It shows that commitment (which is defined as an individual's social investments in a conventional line of action) is strongly correlated with deviance in the Pilrig sample. The diagram illustrates that a moderately strong negative correlation exists between each of the three indicators of commitment ('marks in school', 'aspiration for higher/professional education' and 'family *Izzet*') and deviance. However, the diagram shows a different picture of the relationships between (inhibitive) involvement (an individual's participation in those conventional activities that strengthen his/her social bond to society's conventional order) and deviance. While 'participation in the Mosque/community activities' has a very strong negative correlation with deviance, the correlation between the 'amount of time spent on homework' and the dependent variable is weak. But the third indicator of involvement, or 'feeling of nothing to do', is not correlated with deviance in the Pilrig sample at all.

Finally, Diagram 4 shows that the relationship between belief, or the moral validity and acceptance of rules/social norms, and deviance among the Pilrig boys is even stronger than that between both commitment and involvement and the dependent variable. Both belief in 'the following of Islamic teachings' and belief in the principle of 'being honest with all people' are very strongly and negatively correlated with deviance. But the correlation between 'feelings of guilt' (after behaving dishonestly) and deviance among the Pilrig boys is only moderately strong (and negative).

Thus, it is generally concluded that those Pilrig boys who were less attached to parents and teachers, who were less committed to a conventional line of action, who participated less in school and community-related activities and who accepted the moral values of their community, and of the wider society to a lesser extent were much more likely to be among the deviants. These conclusions support Hirschi's social control theory, accord-

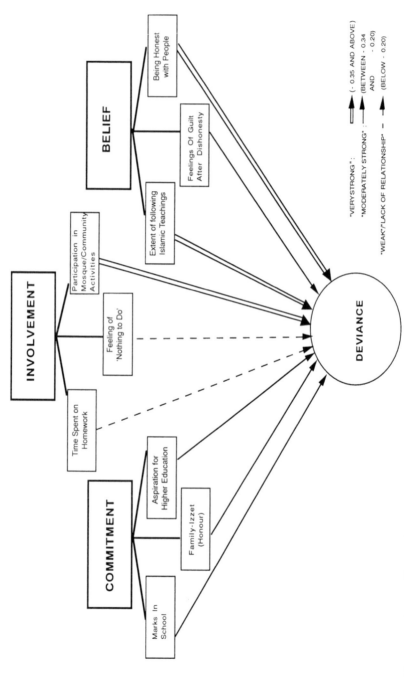

Diagram 4 - Commitment, Involvement, Belief and Deviance

ing to which individuals whose social bonds to the community's conventional order are weak or broken are more likely to get involved in crime and deviance.

This study as a whole shows that the apparently separate themes of 'social control' and 'social deviance' are closely interrelated. It shows that the agencies of social control in Edinburgh's Pakistani community - the family, the *Biraderi*, the Mosque and the P.A.E.E.S. - define what deviance in this particular religio-cultural community is. At the same time, repeated deviance from the community's norms prompts its agencies of social control to tolerate and even redefine deviance. These social processes, in turn, are expected to stimulate social change and pave the way for cultural and normative innovations - innovations that would, in a normal social interactive environment, result in the gradual integration of important aspects of ethnic sub-cultures into the dominant culture of the wider society.

However, exclusionary practices and discrimination against Edinburgh's Pakistani population have not only slowed down their integration, but have created a need for them to strengthen and even revive their traditional cultural institutions. Such practices have, indeed, gradually created the boundaries of an emerging 'closed' community - a community in which they find *inclusion* and acceptance. The dynamics of social control and deviance appear to be at work only within the social and cultural context of this sub-society which has little positive interaction with the wider *exclusive* society.

Bibliography

Abubakrah in Albaihaqi, cited in *As-Siratun Nabawieyah* (1975), Beirut : Islamic Book Co., Ltd.

Agnew, R. (1985) 'A Revised Strain Theory of Delinquency', *Social Forces* 64 : 151–67.

Ahmed, A. (1992) *The Times Saturday Review*, May 2.

Akhbar-e-Watan, 19.11.1989, Glasgow.

Anderson, S. et al (1990) The Edinburgh Crime Survey, Edinburgh: The Scottish Office.

Annual Report of The Glasgow Sailors' Home (1867) Glasgow.

Anwar, M.
(1978) *Between Two Cultures*, London : Community Race Relations Commission.
(1979) *The Myth of Return : Pakistanis in Britain*, London : Heinmann.
(1985) *Pakistanis in Britain*, London : New Century Publishers.
(1986) 'Young Asians Between Two Cultures' in *Race And Social Work*, Ed. Coombe, V. and Little, A., London : Tavistock.

Appignanesi, L. and Maitland, S. (1989) *The Rushdie File*, London : Fourth Estate Ltd.

Armstrong, B. (1989) *People Without Prejudice? : The Experience of Racism in Scotland*, London : Runnymede Trust.

Bailey, F. (1971) *Gifts and Poisons : The Politics Of Reputation*, Oxford : Blackwell.

Becker, H.
(1963) *Outsiders: Studies in the Sociology of Deviance*, New York: Free Press.
(1970) 'Notes on the Concept of Commitment', *Sociological Work*, London : Allen Lane.

Becker W. (1964) 'Consequences of Different Kinds of Parental Discipline' in *Review Of Child Development Research*, Ed. by Hoffman, H. and Hoffman, L., New York : Sage.

Beirstedt, R. (1970) *The Social Order*, New York : McGraw-Hill.

Bell, C. (1976) 'Community, Community, Communion, Class and Community Action' in *Social Areas in Cities II : Spatial Perspectives on Problems and Policies*, Ed. Herbert, D. and Johnson, R. London : John Wiley.

Bell, C. and Newby, H. (1971) *Community Studies*, London : George Allen and Unwin.

Bender, T. (1978) *Community and Change in America*, New Brunswick, N.J. : Rutgers University Press.

Bergalli, R. and Sumner, C. (1997) *Social Control*, London: Sage

Berkowitz. L. (1973) 'Control of Aggression' in *Review of Child Development Research*, Ed. Caldwell, B. and Riecute, Chicago : University of Chicago Press.

Black, D.
(1976) *The Behaviour of Law*, New York : Academic Press.
(1984) 'Social Control as a Dependent Variable' in *Toward a General Theory of Social Control* (Vol. 1) Black, D., New York : Academic Press.

Blalock, H. (1985), *Social Statistics*, Singapore: McGraw-Hill, Inc.

Blood on Street (1978), London : Bethnal Green and Stepney Trades Council.

Blunt, A. (1969) *The Caste System of Northern India*, Delhi : S. Chand and Co.

Bordua, D. (1969), 'Recent Trends: Deviant Behaviour and Social Control', *Annals of the American Academy of Political and Social Science* 369: 149–63.

Box, S. (1971) *Deviance, Reality and Society*, London: Holt, Rinehart and Winston Ltd.

Braithwaite, J. (1989) *Crime, Shame and Reintegration*, Cambridge : Cambridge University Press.

Briar, S. and Pilavin, I. (1965) 'Delinquency, Situational Inducement, and Commitment to Conformity', *Social Problems* 13: 35–45.

Brown, C.
(1984) *Black and White Britain : The Third PSI Survey*, Aldershot : Gower.
(1985) *Racial Discrimination : 17 Years After The Race Relations Act*, London : PSI.

Burket, S. and White, M. (1974) 'Hellfire and Delinquency : Another Look', *Journal of Scientific Study of Religion* 13 : 455–62.

Cage, R. (1985) *The Scots Abroad : Labour, Capital and Enterprise, 1750–1914*, London: Croom Helm.

Cain, A. (1986) *The Cornchest For Scotland : Scots in India*, Edinburgh : National Library of Scotland.

Campbell, J. (1964) *Honour, Family and Patronage : A Study of Institutions and Moral Values in a Greek Mountain Community*, Oxford : Clarendon Press.

Census For Scotland (1991) Part I, Vol. I : 88, Edinburgh : HMSO.

Cernkovich, S. et al (1987) 'Family Relationship and Delinquency', *Criminology* 25 (2) : 295–321.

Chambers Community Consultants (1989) *Fear and Crime in the Inner City*, Leicester : Chambers Community Consultants.

Chambliss, W. (ed.) (1973) *Sociological Readings in the Conflict Perspective*, Reading, Mass: Addison-Wesley.

Chan, J. (1981) 'From Hobbes to Marx : A Study of Man, Society and Criminality', *Canadian Criminological Forum* 3, Spring.

Clark, J. and Wenninger, E. (1962) 'Socio-Economic Class and Area as Correlates of Illegal Behaviour Among Juveniles', *American Sociological Review* 27 : 826–34.

Clayton, R. (1969) 'Religious Orthodoxy and Premarital Sex', *Social Forces* 47 : 469–74.

Clinard, M. and Meier, R. (1985) *The Sociology of Deviant Behaviour* (6th Ed.), New York : Hart Rinehart and Winston.

Cloward R. and Ohlin, L. (1960) *Delinquency and Opportunity: A Theory of Delinquent Gangs*, New York: Free Press.

Cochran, J. and Akers, R. (1989) 'Beyond Hellfire : An Exploration of The Variable Effects of Religiosity on Adolescent Marijuana and Alcohol Use', *Journal of Research in Crime and Delinquency* 26 (3) : 198–225.

Cohen, A.
(1955) *Delinquent Boys*, New York: Free Press.
(1966) *Deviance and Control*, New Jersey: Prentice-Hall, Inc.

Cohen, S. (1985) *Visions of Social Control*, Cambridge : Polity Press.

Constitution of The Pakistan Association, Edinburgh and The East of Scotland (1971), Edinburgh (and its Amendments 1986; 1988).

Cook, D. and Hudson, B. (1993) *Racism and Criminology*, London : Sage.

Cook, et al (1983) 'The Distribution of Power and Exchange Networks : Theory and Experimental Results', *American Journal of Sociology* 89 (2) : 275–305.

Cook, K. (1982) 'Network Structures From An Exchange Perspective' in Marsden, P. et al (eds.) *Social Structure and Network Analysis*, Beverley Hills, CA : Sage.

Cooley, C.

(1902) *Human Nature and Social Order*, New York: Charles Scribner's Sons.

(1914[1909]) *Social Organisation*, New York : Charles Scribner's Sons.

(1918) *Social Process*, New York : Charles Scribner's Sons.

Coser, Rose-Laub (1961) 'Insulation From Observability and Types of Social Conformity', *American Sociological Review* 26 : 28–39.

Commission for Racial Equality

(1990a) *Ethnic Minorities and The Graduate Labour Market*, London : CRE.

(1990b) *Out of Order : Report of A Formal Investigation Into The London Borough of Southwark*, London : CRE.

(1990c) *Racial Discrimination in An Oldham Estate Agency*, London : CRE.

(1990d) *Sorry, It's Gone : Testing For Racial Discrimination in The Private Rented Housing Sector*, London : CRE.

(1991) *Equality in Housing : Code of Practice For Elimination of Racial Discrimination and The Promotion of Equal Opportunities*, London : CRE.

(1992) *Race Through The Nineties*, London : CRE.

Cuneo, C. (1978) 'A Class Perspective on Regionalism' in Glenday, H. et al (eds) *Modernization and The Canadian State*, Toronto : Macmillan.

Dalton, M. and Daghlian, S. (1989) *Race and Housing in Glasgow : The Role of Housing Associations*, London : CRE.

Davis, N. (1972) 'Labeling Theory in Deviance Research: A Critique and Reconsideration', *Sociological Quarterly* 13: 447–74.

Delaney, C. (1987) 'Seeds of Honour, Fields of Shame' in *Honour and Shame and the Unity of the Mediterranean*, Ed. by Gilmore, D., Washington : American Anthropological Association.

Dixon, B. et al (1987) *A Handbook of Social Science Research*, Oxford : Oxford University Press.

Dinitz and Pfau-Vincent, S. (1982), 'Self-Concept and Juvenile Delinquency: An Update', *Youth and Society* 14: 133–58.

Ditton, J. (1977) *Part-Time Crime*, London : The Macmillan Press Ltd.

Doo, L. (1973) 'Dispute Settlement in Chinese-American Communities' 21: 627–63.

Downes, D. and Rock, P. (1982) *Understanding Deviance*, Oxford : Oxford University Press.

Duffee, D. (1980) *Explaining Criminal Justice : Community Theory and Criminal Justice Reform*, Cambridge : Gunn and Hain.

Dunlop, A. (1988) *Aspect of Scottish Migration History with particular emphasis on Contemporary Pakistani and Bangladeshi Migration*, M.Lit Dissertation, Department of Sociology, University of Glasgow.

Dunlop, A. and Miles, R. (1990) 'Recovering The History of Asian Migration To Scotland', *Immigrants and Minorities* 9 (2) : 145–67.

Durkheim, E.

(1915) *The Elementary Forms of Religious Life : A Study in Religious Sociology*, Translated by Swain, J., London : Allen and Unwin.

(1933) *The Division of Labour in Society*, Translated by Simpson, G., New York: The Macmillan Company.

(1951) *Suicide*, translated by Spaulding, J. and Simpson, G., New York : Free Press of Glencoe, Inc.

Edinburgh Evening News (1927), June 3.

Edinburgh Evening News (1989), June 12.

Edwards, A. (1988) *Regulation and Repression : The Study of Social Control*, Sydney : Allen Unwin.

Eglar, Z. (1960) *A Punjabi Village in Pakistan*, New York : Columbia University Press.

Elahi, K. (1967) *Some Aspects of Social Adaptation of Pakistani Immigrants in Glasgow*, Unpublished M.A. Dissertation, The University of Edinburgh.

Ellon, R. (1984) *Ethnographic Research : A Guide to General Conduct*, London : Academic Press.

Elliott, D. (1962) 'Delinquency and Perceived Opportunity', *Sociological Inquiry* 32: 216–27.

Elliott D. et al

(1985) *Explaining Delinquency and Drug Use*, Beverley Hills : Sage.

(1989) *Multiple Problem Youth*, New York : Springer-Verlag.

Employment Gazette (February 1991)/Ethnic Origins and The Labour Market'.

Erickson, R. (1977) 'Social Distance and Reaction Criminality', *British Journal of Criminology* 17 : 16-19.

Erikson, K. (1962), 'Notes on the Sociology of Deviance', *Social Problems* 9: 307–14.

Eron, L. et al (1971) *Learning of Aggression in Children*, Boston : Little, Brown.

Ethnic Minorities in Scotland (1991) *Central Research Papers*, Edinburgh : The Scottish Office.

Etzioni, A. (1964) *A Comparative Analysis of Complex Organizations*, New York : Free Press.

European Committee on Crime Problems (1972) 'The Role of the School in the Prevention of Juvenile Delinquency', Strasbourg : Council of Europe.

Farrington, D.

(1973) 'Self-Reports of Deviant Behaviour : Predictive and Stable', *Journal of Criminal Law and Criminology* 64 : 99–100.

(1986) 'Age and Crime' in *Crime and Justice* 7 : 189–250, Ed. Tonr, M. and Morrison, Chicago : University of Chicago Press.

(1992) 'Criminal Career Research in the United Kingdom', *British Journal of Criminology* 32 : 521–36.

Fischer, C. (1982) *To Dwell Among Friends*, Chicago : University of Chicago Press.

Fischer, C. et al. (1977) *Networks and Places : Social Relations in The Urban Setting*, New York : Free Press.

Fisher, S. (1972) 'Stigma and Deviant Careers in Schools', *Social Problems* 20: 78–83.

Fox, V. (1976) *Introduction to Criminology*, New Jersey: Prentice-Hall, Inc.

Fryer, P.
(1984) *Staying Power : The History of Black People in Britain*, London : Pluto Press.
(1989) *Black People in the British Empire*, London : Pluto Press.

Garland, D. (1985) 'The Criminal and his Science', *British Journal of Criminology* 25: 109–37.

Gibbs, J.
(1965) 'Norms : The Problem of Definition and Classification', *American Journal of Sociology* 70 : 586–94.
(1966) 'Conception of Deviant Behaviour: The Old and the New', *Pacific Sociological Review* 9, Spring.
(1981) *Norms, Deviance and Social Control : Conceptual Matters*, New York : Elsevier.

Gilmore, D. (1987) 'Introduction : The Shame of Dishonour' in *Honour and Shame and The Unity of The Mediterranean*, Ed. by Gilmore, D., New York : Academic Press.

Giordano, P. et al (1986) 'Friendship and Delinquency' *American Journal of Sociology* 91: 1170–202.

Ginsberg, N. (1992) 'Racism and Housing : Concepts and Reality' in Rattasani, A. and Skillington, R. (Eds) *Racism and Anti-Racism : Inequalities, Opportunities and Policies*, London : Sage/Open University.

Gluck, S. and Gluck, E. (1950) *Unravelling Juvenile Delinquency*, Cambridge, Mass. : Harvard University Press.

Gold, M. (1963) *Status Forces in Delinquent Boys*, Ann Arbor : Institute for Social Research, University of Michigan.

Gordon, R. (1964) *Assimilation in American Life*, New York : Oxford University Press.

Gordon, R. et al (1963) 'Values and Gang Delinquency', *American Journal of Sociology* 69: 109–23.

Gottfredson, M. and Hirschi, T. (1990) *A General Theory of Crime*, Stanford, California : Stanford University Press.

Gouldner, A. (1968) 'The Sociologist as Partisan: Sociology and the Welfare State', *American Sociologist* 3: 103–16.

Greenberg, D. (1977) 'Delinquency and The Age Structure of Society', *Contemporary Crises* 1 : 189–223.

Greenwood, P et al (1980) Age, Crime and Sanctions : The Transition From Juvenile to Adult Court, Report R-2642-NIJ, Calif. : Rand.

Gurwich, G. (1945) 'Social Control', in *Twentieth Century Sociology*, Ed. Gurwich, G. et al, New York, Philosophical Library, Inc.

Hagan, J.
(1979) 'The Sexual Stratification of Social Control : A Gender-Based Perspective on Crime and Delinquency', *British Journal of Sociology* 30: (1) : 25–38.
(1987) *Modern Criminology*, Toronto : McGraw-Hill.

Hall, S. et al (1878) *Policing the Crisis*, London: The Macmillan Press Ltd.

Hammerton, J. (1983) *Sketches From Glasgow*, Glasgow.

Haney, B. and Gold, M. (1973), 'The Juvenile Delinquent Nobody Knows', *Psychology Today* 7, (No. 4).

Happenstall, M. (1971) 'Reputation, Criticism, and Information in An Austrian Village' in *Gifts and Poison*, Ed., Bailey, F., Oxford : Blackwell.

Haralambos, H. (1987) *Sociology : A New Introduction*, Lanarkshire : Causeway Press Ltd.

Henley, A. (1986) 'The Asian Community in Britain' in *Race and Social Work*, Coombe, V. and Little, A. (eds.), London : Tavistock.

Hetch (1954) *Continental and Colonial Servants in the Eighteenth Century*.

Hillary, G.
(1955) 'Definitions of Community : Areas of Agreement', *Rural Sociology* 20 : 111–23.
(1983) 'Review of Helping Networks (1981) Warren, D., *Social Forces* 61 : 955–57.

Hills, S. (1971) *Crime, Power and Morality*, Scranton, Pa.: Chandler.

Hindelang, M.
(1971) 'Age, Sex and Versatility of Delinquent Involvement', *Social Problems* 18 : 522–35.
(1972) 'The Relationship of Self-Reported Delinquency and Scales of The CPI and MMPI', *Journal of Criminal Law, Criminology and Police Science*, March.
(1971) (1973) 'Causes of Delinquency : Partial Duplication and Extension', *Social Problems* 18 : 471–87.

Hirschi, T.
(1969) *Causes of Delinquency*, California: California University Press.
(1983) 'Crime and The Family', in *Crime and Public Policy*, Ed. by Wilson, J., San Francisco : Institute for Contemporary Studies.
(1986) 'On The Compatibility of Rational Choice and Social Control Theories of Crime' in *The Reasoning Criminal : Rational Choice Perspective of Crime*, Ed. by Cornish, D. and Clarke, R., New York : Springer-Verlag.

Hirschi, T. and Hindelang, M. (1977) 'Intelligence and Delinquency : A Revisionist View', *American Sociological Review* 42 : 571–87.

Hirschi, T. and Stark, R. (1969) 'Hellfire and Delinquency : Another Look', *Journal for the Scientific Study of Religion* 13 : 455–62.

Hobbes, T. (1958) *Leviathan*, Indianapolis : Bobbs-Merrill.

Home Office (1981) *Racial Attacks*, London, HMSO.

Hotchkiss, J. (1967) 'Children and Conduct in a Ladino Community of Chiapas, Mexico', *American Anthropologist* 68 : 711–18.

Janovitz, M. (1975) 'Sociological Theory and Social Control', *American Journal of Sociology* 18 : 82–108.

Janovitz, M. and Street, D. (1978) 'Changing Social Order of The Metropolitan Area' in *Handbook of Contemporary Urban Life*, Ed. by Street, D. et al, San Francisco : Jossey-Bass.

Jeffrey, C. (1960) 'The Historical Development of Criminology' in *Pioneers in Criminology*, Ed. by Manheim, H., London: Steven and Sons Limited, 364–94.

Jeffrey, P. (1976) *Migrants and Refugees : Muslim and Christian Pakistani Families in Bristol*, Cambridge : Cambridge University Press.

Jensen, G. (1973) 'Parents, Peers and Delinquent Action', *American Journal of Sociology* 78 : 562–75.

Jensen, G. and Eve, R. (1976) 'Sex Differences in Delinquency : An Explanation of Popular Sociological Explanation', *Criminology* 13 : 427–48.

Johnson, R. (1979) *Juvenile Delinquency and its Origin*, Cambridge : Cambridge University Press.

Jones, H. and Davenport, M. (1972) 'The Pakistani Community in Dundee : A Study of Growth and Demographic Structure', *Scottish Geographical Magazine* 88 : 75–85.

Jones, T. and McVoy, D. (1994) *Asian Business*, Liverpool, John Moore's University.

Kaplan, H. and Robbins, C. (1983) 'Testing A General Theory of Deviant Behaviour in Longitudinal Perspective' in *Prospective Studies of Crime and Delinquency*, Ed. by Van Dusen and Mednick, S., Boston : Kluwer-Nijhof.

Kent, R. and Urry, J. (1975) *Social Theory as Science*, London: Routledge and Kegan Paul Ltd.

Kelly, D. and Pink, W. (1973) 'School Commitment, Youth Rebellion and Delinquency', *Criminology* 10 : 1473–85.

Kitsuse, J. and Dietrick, D. (1959), 'Delinquent Boys: A Critique', *American Sociological Review* 24: 208–15.

Klein, H. (1967) *Juvenile Gangs in Context: Theory, Research and Action*, Englewood Cliffs : Prentice-Hall.

Kornhauser, R. (1978), *Social Sources of Delinquency: An Appraisal of Analytical Models*, Chicago and London: University of Chicago Press.

Krienken, R. (1991) 'The Poverty of Social Control: Explaining Power in the Historical Sociology of the Welfare State'.
'Theory and Society', *The Sociological Review* 1 : 1–25

Laurmann, E. (1973) *Bonds of Pluralism*, New York : John Wiley.

Lawrence, R. (1985) 'School Performance, Containment Theory, and Delinquent Behaviour', *Youth and Society* 17: 69–95.

Leighton, B. (1988) 'The Community Concept in Criminology : Toward A Social Network Approach', *Journal of Research in Crime and Delinquency* 25 (4) : 375–91.

Lemert, E.
(1951) *Social Pathology*, New York: McGraw-Hill.
(1967) *Human Deviance, Social Problems and Social Control*, New Jersey: Prentice-Hall.

Lerman, P (1968) 'Individual Values, Peer Values and Subcultural Delinquency', *American Sociological Review* 33: 219–35.

Liazos, A. (1972) 'The Poverty of the Sociology of Deviance: Nuts, Shuts and Perverts', *Social Problems* 20: 103–20.

Long, J. (1976) *An Empirical Explication of the Issues in Containment Theory*, Unpublished Ph.D. Thesis: Oklahoma State University.

Maan, B. (1992) *The New Scots*, Edinburgh : John Donal Publishers Ltd.

Maine, H. (1861) *Ancient Law*, London : Murray.

Mankoff, M. (1971) 'Societal Reaction and Career Deviance: A Critical Analysis', *The Sociological Quarterly* 12, Spring.

Mathew, P. et al (1989) *The 1989 British Crime Survey, Home Office Research Study III*, London : HMSO.

Matza, D.
(1964) *Delinquency and Drift*, New York : Wiley.
(1969) *Becoming Deviant*, Englewood Cliffs, N.J. : Prentice-Hall.

McClintock, F. and Avison, N. (1968) *Crime in England and Wales*, London : Heinemann.

McCord, J. et al (1962) 'Some Effects of Parental Absence on Male Children', *Journal of Abnormal and Social Psychology* 64 : 361–69.

McCrudden, C. et al (1991) *Racial Justice At Work : Enforcement of The Race Relations Act 1976 in Employment*, London : PSI.

McEwan, M. and Varity, M. (1989) *Ethnic Minority Experiences of Council Houses in Edinburgh*, Scottish Ethnic Minority Research Unit and CRE.

Mend, G.
(1925) 'The Genesis of Self and Social Control' in *Selected Writings of George Herbert Mead*, Ed. Reck, A. (1964), Indianapolis : Bobbs-Merrill.
(1934) 'Mind, Self and Society' in *The Standpoint of a Social Behaviourist*, Ed. Morris, C., Chicago: University of Chicago Press.

Meire, R. (1982) 'Perspectives on The Concept of Social Control', *Annual Review of Sociology* 8 : 35–55.

Merry, S.
(1979) 'Going To Court : Strategies of Dispute Management in An American Urban Neighbourhood', *Law and Society Review* 13 : 891–925.
(1981) 'Racial Integration in An Urban Neighbourhood : The Social Organisation of Strangers', *Human Organization* 39 : 59–69.

Merton, R.
(1957) *Social Theory and Social Structure* (Revised Ed.), New York: Free Press.
(1959) 'Social Conformity, Deviation and Opportunity Structures', *American Sociological Review* 24 : 177–89.

Metropolitan Police (1990) *Report of the Commissioner of Police of the Metropolis 1989 : We Care For London*, London : Metropolitan Police.

Miles, R. and Dunlop, A. (1987) 'Racism in Britain : The Scottish Dimension' in *Race and Racism : Essays in Social Geography*, Ed. Jackson, P. , London : Unwin.

Miles, R. and Muirhead, L. (1986) 'Racism in Scotland : A Matter For Further Investigation?', *Scottish Political Yearbook*, Ed. McCrone, D., Edinburgh.

Miller, W. (1958) 'Lower Class Culture as a Generating Milieu of Gang Delinquency', *Journal of Social Issues* 14: 5–19.

Mingione, E. (1974) 'Territorial Division of Labour and Capitalist Development', *Current Sociology* 22 : 222–78.

Mitchell, C. (1969) *Social Networks in Urban Situations*, Manchester : Manchester University Press.

Nee, B.V. and De Bary, B. (1974) *Longtime California: A Documentary Study of an American Chinatown*, Boston : Houghton-Mifflin.

Nye, I. (1958) *Family Relationships and Delinquent Behaviour*, New York: John Wiley and Sons.

Nye, I. and Short, J. (1957) 'Scaling Delinquent Behaviour', *American Sociological Review* 22: 326–32.

Nye, M. (1992) *'A Place For Our Gods':* The Construction of A Hindu Temple Community in Edinburgh, Unpublished Ph.D. Thesis, The University of Edinburgh.

Park, R. (1915) 'The City : Suggestions For The Investigation of Human Behaviour in The Urban Environment', *American Journal of Sociology* 20 : 577–611.

Park, R. and Burgess, E. (1921) *The City*, Chicago : Chicago University Press.

Parsons, T. (1937) *The Structure of Social Action*, New York : McGraw-Hill.

Patterson, G. (1980) 'Children Who Steal', in Hirschi, T. and Gottfredson (Eds), in *Understanding Crime : Current Theory and Research*, CA : Sage.

Patterson, G. (1982) *Coercive Family Process : A Social Learning Approach*, Vol. 3, Eugene, Oregon : Castalia.

Patterson, G. and Dishion, T. (1985) 'Contribution of Family and Peers To Delinquency', *Criminology* 23 : 63–79.

Peristiany, J. (1965) *Honour and Shame : The Values of Mediterranean Societies*, London : Weidenfield and Nicolson.

Philips, D. (1987) 'Searching For a Decent Home : Ethnic Minority Progress in The Post War Housing Market', *New Community* 14 : 105–47.

Pitt-Rivers, J. (1965) 'Honour and Social Status' in *Honour and Shame*, Ed. Peristiany, J., London : Weidenfield and Nicolson.

Polk, K. and Pink, W. (1971) 'Youth Culture and The School', *British Journal of Sociology* 22 : 160––71.

Popline, D. (1972) *Communities : A Survey of Theories and Methods of Research*, New York : Macmillan.

Population Trends (1993) No. 72, Office of the Population Census and Advices (OPCS).

Pound, R. (1942) *Social Control Through Law*, New Haven, Conn. : Yale University Press.

Quinney, R. (1970) *The Social Reality of Crime*, New York: Little, Brown and Company.

Race Relations and Muslims in Great Britain (1992) London : The Muslim Parliament of Great Britain.

Racial Harassment Project (1989) *Because their Skin is Black*, Sheffield City Council, Sheffield.

Rankin, J. and Wells, L. (1990) 'The Effects of Parental Attachments and Direct Control on Delinquency', *Journal of Research on Crime and Delinquency* 27 (2) : 140–64.

Reckless, W.
(1962) 'Containment Theory' in *The Sociology of Crime and Delinquency*, Ed by Wolgang, M., Savitz, L. and Johnston, N., New York: John Wiley and Sons.
(1967) *The Crime Problem*, New York: Appleton-Century-Crofts.

Reiss, A. (1951) 'Delinquency and the Failure of Personal and Social Controls', *American Sociological Review* 16 : 196–207.

Roshier, B. (1989) *Controlling Crime*, Milton Keynes : The Open University.

Ross, E. (1901) *Social Control : A Survey of The Foundations of Social Order*, New York: Macmillan.
Runnymede Trust (1991) *Race and Immigration*, Bulletin 247, London : Runnymede Trust.
Rushdie, S. (1989) *The Satanic Verses*, London : Viking/Penguin.
Rutter, M. and Giller, H. (1983) *Juvenile Delinquency : Trends and Perspectives*, Harmondsworth : Penguin.
Salter, J. (1873) *Missionary to Asiatics in England*, London : Seeley, Jackson and Halliday.
Sampson, R. and Laub, J. (1993) *Crime in the Making*, Massachusetts: Harvard University Press.
Schur, E. (1971) *Labeling Deviant Behaviour*, New York: Harper and Row.
Scottish Office Report (1991) *Ethnic Minorities in Scotland*, Edinburgh : The Scottish Office.
Sears, R. et al (1957) *Patterns of Child-Rearing*, Evanston, Ill. : Row, Peterson.
Seltiz, J. et al (1965) *Research Methods in Social Relations*, Kent : Methuen and Co. Ltd.
SEMRU (Scottish Ethnic Minorities Research Unit [1987]) *Ethnic Minorities Profile*, Vols. II and III, Edinburgh : Edinburgh College of Arts.
Shaw, A. (1988) *A Pakistani Community in Britain*, Oxford : Basil Blackwell.
Shaw, C. et al (1929) *Delinquency Areas*, Chicago : University of Chicago Press.
Shaw, C. and Mackay, H.
   (1931) *Social Factors in Juvenile Delinquency*, Vol. 2 of *Report on The Causes of Crime, National Commission of Law Observance and Enforcement*, Washington, D.C. : Government Printing Office.
   (1942) *Juvenile Delinquency and Urban Areas*, Chicago : University of Chicago Press.
Sheu, C.-J. (1983) *Assimilation, Adaptation and Juvenile Delinquency Among Chinese Youths in New York Chinatown*, Unpublished Ph.D. Thesis, State University of New York at Albany.
Short, J. (1964) 'Gang Delinquency and Anomie' in *Anomie and Deviant Behaviour*, Ed. by Cunnard, M., New York : Free Press.
Skillington, R. (1996) 'Race' in *Britain Today* (2nd edition) London: Open University.
Skillington, R. et al. (1992) 'Race' in *Britain Today*, London: Sage/Open University.
Smith, S. (1989) *The Politics of 'Race' and Residence*, Oxford : Polity Press.
Strivastava, S. (1975) *The Asian Community in Glasgow*, Unpublished Ph.D. Thesis, University of Glasgow.
Sumner, W. (1906) *Folkways*, Boston : Ginn and Company.
Sutherland, E. (1924) *Criminology*, Philadelphia : Lippinstock.
Sutherland, E. and Cressey, D.
   (1956) *Principles of Criminology*, Philadelphia : Lippincott.
   (1978) *Criminology* (10th Edition), New York : Lippincott.
Sykes, G. and Matza, D. (1957) 'Techniques of Neutralization: A Theory of Delinquency', *American Sociological Review* 22: 664–70.
Tannenbaum, F. (1938), *Crime and the Community*, Boston: Gunn and Co.

Taylor, I., Walton, P. and Young, J. (1973) *The New Criminology*, London: Routledge and Kegan Paul.

The Independent on Sunday, December 5 1993.

The Independent on Sunday, June 12 1994.

The Los Angeles Times, March 1990.

The Motherwell Times, February 11 1921.

The Scotsman, January 6 1990.

The Scotsman, December 15 1993.

The Times, April 30 1980.

Thompson, W. and Dodder, A. (1986) 'Containment Theory and Juvenile Delinquency: A Re-evaluation through Factor Analysis', *Adolescence* 21: 366–76.

Thrasher, F. (1927) *The Gang: A Study of 1313 Gangs in Chicago*, Chicago: University of Chicago Press.

Tilly, C. (1973) 'Do Communities Act?', *Sociological Inquiry* 43 : 206–40.

Toby, J. (1957) 'Social Disorganization and Stake in Conformity : Factors in The Predatory Behaviour of Young Hoodlums', *Journal of Criminal Law, Criminology and Police Science* 48 : 12–17.

Tockqueville, A. (1945) *Democracy in America*, Garden City : Anchor Books.

Tonnies, F. (1887) *Community and Society*, New York : Harper and Row.

Trice, H. and Roman, P. (1970) 'Delabeling, Relabeling and Alcoholics Anonymous', *Social Problems* 17: 538–46.

Tunley, R. (1962) *Kids, Crime and Chaos*, New York: Dell Publishing Co.

Turk, A. (1969), *Criminality and Legal Order*, Chicago: Rand McNally.

21st Anniversary Celebration of P.A.E.E.S. (1985) : 11–15 May.

Tyler,T. (1990) *Why People Obey the Law*, London: Yale University Press.

Ullah, I. (1958) 'Caste, Patti and Faction in The Life of A Punjab Village', *Sociologue* 8 : 36–46.

Victim Support (1991) *Racial Attacks in Campden, Southwark, and Newham*, London : Victim Support.

Visram, R. (1986) *Ayahs, Lascars and Princes : Indians in Britain 1700–1947*, London : Pluto Press.

Vold, G. (1979) *Theoretical Criminology* (2nd Ed.), New York and Oxford: Oxford University Press.

Vold, G. and Bernard, T. (1 986) *Theoretical Criminology*, Oxford : Oxford University Press.

Wakil, P. (1970) *Pakistan: Sociological Writings*, Vol. 1.

Waldo, G. and Hall, N. (1970) 'Delinquency Potential and Attitudes Toward Criminal Justice System, *Social Forces* 49 : 291–8.

Watson, J. (1975) *Between Two Cultures*, London : Basil Blackwell.

Webber, M.
(1963) 'Order in Diversity : Community Without Propinquity' in *Cities and Space: The Future of Urban Land*, Ed. Wing, L. Baltimore : Johns Hopkins University Press.
(1968) 'The Post-City Age', *Daedulus* 94 : 1093–9.

Weber, M.
   (1964) T*he Theory of Social and Economic Organisation*, Ed. Parsons, T., New York : Free Press.
   (1968) *Economy and Society*, 3 vol., Ed. Roth, G. and Wittich, C., New York : Bedminster.
Wellman, B and Leighton, B. (1979) 'Networks, Neighbourhoods, and Communities', *Urban Affairs Quarterly* 14 (3): 363–90.
Wells, J. and Rankin, L. (1988) 'Direct Parental Controls and Delinquency', *Criminology* 26 : 263–85.
Werbner, P., (1990) *The Migration Process : Capital, Gifts, and Offerings Among British Pakistanis*, Oxford : Berg.
Werbner, P. (1991) *New Community* 17 (3), 331–46.
West, D. (1982) *Delinquency : its Roots, Careers and Prospects*, London : Heinemann.
West, D. and Farrington, D. (1977) *The Delinquent Way of Life*, New York : Crane Rossak.
Wiatrowski, M. (1978) *Social Control Theory and Delinquency*, Unpublished Ph.D. Dissertation, Portland State University, U.S.A.
Wiatrowski, M. et al (1981) 'Social Control Theory and Delinquency', *American Sociological Review* 46 : 525–41.
Wikstrom, P. (1990) 'Age and Crime in a Stockholm Cohort', *Journal of Quantitative Criminology* 6 : 61–84.
Williams, R. (1973) *The Country and the City*, London : Chatto and Windus.
Wilson, J. (1975) *Thinking about Crime*, New York : Basic Books, Inc. Publishers.
Wilson, J. and Herrnstein, R. (1985) *Crime and Human Nature*, New York : Simon and Schuster, Inc.
Wilson, H.R. (1980) 'Parental Supervision: A Neglected Aspect of Delinquency', *British Journal of Criminology* 20 : 203–35.
Wilson, P. (1974) 'Filcher of Good Names : 'An Inquiry into Anthropology and Gossip', *Man* 3 : 102.
Wirth, L. (1938) 'Urbanism As A Way of Life', *American Journal of Sociology* 44: 1–24.
Young, J. (1986) The Failure of Criminology: The Need for a Radical Realism 'in *Confronting Crime*, Ed. Matthews, R. and Young, J. London: Sage Publications Ltd.
Young, P. (1987) 'The Concept of Social Control and Its Relevance to The Prisons Debate' in *Problems of Long-Term Imprisonment*, Ed. Bottoms, A. and Light, Aldershot : Gower.

Index